Foreign Policy of Nepal

Foreign Policy of Nepal

S.D. Muni

ADROIT
Adroit Publishers
New Delhi

ISBN : 978-81-87393-34-4

Revised & Enlarged Edition 2016

Published by

ADROIT PUBLISHERS
4675/21, Ganpati Bhawan, Ansari Road,
Daryaganj, New Delhi-110 002
Phone : 011-23266030

Distributors
AKHIL BOOK DISTRIBUTORS
email: akhilbooks@yahoo.com
akhilbks@gmail.com

Typesetting—Gaurav Graphics, Delhi-110094

E-mail: gauravsingh1908@gmail.com

Printed at: Avantika Printers Private Limited.

PREFACE

The British withdrawal from Asia and the pattern of post-II World War international politics created a situation towards the end of forties which did not leave Nepal to itself, as was the case hitherto. The Kingdom began to feel and react to the changes that were taking place around it. Internally, a "partial revolution" in 1950-51 replaced the century-old Rana oligarchy with the traditionally well-entrenched monarchy which was to become increasingly assertive. Since these changes, Nepal has actively participated in international alfairs. Through this participation, the Kingdom has evolved an image and a pattern of behaviour of its own, the study of which can provide an interesting insight into the process of struggle of a small and new nation state for its security, prosperity and status in the world, dominated by giant and ruthless powers.

The present work is an attempt in the direction of making such a study. It is the revised version of my Ph.D. dissertation on the subject. A chapter of the original dissertation, "The Role of Political Institutions in Foreign Policy Decision-Making" does not find place here, for that would have further added to the length of the volume. A " Post-Script" has been added to update some of the important developments that have taken place after the period covered in the original dissertation. Otherwise the overall organisation, style and approach of the original dissertation have been kept intact.

In pursuing this study, non-availability of the source material presented a difficult problem. The official and public sources of information on the subject in Kathmandu were found to be inadequate and disorganised. The Nepalese Government's excessive pre-occupation with secrecy and closeness, particularly in relation to the Indian students, further aggravated the problem. Access is not allowed even to the proceedings of Parliament of 1959-60, which are otherwise available in the official Nepali daily, *Gorkhapatra* of that period. There was, however,, a redeeming feature; at personal level, most of the Nepali officials and leaders were friendly, understanding and co-operative.

The study was conducted under the supervision of Dr. S.P. Varma, Professor and Head of the Department of Political Science, University of Rajasthan, Jaipur. His kind and personal interest in my work extended much beyond academic supervision. It constituted a perennial source of moral and material support. My acknowledgements are also due to :

Dr. K.P. Karunakaran, now Visiting Professor at the Department of History, University of Singapore,' who guided this study during its early stages;

Prof. Aloo J. Dastur of Bombay University who not only inspired me to undertake research work, but also kept me affectionately encouraging throughout the period of this study;

The Nepali leaders : Sh. B.P. Koirala, Sh. Subarna Shumshere, Sh. Rishikesh Shah, Sh. K.N. Bista, Sh. S.P. Upadhyaya, Sh. Tanka Prasad Acharya, Dr. D.R. Regmi, Dr. K.I. Singh, Sh. Bharat Shumshere J.B. Rana, Sh. Kesar Jung Raimajhi, late Sh. Yogendraman Sherchan, Sh. Girja Koirala and others who very kindly allowed me long sittings with them. Dr. Regmi and Sh. Girija Koirala went even out of the way to help me in making my stay in Kathmandu comfortable and useful;

Sh. Y.N. Khanal, Dr. Mohd. Mohsin, Prof. B.C. Malla, Sh. Chittaranjan Nepali, Sh. Gopal Dass Shrestha for helping me in the collection of material in Kathmandu;

The HMG Ministries of Foreign Affairs, Economic Planning, Home and Panchayat Affairs, Publicity and Information, and Foreign Trade;

The Indian, US, Soviet, British, Pakistani and Japanese diplomatic missions stationed in Kathmandu and Royal Nepal Embassy in New Delhi;

The Sapru House Library, New Delhi, the Central Library of the University of Rajasthan, Jaipur, and their very efficient and helpful staff.

The Madan Purskar, Tribhuwan University, Singh Durbar Rastriya Panchayat and Vir Libraries in Kathmandu.

Prof. Bimal Prasad, Dr. (Mrs.) Urmila Phadnis, Dr. L.S. Baral and Dr. Satish Kumar of the School of International Studies, Jawaharlal Nehru University, New Delhi;

Dr. Leo E. Rose of California University, Berkeley, USA, for his comments and suggestions;

My colleagues and friends at the University of Rajasthan, South Asia Studies Centre, Jaipur;

Dr. (Mrs.) Sita Radhakrishnan and my friend Mr. Oliver Mendelsohn for editing the dissertation;

My wife Anuradha, who shared the "pangs of research" with me throughout the period of study.

Finally, I gratefully acknowledge the grant sanctioned by the Indian Council of Social Science Research, New Delhi, to subsidise the publication of this Ph D. dissertation. Needless to say that responsibility for the facts and interpretations in this study is entirely mine.

S.D. Muni

South Asia Studies Centre
University of Rajasthan Jaipur.

CONTENTS

1

THE BACKGROUND

The geographical confines of present day Nepal are the outcome of a process of annexation and cession initiated in the latter half of the 18th century by King Prithvi Narayan Shah of Gurkha principality. Since his childhood, he had cherished the dream of territorial and political unification of the Kingdom which was then fragmented into various small principalities. After struggling for more than two decades, he brought the whole of Kathmandu Valley under his control by 1769 A.D. and assumed the title of King of Nepal. After Prithvi Narayan's death in 1774, his plans were carried further by his brother Bahadur Shah while acting as Regent to the infant King, and by Prithvi Narayan's son, Ran Bahadur Shah. Regent Bahadur Shah extended Nepal's sway as far as Kumaon towards the west and up to Sikkim in the east. Flushed with success, Bahadur Shah moved towards the north during 1788-89, where he came in conflict with Tibet and ultimately with China in 1791-92. It will be seen in the subsequent pages that this encounter with China checked Nepal's expansion towards the north. Soon after this debacle, Bahadur Shah's political career also came to an end.

After the lapse of about a decade following Bahadur Shah's fall in 1795, Nepal had a strong Prime Minister in Bhim Sen Thapa who came to power in 1806. Under him, Nepal moved towards the south until stopped by the British in 1816. As a result of the Anglo-Nepalese war of 1814-16, Nepal's western, southern and eastern boundaries were more or less fixed and what followed afterwards were only minor adjustments.

FOREIGN POLICY OF THE SHAH RULERS (1742-1846)

Besides initiating the unification and consolidation of Nepal, King Prithvi Narayan Shah also laid down the basic tenets of its foreign policy. Highlighting the principal determinants of this policy he said :

> This Kingdom (Nepal) is like a tarul (a root vegetable) between two stones. Great friendship should be maintained with the Chinese emperor. Friendship should also be maintained with the Emperor of the southern seas (the British), but he is very clever. He has kept India suppressed. He is entrenching himself in the plains.... Do not engage in an offensive attack, fighting should be done on a defensive basis....If it is found difficult to resist in the fight, then even means of persuasion, tact, and deceit should be employed.[2]

Thus Nepal, fully aware of its weakness, was apprehensive of the growing British power in India. The apprehensions were evident in Prithvi Narayan's reluctance to revive trade relations between India and Nepal.[3] He looked down upon the western way of life as a social and religious perversion. He expelled Christian missionaries who had enjoyed the patronage of his predecessors in Kathmandu. He and his successors were averse to the idea of having a British Resident in Kathmandu. Whenever they had to have one as in 1802, he was kept under strict watch and his movements were severely restricted.[4]

Nepal, Tibet and China : 1788-92

Nepal's economic interests in Tibet brought it into conflict with China. During Prithvi Narayan's reign, some difficulties had arisen in the extensive and long standing trade and economic relations between Nepal and Tibet. The difficulties related to the currency and the condition of the Nepali traders.[5] Besides these difficulties, the wealth of the Tibetan monasteries offered an incentive to go to war, and the militant and expansionist mood of the Gurkhas acted as a stimulant for Nepal to launch an attack on Tibet. The war was started in 1789.

Tibet was defeated, and a treaty signed between the two states on 2 June 1789. Under its provisions, besides accepting Nepalese conditions regarding the currency problem, Tibet agreed to pay Nepal Rs. 50,000 in annual tribute and to allow Nepal to maintain its representative in Lhasa.[6] However, except in the year following the conculusion of the Treaty, Tibet did not honour these commitments.

Nepal, feeling deceived, renewed hostilities. Tibet appealed to the Chinese Emperor for help. Encouraged by its suzerain obligations and rights, and religious, economic and social interests in Tibet, China intervened and forced Nepal to yield. Nepal vainly requested help from the British. Under Chinese good offices, Nepal and Tibet signed a Treaty in late 1792. Under the Treaty, Nepal like Tibet accepted Chinese suzerainty and agreed to send a tributary mission to China at 5 years' intervals. The Treaty did not, however, disturb Nepal's favourable position in Tibet and its disputes with the latter were settled to its satisfaction.[7]

The suzerainty clause between Nepal and China remained an agreement on paper only and never became operative. Nepal waged wars and signed peace without referring to China. This situation was largely due to the distance between the two countries and the growing power of the British in India. Tributary missions that went from Nepal to China were more in the nature of embassies from one court to another, than tributes from a subordinate to a master. The pattern of Nepal's relations with China on the one hand and with Tibet on the other, established by the Treaty of 1792, continued unchanged for a long time.

Anglo-Nepalese War and Treaty of Segoitli

In 1792, China could warn Nepal against any encroachment towards the north, but was unable to restrain the Kingdom's martial spirit. Nepal expanded towards the south and in 1814, came into conflict with British power there. The British had their own feud with the Gurkhas, whose obstinacy had put their commercial schemes for the Himalayan States in jeopardy. Besides, there was an acute problem of criminals looting Indian border villages and finding a safe home in the Terai forests and hills of Nepal. The lack of co-operation of the Government of Nepal made it difficult for the British to solve this problem. Thus war was considered the only course of action left, and the Gurkha encroachments gave another excuse to the Brish to embark upon it. Besides resisting the British with its own strength, Nepal sought China's help and approached the Indian princely States in order to forge an anti-British front, but in vain. After initial difficulties the British defeated Nepal and forced the signing of a Treaty in March 1816 at Segouli.

Peace at Segouli proved a costly bargain for Nepal. Its possessions in Sikkim, Kumaon and Garhwal and portions of territory in eastern and western Terai were lost. It was compelled to give up its resistance to the posting of a British Resident in Kathmandu and promised to seek British permission before employing any European.[8] Experiences of the war had far-reaching implications for the future course of Nepal's foreign policy. The Kingdom realised that the British were becoming stronger and more firmly entrenched in India and the prospects of an anti-British front with the Indian princely States were bleak. Even China would not have liked to anta-gonise the British and, therefore, there was no possibility of using China against the British. In fact the Treaty of Segouli laid down the basis of future pattern of Anglo-Nepalese relations.

Anglo-Nepalese Relations after the Segouli Treaty

Notwithstanding its terms and provisions, the Segouli Treaty succeeded only in forcing Nepal to be at peace with the British. It could not make the Kingdom friendly and co-operative. Nepal received a British Resident in Kathmandu, but its powerful and shrewd Prime Minister Bhim Sen Thapa kept intercourse with the British confined to "rigidly defined and closely guarded limits". Commercial and other matters were also not promoted. Further, Nepal did not completely give up its efforts to forge anti-British alliances with the Indian States, China, Burma, and Afghanistan.[9] It persisted in these efforts until the rise of Jung Bahadur in 1846. During the Anglo-Chinese conflict of 1839-42, Nepal sent diplomatic missions to Lhasa and Peking and offered its cooperation. Again when the Sikhs in India lost to the British in 1846, Nepal approached China. Interestingly enough, in all such communications, special reference was made to the acquisitive designs of the British.[10]

However, none of these attempts were successful in stemming Nepal's slow drift into the British sphere of influence. Bar-ring the year 1855-56, Nepal did not attempt to enter into any hostility, military or diplomatic, with China. The British remained its main concern.

China was not unaware of the growing British power in India, with which it also had commercial interests. China also understood that Nepal was ultimately destined to remain under British influence. China's direct interests, however, lay in Tibet and not in Nepal. This was clearly evident in China's hesitation to come to Nepal's aid during the Anglo-Nepalese wars of 1814-16. During the Opium War (1839-42) and in 1846, China's response to Nepalese overtures was discouraging. In 1846 China even counselled Nepal not to attempt any anti-British alliance but, rather, to maintain friendly relations with British India. Further, China refused to give credence to the Nepalese thesis that the British had designs on Tibet. Through this period China was occupied for most of the time with internal troubles and deliberately avoided conflict with foreign powers.

The Chinese and British reluctance to make Nepal an area of conflict between them was, therefore, in conformity with their respective interests. The Indian States were deterred from associating with Nepal's schemes by the fear of adverse British reaction. This severely limited Nepal's manoeuvrability in foreign policy.

FOREIGN POLICY OF THE RANAS (1846-1945)

A significant change both in domestic politics as well as in foreign policy followed the rise of Jung Bahadur Rana in 1846, as the most powerful Prime Minister the Kingdom had ever had. Jung Bahadur came to power from a humble position as the result of a ghastly act of *Kot Massacre,* on 14 September 1846, in which a large number of the nobility was massacred. He pushed the King into the background, brought all the sources of power under his firm control and established a family rule by making the Prime Ministership hereditary, from brother to brother.[11] Jung Bahadur ushered in a new era of friendship, understanding and cooperation with the British.

The principal determinant of Jung Bahadur's policy was his belief in the invincibility of the British in India. He adopted this policy almost out of helplessness. This was evident in his conversation with the then British Resident in Kathmandu, to whom he was reported to have said :

> We know, you (the British) are a stronger power. You are like a lion, we are like a cat, the cat will scratch if it is driven to a corner, but the lion would soon kill the cat. You can force us to change our policy, you can take our country if it pleases you to do so.[12]

There were personal reasons also behind Jung Bahadur's soft attitude towards the British. He had come to power from a very humble position and, therefore, British patronage could prove helpful in legitimizing his authority. Further, most of his opponents, who had fled to India during the *Kot Massacre* were suspected to be actively working against his regime. Their activities could be checked only with the cooperation and help of the British. Lastly British approval was necessary if he were to make good his ambition to acquire the throne of Nepal for himself. All these objectives underlined the need for Jung Bahadur to have extremely friendly relations with the British. Contrary to his predecessors' anti-British activities, Jung Bahadur, in order to prove his sincerity, offered military assistance to the British, whenever an opportunity arose. Such offers by him in 1848 and 1849 were politely declined but when a great military uprising broke out all over north India in 1857, the British accepted his help after initial hesitation. He himself led the troops and helped ensure the success of the operations against "the mutineers".

Jung Bahadur was the first Nepali Prime Minister to visit England which he did in 1850 even at the cost of violating the social taboo against crossing the sea. There he met Queen Victoria. During his tour of the country, he showed great interest in Britain's social, administrative and military organizations. He was so impressed that later, he made earnest efforts to reorganize Nepal on similar lines. In 1862, 1865 and 1874 he expressed his desire to revisit England. But no fresh visit materialized.

The British for their part, favourably responded to Jung Bahadur's friendly overtures. They observed strict non- interference in his domestic policies and extended all possible support to his dominant position in the Kingdom. In return for the services rendered in 1857, he was decorated with the title of 'The Grand Commander of the Order of Bath', and a part of Terai annexed during 1814-16, which now constitutes Nepalganj, was restored to Nepal. In 1856, when Jung Bahadur launched an attack on Tibet, the British permitted not only the transport of Nepalese troops through their territory but also the purchase of arms by Nepal through private sources in India; this in spite of their declared neutrality in the conflict.[13]

Nevertheless, there were reservations in Jung Bahadur's friendly disposition towards the British. He did not favour British interference in his domestic affairs. To ward off such interference, he minimised intercourse with the British Resident and kept him away from the Nepalese politics. He did not cooperate with the British proposals for scientific surveys of Nepal. He showed no interest in the commercial schemes of the British either. Similarly, his attitude towards the questions of boundary settlement and border crimes and extradition proved "non-cooperative and irritating if not unfriendly" to the British.[14]

A plausible explanation for Jung Bahadur's reservations towards the British can be sought in the British attitude towards his political ambitions. Though the British extended all possible support and cooperation to Jung Bahadur's *de facto* supreme authority in Nepal, they firmly and effectively opposed his bid for the throne. The opposition had distressed him considerably. He even desired to secure international recognition for Nepal as an independent State, ruled by his family. Prompted by this desire, he visited France during his trip to England. He had also been maintaining formal customary relations with China. Later he expressed his willingness to meet the Emperors of France and Austria, the Pasha of Egypt and the Czar of Russia in his own independent capacity, but British reluctance stood in the way.

Jung Bahadur's Successors

Jung Bahadur's foreign policy and attitude towards the British were continued even by his successors. The continued friendly intercourse between the two regimes slowly and gradually removed whatever reservations Nepal entertained during Jung Bahadur's period. Enhanced cooperation and mutual goodwill replaced them.

In 1885, the recruitment of Gurkhas for the British army was formally permitted by Bir Shamshere (1885-1901). The settlement of this issue had been pending since 1816. In 1904, Chandra Shamshere (1901-29) helped a British military mission sent to Tibet under Col. Younghusband.[15] Nepal was obliged under the Treaty signed in 1856 to help Tibet against the threat posed by this Mission, but Chandra Shamshere pressurized the Dalai Lama and the Tibetan Kazis to negotiate a settlement with the British, to the latter's advantage.[16] Like Jung Bahadur, he visited England in 1908 and also played host to George the V at a hunting excursion in 1910. During World War I (1914-18), the Gurkha troops fought on the British side and established a reputation for skill, strength and discipline.

Thus, Chandra Shamshere's contribution to pushing Nepal still deeper under British sway was substantial. In return, he was decorated with titles and honours. Nepal started receiving a yearly gift of one million rupees—which still continues—as a mark of gratitude for the services rendered by the Gurkhas in the British army. As a token of respect, the designation of the British representative in Nepal was changed from 'Resident' to the 'Envoy'. The British formally recognised Nepal as an independent and sovereign state under a Treaty of Peace and Friendship signed between the two countries in December 1923. The Treaty enabled Nepal to freely import goods and arms from and through India. The Treaty obliged the signatories to notify each other of any misunderstanding with neighbouring states which was likely to affect their mutual relations. Both parties undertook not to use their territories for purposes contrary to the interests of the other.[17]

Formal recognition of Nepal's independence was further enhanced during Judha Shamshere's reign (1931-45), when in 1934, a British Minister with full diplomatic status was appointed at the Nepalese Court in place of the British envoy. Nepal on its side, established a legation in England and a Consul General in Delhi during the same period. Gurkha troops again fought for Britain and its allies in the Second World War.

However, Judha Shamshere was the last Rana Prime Minister of Nepal whose hegemony remained unchallenged in the domestic sphere. With his fall in 1945, a change in the pattern of Nepal's external relations was in sight.

Nepal, Tibet and China under the Ranas

When Jung Bahadur assumed office, Nepal's relations with China and Tibet had been guided by the Treaty of 1792. The most notable event during Jung Bahadur's time affecting these relations was Nepal's military expedition into Tibet in 1855-56.

Jung Bahadur was quite unhappy about the difficulties faced by the Nepali traders in Lhasa. The displeasure was further enhanced by the harassment the Tibetans meted out to the Nepalese mission carrying five-yearly tribute to China. At home, Jung Bahadur then faced stiff opposition to his pro-British policies and he was aware of the fact that war had often proved to be an effective measure to calm internal opponents. These factors prompted Jung Bahadur to settle his account with Tibet. His resolve was strengthened by the fact that Chinese imperial authority had gone into considerable decline and that at the time, China was engaged in the Taiping rebellion. The British, on the other hand, as noted above, were not averse to the idea of Nepal's influence in Tibet

The Nepali troops moved into Tibet in March 1855. In spite of the difficulties of food supply and reinforcement, they inflicted heavy casualties on the Tibetans. Ultimately, Tibet sued for peace and after protracted negotiations, a Treaty was signed between Nepal and Tibet on 24 March 1856. Under the Treaty, Tibet agreed to pay Rs. 10,000 annually to Nepal who in turn accepted the obligation to come to Tibet's help in case of any foreign attack. Trade matters were settled to the satisfaction of the Nepalese. Finally, both Nepal and Tibet agreed to respect China as before.[18]

The pattern of these relations continued for some years. Tibet paid its tribute until as late as 1953. Nepal maintained friendly relations with China and continued to send "periodic missions" to the Chinese Court which in turn continued to confer titles and honours upon the Kings and the Prime Ministers of Nepal. China was, however, unable to exercise any influence over the Kingdom, mainly because the British would not permit it and China was neither capable nor willing to force the issue. Explaining the British attitude in this regard, Durand, the British Governor-General, observed in 1888 :

> If the Chinese really attempt to establish their influence in Nepal, we must object and receive our relations with that State (which is) not, I think a very difficult matter with Jung Bahadur's descendants under our protection.[19]
> With the British grip tightening on Nepal, China's significance greatly declined. "Tributary" Mission from Nepal last visited China in 1908. A nationalist Government replaced imperial rule in China in 1912, and apparently neither party bothered about the tributes since then.

With the discontinuance of this practice, whatever direct and formal contact Nepal had with China also ceased. In May 1930, a Chinese friendship mission visited Kathmandu but failed to make any notable improvement in their mutual relations.[20] Nevertheless, the conferring of Chinese titles and decorations always gave pleasure to a Rana Prime Minister ; it meant recognition to his authority from China without much to be given in return.

FOREIGN POLICY AND DOMESTIC POLITICS (1945-50)

The end of Judha Shamshere's rule in November 1945, marked

the beginning of the Rana's fall. After him Nepal had only two more Rana Prime Ministers, Padma Shumshere (1945-48) and Mohan Shumshere (1948-51). Their foreign policies, though still motivated by the desire to cling to power, differed from their predecessor's policies. Political developments in the surrounding region, as well as within the Kingdom itself, accounted for the change.

Development in the Neighbouring Countries : India and China

British rule in India had been a decisive factor in enabling the Ranas to retain power. The withdrawal of the British in 1947, thus, made them very uncomfortable. The feeling was exacerbated more by the Government of independent India which wanted the Ranas to accommodate the forces generated by the distinct, albeit slow, political awakening in Nepal, and the resurgence in Asia. Referring to it, Nehru said in the Lok Sabha on 6 December 1950 :

> Three years ago we assured Nepal of our desire that she should be a strong, independent and progressive country.... We pointed out in as friendly a way as possible that the world was changing rapidly, if Nepal did not make an effort to keep pace with it circumstances were bound to force her to do so.

The Government of India's concern over Nepal was increased by the Communist revolution in China in 1949 and the assertion of Chinese authority in Tibet in 1951. In view of these developments Nehru defined India's interests in the following words :

> Our interest in the internal conditions of Nepal has become still more acute and personal because of the developments across our borders, to be frank specially those in China and Tibet. Besides our sympathetic interests in Nepal we were also interested in the security of our own country. From time immemorial the Himalayas have provided us with a magnificent frontier. Of course they are no longer as impassable as they used to be, but are still fairly effective. We cannot allow that barrier to be penetrated because it is also the principal barrier to India. Therefore, much as we appreciate the independence of Nepal, we cannot allow anything to go wrong in Nepal or permit that barrier to be crossed or weakened because that would also be a risk

to our security. (Speech of 6 December 1950)

In the changed context, India wanted a Government in Nepal which was "progressive" in character and was responsive to India's security interests. The existing Government—the Rana oligarchy, was deemed unfit for it. The Ranas, though ready to accommodate the Indian Government's views concerning the security of the sub-continent, were opposed to the idea of reorganizing Nepal's internal political structure in order to make it more representative and broad-based.

The Movement for Democracy in Nepal

Simultaneously with the developments in India and China there was a movement for political liberalization in Nepal. It took an organised form under the name of Praja Parishad in 1935-26 but was crushed by the repressive measures taken by the Ranas in October 1940.[21] The threads of the movement were again picked up in January 1947, when some Nepali young men, residing in India, held a conference at Calcutta and formed the Nepali National Congress (NNC). From this period on, the democratic movement in Nepal received all the blessings and support of Indian leaders, particularly socialists like Acharya Narendra Dev, Jaya Prakash Narayan and Ram Manohar Lohia. The NNC also received moral support and the sympathies of the educated young men in Nepal.

As its first step against the administration, the NNC organised a general strike in Biratnagar Jute Mill in March 1947. Many of its leaders, including President B.P. Koirala, were imprisoned. The strike was followed by a countrywide *Satyagraha*—peaceful disobedience movement in the Gandhian style. The *Satyagraha* had widespread effects and it forced the Government to yield. As a result, Prime Minister Padma Shumshere formed a Reform Committee to suggest administrative changes. He proposed elections for Panchyat and Municipal bodies, and the establishment of an independent judicial system.[22] These reforms were announced in January 1948, but Prime Minister Padma Shumshere was soon forced to resign through internal pressure from the Ranas themselves against his liberal approach.

He was succeeded by the tough minded Mohan Shumshere on 26 May 1948. Earlier, acting in the name of Padma Shumshere, he had declared the NNC illegal.[23] He undertook repressive measures against anti-Rana activities and showed no inclination to implement the reforms initiated by his predecessor. In protest against his action, the NNC decided to launch another countrywide non-violent movement from 1 June 1949. Meanwhile B.P. Koirala, who had been held in custody by the Ranas since December 1948 had begun a fast unto death on I May 1949, protesting against the ill-treatment of political prisoners. His fast continued for 21 days and forced Mohan Shumshere not only to release him but also to assure him that the reforms would be introduced soon.[24] In the light of this assurance the NNC called off its proposed June movement.

During the course of these events, two new parties had been established. One was the Nepali Democratic Congress (NDC) which was established in August 1948 by a few lower ranking (C Class) Ranas and others.[25] Another was the Communist Party of Nepal (CPN) which was founded at Colkata in September 1949 with the blessing of the Indian Communists. With the objective of strengthening the popular movement, the NNC and NDC merged in April 1950 to give birth to the Nepali Congress (NC). D.R. Regmi's faction of the NNC—Regmi defected from the main organisation towards the end of 1947 and called his group as the real NNC—and the CPN, however, preferred to remain separate.

Prime Minister Mohan Shumshere did not fulfil his assurances given to B.P. Koirala about political reforms. In view of his continued indifference, the NC decided to intensify its struggle against the Rana regime. Towards that end, it resolved in late September 1950 at Bairagnia (India) to under-take armed action, having been convinced that non-violent methods would not work.

Ranas' Foreign Policy (1947-50)

The foreign policy of the Ranas underwent a revision in response to the developments at home and around. The new course adopted had two dimensions : First, to seek international recognition of their authority through extension of diplomatic contacts. And secondly, to keep the Government of India in good humour. Explaining this two-dimensional policy of survival, Mohan Shumshere in his first major policy statement said :

> Our relations with India, a big country which has emerged through independence, should be neighbourly and as between two sisters. Such a pure and friendly relationship had existed, and it will always be our effort to strengthen

> it and make it more happy....
>
> In the present times, it is neither wise nor possible for any country to remain completely detached from the worldwide developments. Therefore, we have also adopted the policy of searching friends and establishing diplomatic contacts with various countries.[26]

Earlier in April 1947, while participating in the first Asian Relations Conference, the Nepalese delegate, General Bijoy Shumshere hoped for the strengthening of the "indissolute Indo-Nepalese ties" and added :

> Our presence here will, I hope, lead to a strengthening of our good relations with old friends and to the establishment of goodwill and contacts with the other countries (to) whom we extend the hand of friendship.

Extension of Diplomatic Relations

Taking advantage of the contacts established during the Second World War, Nepal exchanged a goodwill mission with the United States of America in 1946. Both countries signed an Agreement of Friendship and Commerce at Kathmandu on 25 April 1947. It provided for the establishment of diplomatic and consular relations at a later date and mutually accorded "most favoured nation treatment" in trade and commercial matters.[27] Exchange of ambassadors between the two countries was formally announced in early February 1948.

In forging and consolidating their ties with the United States, the Ranas had been well aware of the former's position as the most powerful and advanced nation of the world.[28] The United States on its part welcomed Nepal's cooperation in its global schemes "to defend freedom and peace,"[29] which, if understood in the context of the US cold-war strategy and the "Marshal Plan", meant containment of Communism. Though the Ranas did not appear to be hostile to American overtures, there is no conclusive evidence of any outcome in this context.[30]

After the United States, Nepal established diplomatic relations with France in May 1949. The same year, the Brazilian Minister and the Australian High Commissioner in India visited Nepal and extended the good wishes of their respective governments to the Rana Prime Minister. Nearer home, Nepal sent a representative to attend sri lanka's independence celebrations in

February 1948. A consulate was opened in My anura in 1949, with the objective of looking after the interests of Nepali settlers there.

In the north, Nepal, of course, had long-standing relations with China and Tibet. In December 1946 a Chinese goodwill mission was received in Kathmandu. It was reciprocated in April of the next year, when the possibilities of reviving diplomatic relations were discussed.[31] Nothing materialized, however, as the communist revolution was still on in China. Nevertheless, on all occasions and in all formal utterings, China and Tibet were referred to as Nepal's good friendly neighbours.

Nepal also had long-standing relations with Britain and these relations helped to diversify its contacts with the western countries.[32] However, owing to British withdrawal from the Indian sub-continent, some adjustments were needed between Nepal and Britain. Accordingly, diplomatic relations were formally renewed in 1947 and a new Treaty for the continuation of Gurkha recruitment to the British army was signed in November 1947. Commercial and other relations were also renewed under the Treaty of Perpetual Peace and Friendship signed in Kathmandu on 30 October 1950.

Besides these bilateral relations, Nepal participated in various international conferences and organizations. It sent observers to the Asian Relations Conference held in New Delhi in March-April 1947, to the ECAFE meeting held in Lapstone (Australia) in 1948-49, and to the Asian Conference on Indonesia held in New Delhi in 1949. In February 1949, Nepal applied for membership of the United Nations and pleaded its case strongly. By this time, it had also acquired membership in some of the UN bodies like IFO, ILO and WHO.

Relations with India

The Ranas knew well that because of Nepal's geographical juxtaposition, socio-cultural affinity, economic dependence and similar historical experiences, it was bound to be considerably influenced by its gigantic neighbour, India.[33] The goodwill of the Government of India was necessary for the Ranas to continue in power. Therefore, during 1947-50 Nepal's relations with India constituted the most vital aspect of the Rana diplomacy and efforts for survival in power against the mounting domestic opposition.

With the approach of independence, Nepal decided to exchange ambassadors with India. Under a tripartite Treaty in November 1947, including the British, Nepal allowed India and Britain to recruit Gurkhas for their respective armies. The practice of recruitment had been started by the British long back.[34] Under the new Agreement, the Gurkhas could be used by India in any situation excepting against the "Hindus", "unarmed mob" and "the Gurkhas". It was further agreed that in order to keep the morale of the Gurkha recruits and the Indian armed forces unimpaired, all activities prejudicial to the interests and security of one party should be prevented in the territory of the other. In return for the recruiting facilities, the Government of India undertook to meet Nepal's military needs regarding defence production, army transport planes, civil supplies and training facilities.

The Gurkha troops fought against Pakistan during the Kashmir crisis in 1947-48. A year later, more Nepalese troops were sent under the command af Prime Minister Mohan Shumshere's son to help the new Government of India stem its internal difficulties, particularly in Hyderabad. Such help was assured for future also and the Rana Government often mentioned it to underline its sincerity towards the Government of India.

In July 1950, Nepal signed two treaties with India : a Treaty of Peace and Friendship and a Treaty of Trade and Commerce. Under the former, the two governments in addition to respecting each other's sovereignty and independence also agreed to consult mutually on matters relating to national security. The second Treaty provided for India's direction and guidance in matters of trade and commerce between the two countries. (The details of this Treaty will be discussed later).

The Treaty of Peace and Friendship was based on a similar Treaty signed in 1923. Both the Treaties underlined that "there shall be ever lasting peace and friendship" between the two countries which "acknowledge and respect the complete sovereignty, territorial integrity and independence of each other (Art. I).[35] Another important clause of the 1923 Treaty (Art. 3) which was carried on in the 1950 Treaty (Art. 2), related to the undertaking that each party will inform the other of any "friction or misunderstanding" with other states likely to damage their (India and Nepal) friendly relations. In the new Treaty, however, the scope of the "other states" was limited to the neighbouring countries alone *i.e.*, China and Tibet. The same clause in the

1923 Treaty included a sentence : "...and each to exert its good offices, as far as may be possible, to remove such friction and misunderstanding", which was deleted in the 1950 Treaty. Probably, this sentence was intended to serve the economic and political interests of the British empire, particularly in the trans-Himalayan region. Hence it was considered redundant by the Government of independent India.

In some aspects the 1950 Treaty was a step ahead of the 1923 Treaty. Under the letters exchanged along with the Treaty, Nepal and India agreed, not to :

(i) tolerate any threat to the security of the other by a foreign aggressor. To deal with any such threat the two Governments shall consult with each other and devise effective counter-measures (Paragraph 1, Letters) ;

(ii) ...employ any foreigners whose activities may be prejudicial to the security of the other. Either Government may make representation to the other in this behalf, as and when occasion requires (Paragraph 5, Letters).

Besides, Nepal could also import "material and equipment" necessary for its security through the Indian territory, subject to India's approval (Paragraph 2, Letters). The 1950 Treaty secured "national treatment" for the citizens of one country rseiding in the territory of the other, in matters of residence, property, profession, movement etc. (Articles 6 and 7). It also provided that the Indian Government and people will be treated at par with their Nepalese counterparts and preferentially against foreigners in the field of economic and industrial ventures in Nepal (Paragraph 4, Letters).

Thus under the two Treaties, the Ranas fully accommodated India's security and commercial interests. Prime Minister Mohan Shumshere, however, remained reluctant to concede the persistent demand by Indian leaders for the liberalization of the political and administrative structure of Nepal.[36] It was because of this reluctance that in spite of the well-planned and efficiently executed foreign policy, he could not secure India's sympathy for the Ranas in the anti-Rana struggle which broke out in November 1950.

"Revolution" and the "Delhi Settlement"

(NOVEMBER 1950—FEBRUARY 1951)

After the Bairagnia Conference of September 1950, vigorous

preparations were made by the Nepali Congress to launch an armed revolt against the Ranas. The whole scheme was called into action when on 6 November 1950, King Tribhuwan and the Royal family—save Crown Prince Mahendra's son, Prince Gyanendra—left the palace under the pretext of a hunting excursion and took asylum in the Indian Embassy in Kathmandu. A reference to King Tribhuwan's association with the anti-Rana movement is relevant in this context.

King Tribhuwan's sympathies and tacit support of the anti-Rana uprising date back to the Praja Parishad days of 1935-40.[34] In 1947, during a stay in Kolkata for medical treatment, he established contact with the newly formed of NNC.[38] Since then he continued to take a keen interest in the activities of the NNC and later of the Nepali Congress. As a result, in September 1950, he was charged by the Ranas, albeit indirectly, with having associated himself with an un-successful Nepali Congress 'plot' to kill Mohan Shumshere and several other Ranas.[39] Meanwhile, he had acquainted him-self with the world outside and new political currents through the medium of books and personal association which were managed secretly, in spite of the strict surveillance placed upon him by the Ranas. He also had several meetings in disguise, with two Indian Ambassadors to Nepal, Surjit Singh Majithia and later with Sir C.P.N. Singh.[40] Thus, prompted by a desire to emancipate himself and restore the power and prestige of the King lost to the Ranas by his ancestors, and impelled by the ideas of freedom and democracy imbibed through books, King Tribhuwan was keen to seek an end to the Rana rule in Nepal.

The Royal family's flight infuriated the Ranas. Having failed to secure the King's return from the Indian Embassy, Monan Shumshere summoned the *Bhardari Sabha* (Council of Nobles) on 7 November, dethroned King Tribhuwan and crowned Prince Gyanendra as King of Nepal. The Government of India was undeterred by this change and in the face of Rana opposition, King Tribhuwan was flown by the Indian Ambassador to New Delhi on 11 November where the King and his entourage were received with all the honours due to the head of a sovereign state.

The Nepali Congress was jubilant over the King's act. Almost simultaneously with his arrival in New Delhi, the party began action against the Rana regime, and launched attacks on the Terai of Birganj, Biratnagar, Amlekganj, Bhairawa, and others, from the bases in India. Kathmandu, the capital was the scene of processions and demonstrations loudly "condemning the Rana regime. But soon the agility and energy, with which the offensive was launched, seemed to be losing momentum. The 'revolutionaries' lacked an efficient and well-trained organisation, adequate resources and a unified command as compared to their adversaries, the Rana troops.[41] Nevertheless, the action was important for it brought home to the Ranas the realization that it was no longer possible to bypass the popular aspiration and the forces supporting them.

The Ranas tried to meet the NC action by force of arms and the King's action by opening a diplomatic front. They sought recognition of Gyanendra as King of Nepal, from India, the United States and the United Kingdom. India flatly refused to oblige the Ranas.[42] The United Kingdom, followed by the United States, adopted a "wait and watch" attitude. A British diplomatic mission visited Kathmandu on 3 December 1950 to make an on-the-spot study of the situation. The mission met a hostile mob at the airport, raising slogans in favour of King Tribhuwan.[43] This was hardly a convincing demonstration of the firm control over the situation as claimed by the Ranas. Besides, the British were not in a position to extend recognition against the wishes of the Government of India. This is evident from what R.K. Shah, a former Foreign Minister in post-Rana Nepal, has written:

> The Rana who was an ambassador to Great Britain at the time, told the author that Bevin, the British Foreign Secretary had agreed to recognise the new King and was ready to announce the recognition in Parliament, but the dispatch of a negotiating team by Mohan Shumshere to Delhi after a war of nerves with the Nehru Government, gave the Indian Government a handle to press Great Britain to postpone its act of recognition pending the outcome of negotiations.[44]

The delay in extending recognition by the British proved fatal to the dying spirit of the Ranas, for they depended heavily upon the guidance and advice of the former.[45] Left with no other alternative, they started negotiations with King Tribhuwan under the supervision and mediation of the Government of India.

The first round of the negotiations began in New Delhi on 27 November 1950 and continued for about a fortnight. At the end of it, the host Government presented on 8 December, a memorandum to the Nepalese Government. The terms of the compromise listed in the memorandum stated that the Govern-ment of Nepal should,

(a) convene, at the earliest opportunity, an elected constituent assembly to draw up a constitution for Nepal;
(b) provide some popular representation in the Govern-ment pending the drafting and implementation of a constitution; and
(c) accept Tribhuwan as King of Nepal.[46]

The Ranas considered various aspects and implications of the memorandum. After due deliberations at home, some proposals for constitutional reform were announced on 24 December 1950. But the Ranas' refusal to accept the third proposal led to an-other round of negotiations on 25 December 1950, again in New Delhi. This round concluded on 1 January 1951 in a settle-ment between the negotiating parties. Under this settlement which was called as the "Delhi Settlement", the Ranas agreed to amend their initial proposals for constitutional reforms, accord-ing to the "friendly suggestions" of the Government of India. A week later, Mohan Shumshere announced measures to "set the people on the road of orderly progress towards the goal of a free and independent democracy".[47] These measures, besides proposing an elected Constituent Assembly and popular repre-sentation in the Cabinet, included :

(a) Amnesty to political prisoners and insurrectionists after they had laid down their arms,
(b) A stipulation that there be no restrictions on the formation and functioning of political parties within the provisions of law, and
(c) The continuation of Tribhuwan as King of Nepal and provision for his appointing a Regent during his absence.

It is clear from the declaration that Mohan Shumshere had succumbed to the Indian pressure and agreed to whatever the Government of India had proposed. Explaining the factors that led him to do so, Mohan Shumshere said :

> ...no friendly country having diplomatic relations with us has recognised the new King...mischief-mongers have used the name of the King in the preparation, disturbances, looting, arson, indignity over women, culminating in the taking of many innocent lives, and...according to the friendly suggestions made during discussions by the Government of India.[48]

In accordance with the "Delhi Settlement", King Tribhuwan formed a Cabinet responsible to him on 18 February 1951. The

Cabinet included Mohan Shumshere and B.P. Koirala, as well as other representatives of the Ranas and the Nepali Congress in equal numbers. Thus "the revolution" ended in a compromise and the disturbed situation seemed to be-gradually settled.

Government of India and the 'Revolution"

It has been noted that India wanted a Nepal responsive to India's security needs. This it thought, could be in part achieved if Nepal become a "strong, progressive and stable", political unit. In accordance with this objective, the Government of India advocated a compromise between the Ranas and the 'revolutionaries'. Defining this policy Nehru said :

> We have tried to find a way, a middle way, if you like which will ensure the progress of Nepal and the introduction of some advance in the ways of democracy in Nepal. We have searched for a way which would at the same time avoid the total uprooting of the ancient order.[49]

The rationale of the "middle-way" can best be understood by studying the alternatives to such a policy. When the 'revolution' broke out, the Government of India could either have remained aloof or have aligned itself completely with either of the two contending parties. The first course was not advisable in view of India's vital security interests in Nepal. It was also impracticable looking at the geographical, cultural and social proximity between the two countries.

As for the second alternative, there were many difficulties inherent in supporting either party wholeheartedly. Alignment with the Ranas was incompatible with the ideological attitudes of the leaders of the Indian Government. They stood for freedom and democracy "in the abstract as well as in the guise of a practical, and, in the context of Asia, a necessary step".[50] The Rana rule being a negation of this, many of them advocated use of force in its overthrow. Sardar Patel, for example, urged that Indian forces be sent to Nepal to end the inhuman and cruel rule.[51] Such views were present even outside the government and the ruling party, Congress. Most vocal and active in this respect were the Indian Socialists who warned the Indian Government to make no attempt,

> to abort this ever widening and unbeatable revolt of the Nepali people against their usurpers. Ranas of Kathmandu

> are a weak tyranny, for they are not only usurpers but are also unable" to exercise effective governmental or military power. Unsupported by India, their end is beyond doubt.[52]

The Government of India also believed that since the situation had been disturbed, "a return to the old order will not bring peace and stability in Nepal".[53]

On the other hand, an all-out support of the 'revolution' would have been contrary to the objective of maintaining peace and stability in Nepal. Such support would certainly have caused an abrupt and total breakdown of the century-old administrative machinery of the Kingdom. This was bound to result in chaos and confusion, creating a situation vulnerable to the forces harmful to the interests of both India and Nepal.

The Government of the Ranas being a constitutional and legal government, an open participation of the Government of India in its overthrow would have made the latter guilty of gross violation of international law and practice. Since India professed itself a champion of these standards, any act in their defiance could also damage its international prestige. A tirade against India in this context, had already been launched in the western press.[54] The Government of India's active support to the Nepali Congress might have made the Ranas desperate and pushed them closer to the United Kingdom and the United States, enhancing Western influence in Nepal. Nehru expressed a strong disapproval of this influence saying :

> Frankly, we do not like and shall not brook any foreign interference in Nepal. We recognize Nepal as an independent country and wish her well, but even a child knows that one cannot go to Nepal without passing through India. Therefore, no other country can have as intimate a relationship with Nepal as ours is. We would like every other country to appreciate the intimate geographical and cultural relationship that exists between India and Nepal.[55]

The Indian leaders further knew that the Nepali Congress movement lacked ideological coherence, a sound economic programme, adequate political schooling and unity of purpose. In these circumstances it would have been unwise to give all support to this body through complete alignment.

Thus the 'revolution' created a very complicated situation

for the Government of India. Indian objectives *vis-a-vis* Nepal were ambivalent. The Government of India wanted democratic processes to be initiated in Nepal, but could not permit an uprooting of the existing order. India claimed "keen and personal" interests in Nepal's internal conditions but a sense of international morality inhibited it from pursuing this interest. Ideological fervour prompted professions of points of view that in the face of hard realities had of necessity to be toned down.

An adequate answer to these conflicting demands was sought through the policy of "middle-way". The central theme of this policy was that there should be peaceful and gradual democratization by evolving a workable compromise between the Ranas and the popular forces. The execution of this policy aimed at pressurizing the Ranas as well as the 'revolunaries', and limiting their respective spheres of activity, so as to allow accommodation of each other.

In this process, the King acquired an important place. The King had enjoyed a very significant and time-honoured position in Nepalese society, but his prestige and power had suffered a great deal under the Ranas. India considered any help to augment the King's efforts to regain his lost prestige and power from the Ranas as worthwhile. Besides weakening the Ranas, who had shown an uncompromising love of power, it could ensure in the King a powerful ally for the Government of India. Further, King Tribhuwan was by no means a traditional monarch. He was favourably disposed towards modern ideas of freedom, progress and equality. He himself was, therefore, a compromise between change and the *status quo.* The Ranas had not disowned the institution of monarchy and the 'revolutionaries' were only too willing to have King Tribhuwan on their side. In the light of these factors, the Government of India extended its support to the King. Here it should be recalled that the Government of India had arranged King Tribhuwan's escape, refused to recognise his dethronement and made it difficult even for the United Kingdom and the United States to do so. How important these acts proved in the ultimate resolution of the crisis was evident in Mohan Shumshere's January declaration (n. 47).

The Government of India's attitude towards the 'revolution' constituted the other dimension of the execution of the "middle-way" policy. Its moral support to the popular cause was unqualified and unequivocal. But in material terms, the support was lukewarm. Making clear the Government's thinking on this question, the then Education Minister of India, Maulana Abul

Kalam Azad stated soon after King Tribhuwan's escape to the Indian Embassy :

> Although we cannot interfere in the internal affairs of Nepal, we have to take cognizance of any discontent that arises there. Nepal is India's neighbour and any crisis there may endanger India's freedom. It is imperative, therefore, that the present Nepalese crisis should be resolved peacefully and without resort to arms.

He further added :

> It is amazing that in the middle of the 20th century naked aristocracy should reign supreme in any part of the world. It is unthinkable and intolerable. There is not even one Indian who today does not sympathise with the cause of the Nepalese people.[56]

Accordingly, whereas the Indian Government hinted that tacit approval would be given to limited NC action against the Ranas, it refused to allow purchase of arms through official or open channels for that action.[57] The Nepali Congress established its bases of operation in Indian territory but the Government of India tried to impress upon the Ranas that they were not encouraging this action.[58] Similarly, the money collcted by the Nepali Congress from the Birganj Treasury, after its fall, was seized by the Government of India. B.P. Koirala, M.P. Koirala and Subrana Shumshere, who were carrying this money, were held up at Palam, at a time when the activities of the Nepali Congress were going on briskly. All these weighed heavily against the smooth and effective conduct of the NC operations. Besides this, on the diplomatic level, no NC representative was included in the negotiations leading to the "Delhi Settlement". This greatly weakened the role which the Nepali Congress could otherwise have played and the influence it could have exercised on the terms of the final settlement.

Though fraught with apparent contradictions, the "middle-way" policy achieved its immediate objectives. It enabled the Government of India to play a decisive role during the 'revolution'. As a result of this, all the concerned agreed upon a compromise, proposed under this policy. The influence thus exercised secured an important say for the Government of India in future also, because all the three, the Ranas, the King and the Nepali Congress, emerged as the main contenders for power in the Kingdom.

Notes

1. Naraharinath Yogi and Baburam Acharya (ed.), *Rastrapita Sri 5 Bada Maharaja Prilhvinarayan Shah Dev ko Divya Updesh* (Divine Counsel of father of the nation His Majesty King Prithvi Narayan Shah Dev), Kathmandu, 1953, 15-16.
2. The British sent a mission under James Logen in 1769 to persuade Prithvi Narayan to revive customary commercial relations between India and Nepal. The Mission was not received well in Kathmandu. See Logen's "Memorandum on Trans-Himalayan Trade of Bengal and Gurkha conquest of Nepal" quoted in N.L. Chatterjee, *Vereht's Rule in India,* Allahabad, 1939.

   In a letter to the Dalai Lama of Tibet Prithvi Narayan asked for his cooperation in forbidding the East India Company to have direct trade relations with Tibet. Percival Landon, *Nepal,* Vol. I, Lonaon, 1928, 67; also see *Divya Updesh,* n. 2, 18-19.
3. Landon, n. 3, 73.
4. Col. Kirkpatrick, *An Account of **the** Kingdom of Nepal,* London, 1822; also Landon, n. 3, Vol. II, Appendix XXI, 275-82.
5. Leo E. Rose, *The Role of Nepal and Tibet in Sino-Indian Relations,* (Unpublished thesis, University of California, 1960), 79 (Microfilm in ICWA Library, New Delhi).
6. Terms of the Treaty, General Pudma Jung Bahadur Rana (Ed. A.C. Mukerjee), *Life of Maharaja Sir Jung Bahadur of Nepal,* Allahabad, 1909, 7-8.
7. Text of the Treaty, in C. Y. Aitchison, *A Collection of Treaties, Engagements and Sunnuds relating to India and Neighbouring Countries,* Vol. XIV, Calcutta, 1929, 35-69 ; Narhari Nath Yogi (ed.), *It'has Prakash ma Sandhi Patra Sangrah* (Collection of Historical Treaties and Papers), Part I, Banaras, 1965.
8. Kanchanmoy Mojumdar, *Indo-Nepalese Relations 1837-77* (Unpublished Ph.D. Thesis, Indian School of International Studies),. New Delhi, 1962, 37, 50, 120-33 and 164.
9. Mang-Pao, *Si tsang-tsou-shu* (West Tibet Memorial Reports) Chuan, 3, Correspondence with the King of the Gurkhas. Referred in Rose n. 6, 294 ; *Ch'ou-Pour-I, Wu Shih-no* (Documents concerning management of foreign affairs), referred in *ibid.,* 310.
10. General Pudma Jung, n. 7, 63-77; also see, Landon, n. 3.
11. Resident to the Government, 6 July 1864. *Foreign Department Political Proceedings,* quoted in Mojumdar, n. 9, 396.
12. Apprehending Russian designs on Tibet, and being themselves engaged in the Crimean War, the British in fact favoured Nepal to assert itself in Tibet. Rose, n. 6, 330-31.

13. Mojumdar, n. 9, 358.
14. Younghusband's mission was sent in 1903. Its objectives were to counteract Russian designs on Tibet and also to extract political and commercial concessions from the latter. For details, see Sir Francis Younghusband, *India and Tibet,* London, 1910, Chapters X and XII.
15. Landon, n. 3, Vol. II, 109-110 ; Younghusband, n. 15, 135-36. As a result of the success of this Mission, the Chumbi Valley trade route between Tibet and India (British) was opened. This in the long run damaged Nepal's own economy and its position as a link between the two.
16. Text of the Treaty ; Narhari Nath Yogi (ed.), n. 8, Part I, 147-49. In an exchange of letters following the Treaty, the Prime Minister of Nepal had agreed to inform beforehand the British envoy at the Court of Nepal about the details of the goods imported through India.
17. Details in General Pudma Jung, n. 7, 172-91.
18. Quoted in Rose, n. 6, 419.
19. The mission was led by Pa Ue Sun, with Daniel J. Lee accompanying as the British Secretary. The latter had an interview with the then Prime Minister of Nepal and quoted him as saying "Tibet has blocked our way to China". Daniel J. Lee, "Nationalist China re-establishes relations with the Kingdom of Nepal", *The China Weekly Review,* Vol. 55, No. 427, December 1930, 148-49.
20. For details of the Praja Parishad Movement, see D. R. Regmi, *A Century of Family Autocracy in Nepal* (The Nepali National Congress, 1950), 235-55.
21. *Gorkhapaira, 4 Jaistha* 2004 (16 May 1947).
22. Even before resigning formally on 26 April 1948, Padma Shumshere retired to India in February 1948. Since then Mohan Shumshere had been acting as the Prime Minister in his name. The NNC was declared illegal on 18 April 1948. Sharma, n. 1, 391.
23. *Ibid.,* 399. Also, *Nepal Today,* 5th issue, July 1949.
24. Classification of the Ranas in A, B and C categories had been done by Chandra Shumshere. It established in descending order the position of various members of the Rana familv in the power hierarchy. C category being the lowest, its members were denied higher positions and hence were disgruntled. For the classification, see Landon, n. 3. The Rana leaders of the NDC were Subarna Shumshere and Mahabir Shumshere, both of whom had considerable property in India. The others included

Mahendra Bikrarn Shah and S. P. Upadhyaya.

25. Text of the speech, *GorkhapUra,* Vol. 48, 14 *Jaistha* 2005 (May 1948) (Sindure Jatra Special Number).

26. Text of the Agreement, *Treaties and Other International Acts Series, 1585,* Department of State, Publication 2858, Washington, 1947.

27. Text of the Nepalese Ambassador's speech while presenting his credentials to the American President, in *Gorkhapatra,* Vol. 47, No. 132, 18 *Falgun.* Also see *Nepal ra Amarica* (Nepal and America), *Gorkhapatra,* Vol. 46, 4 *Mara* 2003 (November 1946); "Nepal ko Parrastra Niti" (Foreign Policy of Nepal), *Gorkhapatra,* Vol. 57, No. 58, 9 *BhaJra* 2004 (August 1947).

28. President Truman's reply to the Nepalese Ambassador's speech on the occasion of the presentation of his credentials, in *Gorkhapatra,* Vol. 47, No. 132, 18 *Falgun* 2004 (February-March 1948).

29. *Gorkhapatra,* Vol. 49, No. 88, 9 *Magh* 2005 (December 1948) Editorial.

    Some reports published in Indian papers to the effect that Nepal had leased some land for 30 years to the United States for the purpose of establishing military bases against the Commu-nist countries, were strongly resented and sharply denied officially in Kathmandu, *Gorkhapatra,* Vol. 48, No. 32, 17 *Ashad* 2005 (June- July 1948).

30. *A. S. Bhasin (ed.),* Documents on Nepal's Relations with India and China, 1949-66, *New Delhi, 1970, 8.*

31. For a brief note on the triangular friendship among Nepal, Britain and the United States, see *Gorkhapatra,* Vol. 46, No. 56, 23 *Kartik* 2003 (November 1946).

32. Nepalese Ambassador to India, Maj. General Bijoy Shumshere in a press interview, *New York Times,* 18 Apiil 1950. This consciousness had been reflected in all the other formal or informal policy pronouncements of the Ranas. For example, see *Gorkhapatra,* Vol. 47, No. 27, 21 *Jaishta* 2004 (June 1947).

33. For details see Ashad Husain, *British India's Relations with the Kingdom of Nepal, 1857-1947,* Allen and Unwin, London, 1970, 234-54.

34. References to the Treaty of 1950 are based upon the Text of the Treaty and the letters exchanged along with it supplied in cyclo-styled form by the Indian Embassy, Kathmandu. See appendix V.

35. Mohan Sumshere had convened a Legislative Assembly on 22 September 1950 as a fake attempt to implement the reforms introduced by Padma Sumshere. But this attempt fell very short of the expectations of the Nepali Congress and the

Government of India. Anirudha Gupta, *Politics in Nepal,* Allied Publishers, Bombay, 1964, 41-42.

36. Tanka Prasad Acharya, the then President of the Praja Parishad disclosed to the author in an interview that in their activities they had the blessings and support of King Tribhuwan. Also Sharma, n. 1, 376 ; Regmi, n. 21, 249-50 ; Bhola Chatterjee, *A Study of Recent Nepalese Politics,* Calcutta, 1967, 31.

37. The contact was said to have been established through Subarna Shumshere, a 'C' Class Rana who accompanied the King in some official capacity. Sometime later he resigned from his services to the Ranas, became one of the founder member of the NDC and later a top-ranking leader of the Nepali Congress (n. 25) ; Chatterjee, n. 37, 38-39.

38. Sometime in August-September 1950, Ganeshman Singh and a few others, were entrusted by the Nepali Congress with a mission to subvert the Rana rule. It could not succceed and Ganeshman with his associates, were arrested and sentenced to death in the later half of September. King Tribhuwan refused to sign their death warrant in spite of the Rana intimidation. This convinced the Ranas of his association with the plot. *Ibid.,* 79-82, 96.

39. For a lively account of King Tribhuwan's clandestine anti-Rana activities, see L. Er ka, *The King in the Clouds,* London, 1958.

40. For further details of the activities of the revolutionaries, see Sharma, n. 1, 107-15; Ram Hari Joshi, *Nepal Ko November Kranti Sansmaran* (November Revolution of Nepal : Memoirs), Patna, 1952 ; K.P. Srivastava, *Nepal Ki Kahani* (The story of Nepal), Delhi, 1955, 148-63 ; Chatterjee, n. 37, 103-37 ; Fanishwar Nath Renu, *Nepal Ki Kranti, Dinman* (Hindi weekly), New Delhi, July-September 1971 ; Ganeshman Singh, "2007 Sal: EK Vihangam Dhristi" (Year 2007 *i.e.* 1950-51 A.D., An overview), *Tarun* (Nepali) Banaras, Bulletin No. 3 and 4, April and September 1971, respectively.

41. Even before a formal communication to that effect was sent by New Delhi, the Home and Deputy Prime Minister Sardar Patel said, "Where a change in the head of the State has been brought about by force it would be extremely difficult for India to recognise such a change." *The Hindu,* 11 November, 1950. Also see Sharma, n. 1, 416.

The decision was officially communicated to the Rana Government by the Government of India on 22 November 1950, *The Hindu,* 23 November 1950.

42. Sir Ester Denning, the British Ambassador at large in the East, and Frank Roberts, the British Deputy High Commissioner in

India constituted the mission. The demonstration against the mission was so hostile that the Government of Nepal had to use force to disperse it. Sharma, n. 1, 429.

43. R.K. Shah, *Nepal's Foreign Policy* (unpublished), 22.

44. A siege around the Indian Embassy to seek the surrender of King Tribhuwan, was said to have been advised by the British Minister to the Court of Nepal. *Ibid.*

45. Nehru in Parliament on 21 December 1950, *India, Parliamentary Debates,* Part II, Vol. VII, No. 8, 2138-42.

46. English Text of a Declaration by His Highness the Maharaja on *January 8, 1951* (Cyclostyled).

47. Ibid.

48. *India, Parliamentary Debates,* Part II (Lok Sabha), Vol. VIII, 6 December 1950, Cols. 1267-71.

49. *India, Parliamentary Debates,* Part II, Vol. Ill, No. 3, 17 March 1950, Cols. 1697-8.

50. Grishma Bahadur Devkola, *Nepal Ko Rajnitik Darpan* (Nepal's political mirror), Kathmandu, 1960, 37.

51. Ram Manohar Lohia, *Foreign Policy,* 1964, 231.

52. Nehru's speech in Lok Sabha, n. 49.

53. For example, see *The Manchester Guardian,* 24 November 1950 ; *The Economist,* Vol. CLX, No. 5602, 6 January 1951, 27.

54. Nehru's speech, n. 49. This statement was made in continuation of the reference to Nepal's relations with the Western countries. Further, this policy speech followed the visit of a British diplomatic mission to Nepal (n. 43). Nehru's warning was taken seri-ously by the United States and the United Kingdom.

55. *The Hindu,* 11 November 1950.

56. Chatterjee, n. 37, 60-61, 63-96.

57. Instructions were issued to the Governments of the States border-ing Nepal, to take suitable measures to prevent the use of Indian territory by the 'revolutionaries'. It was done in response to a complaint in this regard from the Government of Nepal. *The Statesman,* 13 and 14 November 1950.

2

MAJOR DETERMINANTS AND OBJECTIVES OF NEPAL'S FOREIGN POLICY

Like an individual's social behaviour, the international behaviour of a nation state is the interaction between its organism and the society around. The theoretical layout within which this interaction operates, constitutes the basic frame of the foreign policy of that country. This basic framework is motivated by the needs and aspirations of the state that are further conditioned in expression, by the domestic milieu and external setting. Thus, there are two sets of factors operating throughout the gestation, formulation and execution stages of foreign policy. The factors are the motivational and the structural, *i.e.* conditioning. The resulting outcome of inter-action between these two types of factors is expressed in terms of the policy objectives in general and decisions in particular. Within this framework, the determinants and objectives of the foreign policy of Nepal will be discussed below. For this purpose, the chapter is divided in four sections: motivations, conditioning factors, policy objectives and the operational frame of the policy.

MOTIVATIONS

There were three principal motives at play behind the evolution, content and execution of Nepal's foreign policy. Borrowing George Liska's expression, the motives may be termed "security, stability and status".[1]

The 'security' motive has two dimensions, the preservation

of independence in taking and implementing decisions, and the preservation of territorial integrity. The first dimension has a political connotation and its task can be described as one of counteracting external political pressures and influences. This may be represented as *Security* (*P*). The second dimension has a military and strategic connotation and its task is the defence against external aggression for the preservation of territorial integrity. This may be represented as *Security (T).*

Similarly, the 'stability' motive has two dimensions : first, stability of the domestic power structure in which every ruling group will have the highest stakes, and secondly, stability through economic development. These aspects may be represented as *Stability (P)* and *Stability* (E) respectively. Foreign policy has often been used as an important instrument to ensure and consolidate both the aspects of 'stability', especially in under-developed and unstable political systems.

The 'status' motive is psychological in nature. Nepal's long history of isolation, its somewhat dubious independence and sovereignty *vis-a-vis* the British Empire, its new entry into international politics after the Second World War, and its diffused identity with and excessive dependence upon India, all contributed to the emergence and growth of this motive.

As spelled out above, these three basic motives do not give a clear picture of the formulation of Nepalese foreign policy. Thus, some reference should be made to the basic needs of Nepal which find their expression in one form or an-other in its foreign policy. As motivations, these needs operate upon the structural factors and after permeating through them, getting restrained or accelerated or both—break into clearly defined policy objectives. Therefore, to understand them in proper perspective a study of the structural or the conditioning factors is called for.

CONDITIONING FACTORS

Conditioning factors of a foreign policy can be said to fall into two broad categories. In the first category can be included the constants, that is, the factors having a permanent and stable character like geography, history, and the general socio-cultural structure. In the second come the variables, that is, the factors which are comparatively recent in origin and which are continuously changing. Examples of such variables are the phenomenon of nationalism and the political system of the moment. By virtue of their rigidity, factors of the first category remain constant in their influence on foreign policy. Policy-makers have to accept them as such, given, whatever course of action they pursue. Factors of the second category are, however, susceptible to manipulation by policy-makers and so their influence on foreign policy will vary in character and content.

A. Constant Factors

Geographical determinism

Nepal's discomfiture resulting from its location, size and topography, has had an important bearing on its foreign policy. The Kingdom lies between Asia's two major powers and land-masses, India and China. Its northern border runs along the Tibet region of China, passing through the world's highest mountain ranges, the Himalayas. The mountainous border is perforated by narrow passes which, with the exception of the Kerong and Kutti passes, are higher than 17,000 ft., and impassable for the best part of the year. Thus the Himalayas forms a natural "zone of protection" which has shielded Nepal from, military invasion and socio-cultural and political influences coming to the Kingdom from the north. The technological revolution in methods of warfare, and new means of transport and communication may reduce the importance of the Himalayas as a natural barrier but their shielding effect will never be wholly displaced.

In the West, the South and the East, Nepal is respectively flanked by Uttar Pradesh, Bihar and Bengal and Sikkim(States of India). its south-east is separated from Bangla Desh (former East Pakistan) by a narrow strip of Indian territory in West Bengal. The border with India is not a natural one though long patches of thick forests lie between the two nations. The border runs through the inner periphery of the open and extensive Indo-Gangetic plain, and constitutes what can be called a "zone of exposure". This makes Nepal and India easily accessible to each other. As a result, the exchange of socio-cultural and political influences between the two countries has been greatly encouraged and facilitated. Nepal also has close access to the sea in the south.

The zones of "protection" and "exposure" that insulate Nepal in the north and the south respectively, have long played an important role in determining the form and content of the Kingdom's relations with its neighbours. Whereas intercourse with India has been varied and extensive, that with the northern neighbours, Tibet and China, it was comparatively restricted and formal in nature. Nepal's perception of its neighbours that has emerged out of this history dominates the foreign policy thinking in Kathmandu even today.

Size is a relative factor. Nepal is very small as compared with its immediate neighbours, India and China. It is even smaller than the adjacent Indian States of Bihar and the Uttar Pradesh in the south and the Tibet Region of China in the north. But it is similar in size to Bangla Desh. Bhutan is smaller than Nepal. Thus smaller than its immediate neighbours, Nepal is bigger than those which are not far off. The consciousness resulting from its size, is clearly evident in Nepal's relations not only with its neighbours but also with various other countries of the world.

Topographically Nepal can broadly be divided into three regions : (1) The Himalayas ; (2) the central hills and valleys; and (3) the Terai. The Terai extends along the length of the country in the south and varies from 16 to 20 miles in breadth. The other zones comprise hills varying from 2,000 ft. to 29,000 ft. in height. The height increases as we move north-wards. Except for the Terai, therefore, the country is mountainous. This has created a problem of transport and communication between the centre and other parts of the country as also between the parts themselves. Besides marring the efficiency and control of the central administration over the rest of the country the mountains have created problems of national integration. Further, they also hinder defence mobility but at the same time the difficult and hostile terrain in itself acts as a defensive measure against an invading army.

Historical background

We have dealt with the historical background of Nepal in the first chapter. Nonetheless, even at the risk of repetition, certain features of the background need to be recalled here, for they have made an imprint on the present day foreign relations of the Kingdom.

In the first place we noted Nepal's paternalistic attitude towards weak Tibet. This attitude, combined with the military adventurism of the rising Gorkhas, led Nepal to launch military campaigns against Tibet in the 1790's and again in 1856. On the first occasion, China intervened on Tibet's behalf and forced its own suzerainty over Nepal. Although Chinese suzerainty remained vague and nebulous in practice, Nepal never challenged it. Perhaps, an appearance of friendly ties with China was considered diplomatically useful for the Kingdom. Besides, Nepal was fearful of China having experienced China's military strength in 1792.

The fear was perpetuated as a result of Nepal's association with the British who often looked towards China with suspicion and apprehension and occasionally tried to use Nepal to further their trans-Himalayan policy. Nepal had military encounters with British India in 1814-16 and suffered heavy defeat. To avoid any possibility of further Anglo-Nepalese conflict the British not only diverted the war potential of Nepal in the form of Gorkha recruitment for their army, but also, endeavoured to encourage economic and cultural intercourse between the two Governments. The most favourable period for such inter-course began with the rise of the Ranas in 1846. It continued for more than a century during which all scars of the Anglo-Nepalese wars of 1814-16 and the mutual ill-will and suspicion existing before that were wiped off. It should, however, be kept in mind that fear of political interference from the South could never be eliminated completely from Nepal. A very important reason was that though the British scrupulously practised non-interference in the domestic affairs of the Kingdom, its rulers always lived under the possibility of such interference.

In this context, Nepal's desire for independence needs mention. It is true that the treaties with China in 1792 and 1856 and with the British in 1816, compromised its sovereignty and independence to some extent. But it always showed in-difference towards the unfavourable clauses of the treaties with a distant power, China. Towards the British also, Nepal never reconciled itself to a subordinate position. Since the unification of Nepal under Prithvi Narayan Shah, we find the Nepali statsmen meticulously trying to keep British hands off their inteinal matters. Though at times, British support was sought by particular groups or individuals, to increase their political weigit in domestic fights, any foreign meddling in its affairs was resisted. To preserve the independence, the Nepali leaders alternately followed policies of isolationism and balance of power The names of Bahadur Shah and Bhim Sen Thapa may be recalled for reference.

The Ranas also maintained a similar stance. They left their foreign policy to the care of the British but maintained their independent sway over domestic politics. They also achieved revision of the 1816 Segouli treaty by the British in 1923, by which Nepal's independence and sovereignty were recognized. Rightly then a Nepali statesman R.K. Shah has observed :

> Friends by necessity we may choose to be, but the status of slave we shall never own. This has been the watch-word of the Nepali statesmen and military leaders in the grave hours of national emergency and crisis. History shows that the Nepalese have been highly sensitive to the question of national honour and prestige and have always in the past stood as a solid block in defence of their freedom and frontiers.[2]

Socio-cultural composition

The social and cultural make-up of Nepal broadly parallels its physical division into three parts. The frontier regions in the north and south possess a large measure of social and cultural identity with the areas directly adjacent to them. Ethnically, the northern hill people belong to the Mongoloid stock, whereas the Terai people in the south, it is generally held, belong to the Indo-Aryan race. The languages spoken in the different regions are varied and numerous. However, those dominant "in the hills—Limbu, Gurung, Tamang, Sunuwar, Raikirat are some—are said to be of the Tibeto-Burmese group. Those dominant in the Terai—Bhojpuri, Abadi, Maithili, Tharu and Hindi—are of the Indo-Astroloid group and are prevalent in the adjacent Indian provinces of Bihar and the U.P.[3]

Again, the social pattern—caste structure, social values and norms—of the northern and the southern regions of Nepal correspond to that of their respective neighbourhood. Finally, two dominant religions are practised in the Kingdom, Hinduism and Buddhism. Hinduism is present everywhere but its concentration is more in the Terai and as one goes up towards the north, Buddhism starts appearing as an important cultural determinant.

A synthesis of two cultural currents exists in Nepal. One comes from India and the other from across the Himalayas. This synthesis is especially evident in the central region, the Kathmandu valley. Since long past, the Hindu rulers of the valley have had Buddhist subjects, the Newars, and through centuries of co-existence, the two religious groups have influenced each other. The Newars, on the one hand, adopted the Hindu caste system, but did not allow it to retain its complex characteristics like untouchability. The Kings, on the other hand, while retaining their loyalty to Hindu social customs and religious practices, established a happy rapport with the sentiments of their subjects and participated in the latter's social and religious functions.

Nepalese society is, in short, a plural society. The diversity of its cultural and social life originated from isolation enforced by the rigid physical divisions. It was also due in part, to the entry of two different peoples and cultures from different directions and the emergence of a third resulting from their diffusion into each other. But since people and the cultural currents could enter Nepal more easily from the South, the Southern influence became dominant in the Kingdom's socio-cultural composition. Its social and cultural festivals, for example, Vijay Dashmi, Diwali, Holi and Shivaratri, and the style of their celebration, are evidences of this fact. Further the national language, Nepali, is written in Devnagari, an Indian script, and closely resembles Hindi. However, with the present wave of Nepalese nationalism, it is the distinctive aspects of the Nepalese culture that are emphasized and stressed.

Economic background

Nepal is an exceptionally poor country. Indeed, it stands at the very bottom of international economic stratification. And its position was even worse during the rule of the Ranas. Two factors account for this poverty: an imbalanced economy and an inadequate economic environment. The imbalance results from the predominance of agriculture, which contributes a comparatively small share to the national product. Whereas 93 to 94 per cent of the population was engaged in agriculture, contribution from this sector amounted to only 63 to 64 per cent of the gross national product. This poor ratio was largely due to highly conservative methods of cultivation. In the post-Rana period, attempts have been made to modernise agriculture, but progress has not yet been of much significance. Industrialization seemed a possible route to economic advancement and efforts have been made in this direction. In 1966, the industrial complex, while employing only 2 per cent of the population, contributed 12 per cent of the gross national product. But the infrastructure, required to move the economy towards industrialization, has been almost non-existent.

In the first place, there are no adequate facilities for transport and communication. Transportation by air and train is woefully inadenale, and the road mileage is lamentably poor. This has hampered the movement of goods and agricultural products from one part of the country to the other. As a result the surplus of the Terai finds an easy way to the bordering Indian markets, leaving the hills deficient and consequently causing the movement of population from the hills to the Terai in search of work and food. Besides, the agricultural products are mostly foodgrains and not the cash crops that can feed industries. Jute and sugarcane produced in the Terai were not sufficient to run mills to their full capacity. And to make matters worse, there were very few sources of energy. Coal and oil are absent in Nepal and hydro-electric power has not been harnessed because of the high cost of construction of dams and generators.

Internal resources to remedy these inadequacies and im-balances have been lacking. The government has had no money to undertake construction of the economic infrastructure nor has it had a proper administrative organization to respond to the demands of economic regeneration.[4] For all this, therefore, reliance had to be placed on foreign assistance in the form of aid, loans, technical assistance and private capital.

B. Variables

Nationalism

The origins of Nepali nationalism have been traced to the days of Prithvi Narayan Shah. As noted already, he brought about the territorial and political unification of the country and tried to create among its inhabitants a feeling of unity. His approach was, however, limited to the territorial and political components of nationalism. Its social, economic, cultural and intellectual planes were not even touched. Whatever this, "feeling of oneness" might be, it declined after Prithvi Narayan Shah and vanished altogether with the rise of the Ranas.

The revival of nationalism in Nepal has come about during the post-II World War period. It came as a by-product of the general resurgence of Asia, which in turn owed much to the withdrawal of the British from the Indian sub-continent. The new Nepali nationalism found expression in the anti-Rana movement. Nepali statesmen and scholars tend to compare the anti-Rana movement with the anti-British movement in India. But there were differences in the goals and institutional make-up of the two movements including the significant difference that the Ranas were not a foreign power as were the British.

The Nepalese movement was in any case less comprehensive

in its approach and scope than the Indian movement. The Terai was the epicentre of the anti-Rana movement which failed to mobilize the other regions, particularly, the northern hills effectively. The result of this imbalance was that as soon as the objective of overthrowing the Ranas was achieved, the national focus was left hanging in a void.[5] The situation led to confusion and chaos in the political, social and economic life of the Kingdom.

When the Nepali Congress was elected to power in 1959, it tried to arrest this trend. The party talked about socialism and parliamentary democracy as the slogans for national construction and tried to generate the forgotten "feeling of oneness", the sense of common identity and interests. The Nepali Congress sought to provide equitable representation to various regions in the central administration. In fact, all these measures had been mooted much earlier, but none were made effective. The efforts of the Nepali Congress had only begun to take shape when the government was dismissed by King Mahendra in December 1960.

Since his assumption of power in 1955, King Mahendra had been trying to assert the role of monarchy in the political structure of Nepal, and also to consolidate the monarchy as one of the symbols of nationalism. The monarchy of old had, in fact, been the most important symbol of nationalism in Nepal. The name of Prithvi Narayan Shah may be recalled in this context. Even in the days of his political eclipse, the King—the manifestation of Lord Vishnu—continued to remain an object of devotion and reverence for Nepalis. The role played by King Tribhuwan in the anti-Rana movement and the respect and importance he continued to command in spite of his reluctance to assert his position, provide further evidences of the influence of the monarchy.

King Mahendra's efforts to identify himself with Nepal's nationalism became even more vigorous after his 'takeover' from the Nepali Congress government. He described his 'takeover' as the fulfilment of his "ultimate responsibility for protecting national unity, nationality and sovereignty...."[6] While elaborating on the point, he underlined the idea that the nationalism which he was going to invoke was a "new consciousness", wider in base and comprehensive in its meaning. In his first policy statement after the 'takeover', he said on 5 January 1961 :

> We have been able to overcome great difficulties and

> calamities in our national history because of our patriotism, national pride and discipline. We have to create a new consciousness in the people so as to enable the country to meet the demands of the time. We have to enthuse them anew for development, construction and increased production. To fulfil our selfless and sacred desire to bring about this mental and spiritual regeneration in the task of all round development of the nation under our leadership, we invite the active co-operation of all....

In pursuit of these sentiments, the King introduced a new panchayat system. The world 'democracy' was, however, retained to qualify the system. The importance and mass appeal which the concept and slogan of democracy had acquired in the post-Rana Nepal, could not be undermined. The panchayat system was described as being "based on the bedrock of popular feelings and aspirations and having for its sole aim the establishment of a democracy suited to our national genius".[7] The "panchayat philosophy" later came to be termed "Nepalism" by the then Minister of National Guidance, Vishwa Bandu Thapa. Those who challenged the efficacy of the new system or the position acquired by the King under it —the members of the Nepali Congress, the Gorkha Parishad and the Communist Party, mostly exiled in India—were dubbed as "anti-nationals". Nepal's strong official and popular protests to the Chinese Government for the show of impertinence towards King Mahendra's portrait in the Chinese stall in a Kathmandu exhibition in May 1967 was another instance of close identification between the King and Nepali nationalism.

Thus the 'monarchy' and 'democracy', two most important features of the Nepali political system provided the symbols of nationalism too. On the cultural side, there was little to be mobilized to cultivate nationalism because diversity, and not unity, had been Nepal's characteristic feature. Hinduism, for example, was the religion of the majority but could not provide a base for nationalism since it left out the Buddhist and the Muslim sections of the society. Nevertheless, emphasis has always been on the synthetic aspects of their culture. Besides this, the stress upon the national language—Nepali—also needs mention in this context.[8]

Not many socio-cultural symbols including religion, could invoke a satisfactory and true sense of separate and distinct national identity in Nepal since the origin of these symbols could be located in India or China. The Kingdom's cultural and social proximity being far more intimate and extensive with India, the thrust of nationalist sentiments and the urge for a separate identity led it to assert itself *vis-a-vis* the latter. Such assertion received further impetus from the awareness of the recent past when Nepal was virtually an ally of British India. The nationalist Government of India was also destined to exercise considerable political influence in Nepal as became evident during the anti-Rana revolution. The psychological need to assert against India was, therefore, greater and all the more persistent.

International milieu

The British withdrawal from the Indian sub-continent in 1947 did not appear to have made any immediate impact on Nepal's position in the region. The situation was, however, radically altered within a couple of years, when the new communist regime in China moved its troops into Tibet in October 1950 and ultimately established its hegemony there. The country most alarmed and directly affected by these developments was India, which quickly moved to protect its strategic stakes in Nepal and the other two Himalayan Kingdoms of Bhutan and Sikkim. Nehru's loud claims of India's "keen and personal interest" and "special position" in Nepal as discussed in the previous chapter resulted from these security and strategic considerations.

China did not disturb India's moves in Nepal in the beginning. But, from 1956 gradual attempts became evident on China's part to put up a diplomatic offensive against India's "special position" in the Kingdom. A workable rapport between Nepal and China seemed inevitable. With the growth of hostilities between India and China, Nepal was dragged into the politics of cross-diplomatic currents between its two powerful neighbours.

Nepal's enhanced strategic position owing to its location *vis-a-vis* a giant communist power led to powers outside South Asia, also taking an interest in it. The Kingdom represented an important link in the US objectives of containing communism on all fronts. India's refusal to toe the US approach to communist powers and to China in particular, enhanced American interests in Nepal. The USSR had been watching the situation in Nepal till 1955, when after initial hesitations, it entered into the Kingdom diplomatically. The regularization of diplomatic relations between China and Nepal in 1955 and 1956, and the increase in the Chinese activities that followed, further entrenched US and Soviet interests in Nepal.

Nepal sought to steer a passage through the pressures and counter-pressures exerted by the major powers in the region and by the more distant super powers. What complicated the situation further was that the balance between regional powers did not get established nor for that matter, the character of "cold-war" politics and the initial bipolar structure of the super powers. China has been moving fast closer to the status of a super power. The equations and equilibrium amongst the big powers in the world have been changing since then. Nepal obviously could not afford to be indifferent towards these changes in its foreign policy formulations.

The post-II World War phenomenon of Asian resurgence was an equally important factor. The emergence of a group of independent nations in Asia freed from the yoke by the withdrawal of colonialism, made a significant impact on the dynamics of world politics. The substitution of the old orders by the new in these new nations as a result of the resurgence released powerful demands for social modernization and economic prosperity. And these demands invariably found their expression in the foreign policies of these resurgent nations, and so it was with Nepal.

OBJECTIVES

Security and preservation of independence

Corresponding to *Security* (*T*) and *Security* (*P*) motives mentioned earlier, the preservation of territorial integrity and political independence is the first and the most important objective in the foreign policy of a nation, particularly one whose independence is new. Though Nepal's independence in theoretical and legal terms was not new, it had lived under the dark shadow of British Imperial authority in India. Further its entry into world politics was only a post-II World War development and its suspicion of the big powers and colonial rulers was strong.[9]

Nepal did not envisage a military threat to its independence from the major powers. The threat was considered to be more political in nature, one of "direct and subtle interference" of the big powers in the affairs of small countries.[10] Asserting his country's love for independence, Prime Minister B.P. Koirala told the UN General Assembly in October 1960:

> My country is fiercely proud of its independence which we never wholly lost ... Like other countries now represented here, we prefer to estimate ourselves the strengths and weaknesses of other social systems and to choose our own. We do not wish to be battered by propaganda or to have our minds made up for us, or to reach our decisions in an atmosphere of suspicion and hatred. We do not want to be absorbed into the cold war or to become a tool of any power bloc.

The threat to Nepal's independence was obviously more imminent from its direct neighbours, and this threat was both military and political in nature. But in the light of the background of geographical determinism, historical perspective and socio-cultural affinities which have been discussed, two deductions can be made :

1. From China, the nature of the threat was considered to be of a politico-military nature.
2. From India, it was largely of a political nature.

To meet the military aspect of the threat, Nepal instituted its defence arrangements with India and the Western powers (This will be discussed later). To ward off the threat of political interference, Nepal pleaded for observance of the principle of absolute non-interference in matters internal to a nation. This principle was repeatedly asserted by Nepal in various forums, the National Legislature, the United Nations and a number of international conferences. During their official state visits abroad, the Nepali leaders and statesmen lauded the principle which also finds a place in the treaties, agreements and joint communiques signed by Nepal.

A very important aspect of the objective of preservation of independence was the quest for international recognition as an independent and sovereign nation. It reflected the 'status' motive of Nepal. As a first step in this direction, Nepal bade adieu to its old policy of isolationism, for this policy was considered to be "fraught with many dangers, including the danger of losing Nepal's political entity".[11] King Mahendra observed more generally that due to the "introvert civilization...and... contemplative bent...to keep to oneself...Asia shrank closer into its own narrow, individualistic empire illumined by its egoism only".[12] To avert this danger, Nepal made a "deliberate entry" into the comity of nations and followed an "open door" policy.[13]

This open door policy in place of the old isolationism, was partly in view of the international milieu around Nepal. The claims and demands made on Nepal because of its newly enhanced strategic significance as well as from rising expectations within Nepal itself, no longer permitted an isolated existence.[14] The compulsion was evident in King Tribhuwan's address to the Second Advisory Assembly on 7 June 1954 in which he said that "it is an undeniable fact that no nation can, in the context of the modern world, lead an isolated existence."

In accordance with the policy of "open door" participation, Nepal expanded its diplomatic contacts. In 1950-51, it had diplomatic relations with only four countries : India, Britain, the United States and France. Today most of the countries have formal diplomatic relations with Nepal with a number of Nepalese diplomatic missions working abroad as well as a number of foreign diplomatic missions stationed in Kathmandu. In 1955, the Kingdom secured membership in the United Nations six years after its initial request. The Kingdom also joined regional organizations like the Colombo Plan and the Asian Development Bank, and took part in regional conferences of Asian and developing nations at Bandung, Belgrade and Cairo. While leaving for Belgrade as the leader of the Nepali delegation in 1961, King Mahendra told his country "...ever bearing in mind that the disappearance of Nepal's sovereign entity will mean an end to the existence of every Nepali and that we rise or fall with our country, we are this day leaving for Belgrade."

At all these places, the Nepali delegations stressed the independence and sovereignty of their country, and reiterated the need for strict observance of the principle of non-interference in the domestic affairs of another nation. Nepal was also identified with the Asian, African and all small nations. The speeches made at successive conferences reveal that Nepal's style of participation in such gatherings underwent a marked change. From 'shy' and 'modest' respectively in the Asian Relations Conference in 1947 in New Delhi and Bandung in 1955, it became 'active' and 'confident' in the non-aligned summit conferences at Belgrade (1961), Cairo (1964) and Lusaka (1971), and at preparatory meetings in 1965 for the Afro-Asian Conference at Algiers (1966). The same was true of Nepal's participation in the United Nations. This gradually increasing participation in international politics appears to have contributed to the enhancement of Nepal's prestige and to have satisfied its quest for recognition. In his message to the nation on the first anniversary of the "takeover" King Mahendra said in December 1961 :

> In furtherance of our policy of friendship with all countries, this year we participated in the Conference of Heads of States and Governments of non-aligned nations at Belgrade, and we paid state visits to Pakistan, the People's Republic of China and the People's Republic of Mongolia. By these visits Nepal and the Nepalese have become better known to the people and the governments of those countries, and we feel that we have benefited much from personal contacts with the leaders of these different countries....We feel that our prestige at the United Nations has risen because of our sustained policy of friendly relations with all countries....

Y.N. Khanal after attending the Bandung Conference as a member of the Nepali delegation said that the participation in the Conference brought honour to Nepal and enhanced its prestige.[15]

Economic Development

The objective of economic development in Nepal's foreign policy had priority over the quest for international recognition through the extension of diplomatic contacts. The priority was evident in the fact that the amount of likely inflow of economic aid and assistance formed one of the important criteria in Nepal's expanding diplomatic contacts during the early years.[16] Further, the establishment of the Nepalese missions abroad had been guided by the considerations as to whether it was to be beneficial economically and whether Nepal could afford the expenditure involved in foreign exchange.[17]

Nepal highlighted the disparity not only between the developed and the developing countries, but at "all levels between countries at different stages of economic development." It analysed this question in a somewhat Marxist framework and held that the economic disparity in the world at large, as within a single nation, was the major source of tension and friction.[18] It also held that the richer nations owed an obligation to help the poorer ones and that economic aid was "not a benevolent act of charity" on the part of the 'have' nations towards the "have-not nations".[19] A Nepali Prime Minister attacked under-development with emotional intensity saying, for example :

> Is it necessary for some people as for some nations to continue to be poor in order that other people as other nations can continue to be rich? Does the starvation of a part of humanity always stare us in the face? Is it too much to hope that the United Nations will pool to- gather all the human material and technological resources available at present and use them most effectively to raise the living standards of the people of the under-developed countries?[20]

This way, the need for international cooperation was stressed. In practice, Nepal tried to mobilize this cooperation at three levels : bilateral, regional and international. The objective was to create favourable conditions for aid, trade and the inflow of foreign private capital to help industrialization.

World Peace

World peace is an avowed objective of every foreign policy. For Nepal it reflected a sense of realism too behind the facade of international rhetoric. In the latter sense, world peace was desired as a necessary condition for preserving independence and working for economic development. Nepal subscribed to the well-known Asian slogan that "peace and prosperity are indivisible", and that any disturbance anywhere was likely to affect adversely, the process of reconstruction in a small, weak and poor country.

The danger to world peace was primarily from the tension created by the super-power rivalry. Nepal always pleaded that this tension be reduced gradually and eliminated ultimately. It welcomed every sign of improvement in the relations between the super-powers. To expedite the *detente* and consolidate it, Nepal also advocated extension of the "area of peace" and the "zone of non-commitment". With this goal in mind the Kingdom refused to subscribe to the idea of forging a "neutralist bloc" as such. The danger to world peace was considered also to be inherent in the existing economic and power disparities among the nations. In that context, King Mahendra held that world peace would not be achieved :

> Unless interference and encroachment are fully stopped, unless defence expenditures are reduced and diverted to development and unless the developed countries help the developing countries in a really disinterested manner and in man's pursuit of peace and happiness.[21]

A very important dimension of world peace for Nepal was peace in the neighbourhood. There again it pleaded for cordial relations and better understanding between its neighbours, India and China on the one hand, and India and Pakistan on the other.

Another source of danger to world peace was from the arms race in conventional and nuclear weapons. Besides perpetuating the tension and mutual suspicion, the race was responsible for the increased sense of insecurity in the world. It also consumed a substantial part of the world's resources and talent which, if used otherwise, could eliminate poverty and ensure better conditions of living. This, in course of time, would remove another cause of tension and unrest in the world.[22] Guided by these considerations Nepal advocated drastic reduction of all arms and continued to welcome and encourage every modest step taken in the direction of disarmament and nuclear non-proliferation.

Anti-Colonialism, Anti-Imperialism and Racialism

Related to the longing for world peace and in tune with its identification with the Asian community, was Nepal's objective to further the cause of anti-colonialism, anti-imperialism, and anti-racialism. Like any other Asian country, Nepal had been very vocal on these issues and rendered its uncompromising support in favour of the movement towards them. It considered imperialism and colonialism to be "unmixed evils" because they envisaged social and political orders which legitimized the domination of man over man and country over country. Racialism on the other hand was an atrocious negation of the fundamental human values. In these policies Nepal saw a threat to world peace and, therefore, viewed the movements for their elimination as a part of the wider movement for world peace.[23] For the success of these movements, Nepal consellled decency and justice to the colonial and racial powers on the one hand and called for Afro-Asian unity and solidarity in all the available national and international forums on the other.

Identity with Smaller Nations

While talking about world peace or disarmament or anti-colonialism, anti-imperialism, anti-racialism and human rights, Nepal did not, even for a moment, forget about its size and strength. It was well aware of the fact that due to its small and weak stature, by itself, it was incapable of contributing anything towards the fulfilment of these objectives. Therefore, it decided to throw its weight with the new, small and like-minded nations. Establishment of identity with this group of nations, thus became another important objective of Nepal's foreign policy.

The credit for introducing emphasis and increased awareness about this aspect goes to the Nepali Congress Prime Minister, B.P. Koirala. In his speech in the UN General Assembly in October 1960 he said :

> In welcoming the new members, I have a feeling that we are welcoming nations which have a similar approach to the basic problems of the world today. I speak on behalf of a small uncommitted country which has no pretensions of any kind. When welcoming the new members, we have consciousness of accession of strength of our point.

This strength, Koirala held, had shifted the "centre of gravity of the world politics" from 'big' to the 'small' nations, but unfortunately, the shift had not been realized by the smaller nations themselves.[24] He, therefore, urged them to unite and offer a concerted response to the issues facing the world. This approach on the part of the smaller nations was considered to be the only way in which they could influence world politics.[25] This aspect of identity with the smaller nations was carried further by King Mahendra and his Foreign Ministers and today, this constitutes one of the very important objectives of Nepal's foreign policy.

Strengthening the United Nations

To further these objectives, Nepal looked towards the United Nations as the most important instrument. That was the place where the Kingdom could identify itself with the smaller nations and anti-colonial, anti-imperial and anti-racial forces. There only could it plead the cause of world peace and at the same time get recognition of its independence and sovereignty, as also aid and assistance for its economic development. Reiterating Nepal's faith in the United Nations, Chairman and Foreign Minister Dr. Tulsi Giri stated in the UN General Assembly in 1964 :

> ...I should like to reiterate that the people and the Government of Nepal look upon the United Nations, in great measure as a guardian of the independence and territorial integrity of small nations and as a forum where

small nations can make their own humble contributions to the cause of international peace and prosperity.

Therefore, Nepal saw a clear need for the United Nations to be strengthened. For this, it expressed readiness to fulfil the commitments and obligations resulting from its membership of the Organization and called on all the countries to do the same and have their faith in it.

OPERATIONAL FRAME OF THE POLICY

For the fulfilment of the objectives discussed above, a comprehensive operational frame for the policy, capable of providing due emphasis to each of the objectives, was necessary. The policy options theoretically available to a country like Nepal, in the post-II World War international pattern, were three: *Isolationism,* as chosen by Myanmar, *alignment,* which Pakistan opted for and *non-alignment* as followed by India and several other countries.

The case for isolationism did not exist. Even if Nepal had so wished, the forces released as a result of the domestic political change, Asian resurgence and external pressures could not let it remain isolated.

The option of alignment can be viewed from two aspects: ideological and practical. Ideologically it was incompatible with the mood in the country and the climate around. Any kind of military alliance was looked upon as enslavement in disguise. In 1951, the Nepali Congress—the partner in the then ruling coalition held in a resolution :

> Nepal having gained an important place in the political map of Asia...is watching with vigilance the behind-the-screen moves on the part of different power blocs which have had no direct concern with Nepal before. The people of Nepal shall not only resent but vehemently oppose such unwelcome moves from whatever quarter they come and never allow Nepal to be a pawn in the game of international politics.[26]

The alignment could help improve Nepal's economic and social conditions little more rapidly and could provide a military shield for its frontiers but only at the cost of a "complete moral and material isolation" from the countries around and a compromise with its sense of independence and national pride. Hence it was unacceptable.

From the practical aspect, the case for alignment can be viewed in terms of four specific choices available to Nepal to align itself with. They were : (a) Soviet bloc, (b) Western bloc, (c) China and (d) India. Alliance with the Soviet bloc was not possible for two reasons. First, Nepal and the USSR had no contacts whatsoever, at a time when the latter was forging alliances. Secondly, and this was more important, the image the USSR had of Nepal was one of a country tied to India within the orbit of Western influence in its external affairs. Nepal's participation in the two world wars, on the side of the Western powers—the United Kingdom and the United States—on the one hand and the pattern of its intimate relations with independent India were perhaps the factors that shaped the Soviet Union's perception of the Kingdom. Owing to this perception, the Soviet Union re-peatedly used the Veto to bloc Nepal's entry into the United Nations at a time when alignments and blocs were forged and consolidated.

As noted earlier, the second choice for alignment in favour of the Western powers was very much in the picture during the last days of the Ranas. At that time and later, it could not materialize because of India's resistance—a factor which no government in Nepal could bypass. India's influence on Nepal in this respect was evident in Nepal's strong dis-approval of the military pact and security arrangement, initiated by the Western powers in Asia. Nepal's Foreign Minister D.R. Regmi resenting the Western powers' move for the alliance stated :

> Certain powers are trying to make this area a war base. Nepal which has common frontier with China for about 500 miles has its own strategic importance and so has India. It is in the interest of both that these powers do not succeed in involving Nepal and India in a war cauldron.[27]

D.R. Regmi also criticized the SEATO negotiations taking place in the Philippines in August 1954 and welcomed the Colombo Powers—India, Sri lanka and Indonesia—for their opposition to the western sponsored military alliance in South-east Asia. He said on the occasion: "I particularly appreciate Mr. Nehru's bold stand in this matter. I think it is his stand which has prevented others from falling into the trap."[28]

Regarding the last two choices, neither India nor China was

sponsoring any military alliance against the power blocs. They did not even approve of the idea. Further, in the context of historical, geographical and political factors, it was unthinkable for Nepal to enter into bilateral alliances with China against India. Besides the fact that the diplomatic contacts between China and Nepal were frozen at that time, the latter did not perceive any military threat from India. China on its part was occupied with the still unsettled conditions in Tibet and owing to the political transformation in the mainland only recently achieved, was not in a position to afford confrontation with India.

Nepal's alliance with India to meet any threat from China was both plausible and possible. It was so notwithstanding the factors of Nepal's nationalism, and its search for separate identity. These factors assumed effective proportions only after 1954. Until then, the relations between the two governments were very cordial and the political environment was quite conducive and congenial to moves like alignment. Accordingly, the two countries had arrived at very close understanding on matters of mutual security and defence as underlined in the Agreement on the recruitment of Gurkhas in the Indian Army (1947) and in the Treaty of Peace and Friendship (1950). This understanding and the arrangements evolved in pursuance of it did not constitute an alliance in the formal and legal sense. India was ideologically averse and materially ill-equipped to forge a 'rigid' and 'total' alliance. Moreover, it would have been incompatible with India's global approach which decried military pacts, highlighted non-alignment and endeavoured to extend the "area of peace". A declared military alliance between Nepal and India would have also unnecessarily offended China at that time.

The above specific choices for Nepal's alliance have been discussed largely with the focus on the would be bigger and powerful partner in the alliance and with the presumption that Nepal would have accepted the arrangement. The context of the discussion is hypothetical and is not meant to undermine the ideological moorings and political climate of the would be smaller and weaker partner in the alliance—Nepal. These moorings and the climate were, to repeat, wholly incongruent to the idea of pushing the Kingdom into an alliance.

The arguments that reject the first two options, isolationalism and alignment, by implication provide justification for the third. Non-alignment was held to be capable of catering to the needs—political, economic and psychological—of Nepal without inflicting embarrassment and humiliation inherent in the other two options. It, thus, became the operational frame for Nepal's foreign policy.

Non-alignment

There were three salient features of Nepal's policy of non-alignment. The first was the dynamic and positive nature of the policy. Geopolitical aspects of Nepal suggested that its policy was more likely to be inactive and passive. Werner Levy held that, situated as it is,

> Nepal can afford neither to run counter to the policies of her big neighbours nor hope seriously to affect the policies of any other nation. She does not have the means to enforce an active and relatively independent policy.[29]

Nepali leaders and statesmen, however, thought otherwise. They did not accept that their participation in the international system was passive or devoid of initiative. In his address to the American Senate on 28 April 1960, King Mahendra said:

> Not to be camp follower of any bloc should not mean that we sit on the fence....In this there is not the least strain of passivity, selfishness or escapism. Because we are convinced that this is the correct path, we shall not deviate from it under any circumstances, whatsoever. When choice is between good and the evil, right and wrong, we never faltered, nor did we sit on the fence....

On another occasion, he subscribed to Nehru's slogan : "Where freedom is menaced or justice threatened, we cannot and shall not be neutral."[30]

The contentions of the scholars on the one hand and of the Nepali leaders on the other, present two extremes of the point. A keen observation of the evolution of Nepal's foreign policy since 1951, reveals a compromise of the two. It is true that Nepal till 1954 had very limited contacts with the world outside and was docile and devoid of initiative in its inter-national behaviour. But this is also true that afterwards, its diplomatic contacts extended gradually and it started taking a more active interest in the international events. That though its contribution to and effect on world politics was conditioned by limited means and power-potential, an assertive tendency towards playing a more meaningful and positive role was clearly evident in Nepal's international behaviour. We, therefore, find a shift from a passive and docile to an active and dynamic attitude.[31]

The shift from passivity to dynamism had nevertheless been chequered and severely restricted with regard to Nepal's relations with its neighbours. It was there that the logical implications of its geopolitics were visible. The Kingdom scrupulously refrained from making comments or doing anything which had a bearing on the issues between India and China.

The second salient feature of the policy of non-alignment was that it was an independent policy. Stress on independence is inherent in non-alignment itself. Accordingly, the policy proposed to cherish no preconceived views on the inter-national issues erupting from time to time, neither did it approve of following a particular line under the influence of external pressures. Elaborating upon this theme, Prime Minister B.P. Koirala told the world body in October 1960 :

> If we believe in a policy of non-alignment with any of the power blocs it is because we do not wish to commit our-selves beforehand to support one side or the other, and we wish to retain our independence of judgement in assessing international issues as they arise. In our humble opinion, this is the only way in which we can really be objective and detached in examination of the issues that may confront the world community from time to time. We have never hesitated to pronounce ourselves clearly and unequivocally on what has appeared to be right to us.

He also felt that it was rather convenient and smooth for Nepal to follow an independent course of action for the reason that it had "no disputes and far fewer commitments" as compared to other bigger states.

To a very considerable extent Nepal found India a hurdle in its desire to exercise independence in judgement and decision. There were many reasons for that. First was the hangover of the British (India)-Rana relations. This pattern of relationship continued even when the British had left and also for some years after the Ranas had fallen. There were various factors—personal, political and situational—which contributed to this continuity, and at a time, there existed a strong feeling in the Kingdom that with regard to India, Nepal was in a state of "semi-dependency". To undo this image, there was a clear need to readjust its relations with India. Speaking his mind on this aspect, King Mahendra said in October 1962 :

> Nepal has ever been an independent and peace-loving nation....This country always wishes well to all other countries, never wishes ill to any country. Nepal is always desirous of friendly relations with friendly country India as well, but Nepal is never prepared to play second fiddle to any country and will never lag behind in thinking out ways and means of her own welfare. Nepal, however, wants to maintain in a right manner, cooperation and traditional relations of friendship and goodwill with India. Now we are determined not to become a plaything in the hands of any foreign power.

Similarly, whenever Nepal acted in a way different to what India had done on the international issues, those instances were mentioned with a sense of satisfaction and pride. Its stand on Hungary and grater emphasis on the Tibet issue favouring China's position can be taken as examples.[32]

The third feature of the non-alignment policy was the element of morality in it. With the large number of the newly independent nations adopting non-alignment as the operational frame of their policies, the super powers got suspicious about it. They considered it as a facade for the leanings of these nations towards their rival camp. The Western powers were more pronounced in their criticism of non-alignment. In retaliation to this type of criticism, as well as due to feeble power-potential, higher emotional intensity and sense of cultural superiority over the West, many of the non-aligned Asian states described their policy as morally superior.

In Nepal's case also, we find emotional overtones hinting at the self-imposed moral obligation on its policy to work for world peace. In November 1954, Prime Minister M.P. Koirala observed :

> Today, the world is divided into two blocs. Nepal does not want to join any bloc and according to Gautam Buddha's ideals of peace, unity and non-violence, we have adopted our foreign policy. For having belonged to Buddha's land, on us lies the greater responsibility for peace.[33]

Buddha, the apostle of peace, repeatedly found mention in this context. The ruling party, the Nepali Congress, resolved in May 1960 to give Buddha's message of peace, equality, freedom and fraternity to the world.[34] So did King Mahendra while concluding his speech at the Belgrade non-aligned conference.

A sense of moral obligation for peace in the policy of non-alignment, implying thereby that other policies, of alignment particularly, were morally inferior, was evident even apart from the mention of Buddha. Whereas King Mahendra described the second non-aligned conference as a moral movement for peace, Prime Minister B.P. Koirala in the United Nations in 1960 held that the moral strength of a country like Nepal was great, at least potentially.

However, we find a contradiction in Nepal over this aspect. On the one hand, we have noted above that the leadership in the country held that their policy was morally superior and that it had an obligation to further the cause of peace. On the other hand, high officials in the foreign service opined exactly the opposite. In February 1963 Nepal's Foreign Secretary, General Padma Bahadur Khatri in a radio speech refused to entertain the belief that the moral standard of non-alignment was higher in any way, than that of military alliances. Stating the same point even more candidly, Khatri's successor Y.N. Khanal said:

> There is no truth in the contention that neutralism as such is better than the bloc politics from the moral point of view....In our country there are certain elements who think that neutralism is the height of morality and aligned countries are also immoral.
>
> The basis of the neutral policy of the *(sic)* Nepal is not provided by conceptions like these. Morality is neither an integral part of neutrality nor that of military alliance. Morality is in fact an attribute of the individual.
>
> In the present situation of the world which is divided into opposing camps, Nepal believes in neutralism because it is both practical and suitable for her.[35]

This rejection of the moral aspect in the attitude of the civil servant was of later origin. The contradiction is not easy to account for. Nevertheless, it indicated the growing stress on the realistic and pragmatic approach in the formulation of foreign policy. This, however, is not to say that the attitude of the leadership and the civil servants earlier, was in any way less real and practical.

While studying these features of the Nepalese non-alignment—dynamic approach, independence of judgement and moral superiority—the statements of the policy makers have been surveyed. From this survey, there appears to be some confusion about the semantics of the term "non-alignment". The terms "non-alignment", "neutralism and neutrality" have been used at times as synonyms and at times to mean different things.[36] No effort was visible on the part of the policy makers to distinguish these terms from one another.[37]

Peaceful Co-existence

Peaceful co-existence was the second epithet of the opera-tional frame. Its use came into vogue after the Agreement in 1954 between India and China on *Parichsheela,* the five principles of peaceful co-existence—wherein the term was used first. It was often used simultaneously and at times even in an identical sense with non-alignment. Explaining the relation-ship between the two as understood in Nepal, King Mahendra said : "The principle of peaceful co-existence when used negatively in the sense of military non-involvement becomes one of non-alignment."[38]

Nepal was quite optimistic about the practicability of co-existence. It believed that mutual accommodation and adjustment brought on the basis of mutual tolerance, understanding and interdependence of interests was possible even without the sacrifice of the values and faith cherished individually by the co-existing parties. It believed that as a result of such peaceful co-existence, a synthesis of the values, which are best in the various systems, would evolve.[39] Behind this philosophical approach, Nepal had some pragmatic considerations. She thought that by evolving a code of conduct for international politics, embodying all the essential principles of peaceful co-existence, world peace could be ensured.

In this context the realization of peaceful co-existence between India and China on the one hand and of Nepal with each on the other, was of special significance. In 1954 Nepal cheered China and India when they signed the *Panchsheela* agreement. The then Foreign Minister of Nepal found that Nehru-Chou En lai joint statement released on that occasion was capable as well as suitable to serve as a model for bilateral relations in the world.[40] In the statement, Nepal also saw a guarantee by the two big nations of Asia to the smaller nations that their independence will not be en upon.[41]

Therefore, the signs of a breakdown of peaceful co-existence between India and China found Nepal uneasy and in an awkward position. The situation of actual conflict between its neighbours made Nepal all the more concerned. Expressing this concern, Foreign Secretary Y.N. Khanal stated :

> So far as Nepal is concerned, peaceful co-existence when applied to practical conditions and short of extraneous forces means co-existence between India and China and our own co-existence with both of them. So we have tried to cultivate friendship with them as best as we can. We know that in the present atmosphere of tension between them, ours is an unenviable position, but we are forti-fied in our belief through the realisation that peaceful co-existence is bound to prevail sooner or later, in spite of the complexities of the Sino-Indian differences, because the alternative to it is disaster. Afro-Asian unity within the framework of continuing tension between India and China is in our opinion a mirage....It is difficult to envisage a world or even less an Afro-Asian community in which India or China is completely isolated.[42]

Besides, there was a domestic logic in support of Nepal's advocacy of peaceful co-existence with each of its neighbours. We have noted earlier that Nepal is a mixed society and its people have ethnic and socio-cultural identities with India on the one hand and China on the other. Though the identities with the latter are somewhat weak and less pronounced as compared to that with the former, the fact remains that they exist and that too over a long past. Therefore, for social harmony and domestic peace, friendship and understanding with both India and China was essential for Nepal.

Notes

1. George Liska, *Alliances and the Third World,* USA, 1968, 27.
2. Rishikesh Shah, *Nepal and the World,* Kathmandu, 1955, 27.
3. Stanley Maron, Leo E. Rose and Julian Heyman, *Survey of Nepal Society,* Human Relations Area File, South Asia Project, University of California, 1956 (Typed manuscript at ICWA Library, New Delhi).
4. Y. P. Pant, *Nepal's Economic Development on International Basis,* Nepal Council of Asian Relations and World Affairs, Kathmandu, 1956.
5. Charvak, "Kendra Ko Khoj Ma" (In search of a focus), *Rastrahit,*

Yr. 1, No. 1, 16 *Shrawan* 2009 (July-August 1952), 11.

6. H.M. King Mahendra, *Proclamations, Speeches and messages* (hereafter referred to as *Speeches*), Vol. II, Department of Publicity, Ministry of Information and Broadcasting, HMG, Nepal, Kathmandu, June 1967, 2.
7. *Ibid.*, 19.
8. King Mahendra in his convocation address to the Tribhuwan University on 11 March 1962 said that Nepali, besides being the language of the courts and administration, "expressed our spiritual longings and thoughts abundantly". *Ibid.*, 107.
9. The first commoner Prime Minister of Nepal, M. P. Koirala, held that the Asian countries must unite together as there was a common danger for them to be enslaved again, *The Hindustan Standard*, 25 December 1953.
10. King Mahendra's address to the Second Conference of the Non-aligned Nations in Cairo, October 1964. *Speeches*, n. 6, 227.
11. T. R. Taladhar, *Mahendra, The King of Nepal*, Department of Publicity and Broadcasting, Ministry of Nation Guidance, HMG, Nepal, Kathmandu, 1961,10.
12. *Speeches*, n. 6, 37.
13. Y.N. Khanal, "Nepal's Foreign Policy: Its Content and Execution",. *Souvenir Issue*, Nepal Council of World Affairs, Kathmandu, June 1967.
14. Warren F. Ilchman in his article, "Political Development and Foreign Policy : The Case of India" observed that "Newly in-dependent nations are of necessity bound to participate in an international system", *Journal of Commonwealth Political Studies*,. Vol. IV, No. 3, 1966, 216-30. Also see Werner Levi, "Nepal in World Politics", *Pacific Affairs*, Vol. XXX, No. 3, September 1957, 236-48.
15. *Gorkhapatra*, 13 *Jaistha* 2012 (27 May 1955).
16. King Tribhuwan's speech to the Second Advisory Assembly. Text in *Nepal Marching Towards Progress*, Department of Publicity, Government of Nepal, Kathmanda, n.d.
17. *Rastriya Panchayat: Kariyvahi Ko Sankshipt Viveran* (National Panchayat: Brief description of the proceedings), 22 *Shravan* 2024 (July-August 1967). (See speech of the Deputy Prime Minister and Minister of External Affairs and Economic Planning).
18. *Policy Speech by* Prime Minister B. P. Koirala at the 15th UN General Assembly. Department of Publicity and Broadcasting HMG, Nepal, Kathmandu, n. d., 6.
19. R. K. Shah, the then Foreign Minister of Nepal in his speech to the Indian Council of World Affairs on 10 September 1962 *The Indian*

Express, 11 September 1962.

20. Policy Speech, *n. 18.*
21. *Speeches*, n. 6,40.
22. *Ibid.*, 39.
23. *Ibid.*, 38-39,277.
24. *The Hindu*, 31 October 1960.
25. Policy Speech, *n. 18.*
26. *The Hindu*, 30 May 1951.
27. The Times of India, *21 June 1954.*
28. *The Statesman*, 23 August 1954.
29. Werner Levy, n. 14. Depending on levy's analysis, Peter Lyon included Nepal in the category of the neutral buffer states, which he said, were the states without an active policy at all. *Neutralism* (Cheicester University), 1963, 93. Also see Nicholas Spykeman J., "Geography and Foreign Policy", *American Political Science Review*, Vol. XXXII, No. 2, April 1938, 227.
30. *Speeches*, n. 6, Vol. II, 126.
31. Sayegh in his essay on the "Anatomy of Neutralism" categorised Nepal as a state outgrowing the phase of passive neutralism. Fayez A. Sayegh, (ed.), *The Dynamics of the Neutralism in Arab World*, USA, 1964, 1-102.
32. Y. N. Khanal, *Background of Nepal's Foreign Policy*, Department of Publicity and Broadcasting, Ministry of National Guidance, HMG, Nepal, Kathmandu, n. d.
33. *Hamro Par Rastra Sampark* (Our External Relations), Publicity Department, Central Secretariat, Kathmandu, Nepal, n. d. 57.
34. Kalpana, 11 May 1960.
35. Y. N. Khanal, *Reflections on Nepal-India Relations*, New Delhi, 1964, 8, 50.
36. To take the example of King Mahendra only, he used: "Neutral foreign policy" and policy of "neutrality" in his addresses to the first and the second sessions of the parliament in 1959 and 1960 respctively. *Speeches*, n. 6, Vol. I, 154, 174; 'neutralism' in his speech at the Indian Council of World Affairs, Sapru House (New Delhi) during his official visit to India in April 1962, as well as in his address to the first session of the Rastriya Panchayat in April 1963 (*Speeches*, n. 6, Vol. II, 126, 172-73); "neutrality and non-alignment" together in his first policy speech on 5 January 1961, after the take over and latter in his directives to the Council of Ministers in August 1964 (*Ibid.*, 8, 264); "non-alignment" in his address to the Rastriya Panchayat Sessions

in June 1964, 1965, 1966 and 1967 respectively. *Text of the Address* (unofficial translation) published regularly by the Department of Publicity, Ministry of Information and Broadcasting, HMG, Nepal, Kathmandu; "Policy of neutrality" in his message to the nation on the eve of departure for the Belgrade non-aligned conference but "non-alignment" in the conference (*Speeches,* n. 6, Vol. II, 33 and 40).

37. In answer to a question regarding the kind of neutrality Nepal was thinking of, Prime Minister Tanka Prasad Acharya said in 1956:

    "I do not know how many kinds of neutrality there are. But we want to develop a neutrality under which Nepal will be able to serve the cause of peace and afford sympathy for the oppressed. We do not like the bloc system in human relations between neighbours and nations based on mutual cooperative existence." *The Statesman,* 3 September 1956.

38. Speeches, n. 6, Vol. II, 40.

39. King Mahendra's speech at the World Affairs Council, Los Angeles, during his state visit to the United States in May 1960. Text of the speech in *The Commoner,* 12 May 1960.

40. *The Statesman,* 30 June 1954. It was reiterated by the Nepalese dele-gation at the Bandung Conference. *Asia-Africa Speaks from Bandung,* Ministry of Foreign Affairs, Republic of Indonesia Djakarta, July 1955, 105-7.

41. *The Statesman,* 30 April 1956.

42. Y. N. Khanal, "Nepal and the World Today", *Nepal: Monograph on Nepalese Culture,* Ministry of Information and Broadcasting HMG, Nepal, 1968.

3

THE ERA OF "SPECIAL RELATIONS" WITH INDIA

Nepal's external relations during King Tribhuwan's rule (from February 1951 to March 1955) were dominated by India. The two countries were described as having had "special relations" with each other. The phrase "special relations" was very frequently used by both India and Nepal during this period though later, it became a much despised and maligned expression for the Nepalis. The era of "special relations" constituted an important initial phase in the evolution of Nepal's foreign policy. Therefore, the genesis, growth and decline of "special relations" that Nepal had with India need our attention before other substantive aspects of Nepal's foreign policy are taken up.

GENESIS OF "SPECIAL RELATIONS"

There were various factors that accounted for "special relations" between Nepal and India. There were the constant factors like geographical contiguity, strong socio-cultural and ethnic identities between the two countries, and Nepal's excessive economic dependence upon India. However, there was something more than these factors during King Tribhuwan's period that accounted for the pattern of "special relations". These additional factors were the legacy of the Rana regime and the domestic and external milieus obtaining at that time in the Kingdom.

Legacy of the Rana Regime

The pattern of "special relations" between Nepal and India

during King Tribhuwan's period was not wholly new. The relationship existing between the Rana rulers of Nepal and the British in India was basically the same and had the germs of the "special relations". It may be recalled here that the Ranas were very favourably disposed towards the interests and objectives of the British. The latter's withdrawal from the sub-continent did not make any substantial difference in the situation because the Government of independent India only stepped into the British shoe so far as India's defence mechanism and political interests in the Himalayan region were concerned. Nepal occupied a significant position in that context more so in view of the developments in China and Tibet.

The Ranas on their part were found to be too willing to adjust Nepal to suit India's interest in the changed context. This was evident in the Agreement on Gurkha recruitment and in the Treaties of Peace and Friendship and of Trade and Commerce of 1950 between Nepal and India. As discussed in Chapter 1, it was clear from these Treaties and Agreements that Nepal had joined India in a unified system of defence and had agreed to subject its external affairs and external trade to India's guidance.

Domestic Political Scene

The domestic political scene that followed after the fall the Ranas in Nepal further consolidated the pattern of "special relations" established between Nepal and India by the Treaties and Agreements. Unlike the Ranas, the new leadership—King Tribhuwan and the Nepali Congress leaders—were not apprehensive of the Government of India. Instead they were indebted to it for its role in bringing about the fall of the Ranas and in the consequent ascendance to power of the new Nepali elite. Therefore, the King and the party leaders looked towards the Indian Government and leaders with respect and admiration for the latter's rich political experience and democratic ideals, and derived inspiration and guidance from them.

Besides their psychological and political affinity with the Indian leaders, the Nepali leaders had to face many problems created by the new political and social order emerging in the country. There were problems of political stability, of law and order, of having an efficient administration which could respond to the growing demands of society, of constitutional and economic development and of international relations. The new leadership had little political experience and even less indigenous resources and skill to solve these problems. Hence they were compelled to look towards India for help and guidance which was readily forthcoming in view of India's own stakes in the "stability and progress" of the Kingdom. Pointing out the need for external help in Nepal's progress, King Tribhuwan, in a New Year (Nepali) broadcast in April 1953 stated :

> I want to make a particular mention of our very cordial and affectionate relations with our neighbour, India. We are akin to each other in so many spheres : religious, social, geographical, historical and so forth. Even Nepal's democracy is the result of an inspiration from India.

This led to extensive intercourse between the two Governments in various fields : political, administrative, cultural and economic, and with it grew Nepal's dependence upon India. The increased rapport between the two sides that resulted from this created a conducive environment for the "special relations" to flourish.

External Milieu

A very important factor which sustained the "intimate" relations between India and Nepal was the absence of any external interference. China's position in Tibet was unsettled and its claims there were largely unrecognized by the inter-national community. The outbreak of hostilities in the Indo-China region that took place simultaneously created new problems In this situation, China needed India's goodwill and support. Any attempt by China to question India's position or interest in Nepal was likely to invoke strong reaction and, therefore, would prove contrary to its objective of befriending India. Even its desire to establish formal diplomatic relations with Nepal would have been unwelcome, since the Nepali leaders were apprehensive of China because in 1939 Mao had listed Nepal as a "tributary state"[1] and in 1950, China had declared its objective of liberating Nepal after liberating Tibet.

India was no less interested to cooperate with China, an emerging major Asian power, to stabilize the regional politics in order to carry on the process of internal reconstruction and to realize the dream of "Asia for the Asians". Both India and China, therefore, avoided the issues which were likely to bring them in confrontation with each other.

China was not happy with the privileges enjoyed by India and Nepal in Tibet.[2] Yet it did not disturb Nepal's position in Tibet until 1956. This was evident in the fact that the Nepali traders in Tibet were not only allowed to continue their business smoothly but offered incentives in the form of loans and advance payments to increase the volume of trade since the demand of essential goods had increased due to the presence of the Chinese and the dislocation of the local trade there.[3] The reported attempts to "squeeze out" Nepali traders from Tibet, were contradicted promptly and strongly by the Government of Nepal.[4] The Nepalis, who left Tibet during this time did so under the panic caused by the Chinese action in Tibet and indefiniteness about the future.

Apart from the position of the traders, Tibet sent its tributary mission to Nepal in January 1952 as had been the practice since the signing of the 1856 Treaty. This was in gross disregard of China's warning to Tibet against sending such missions.[5] Two months later, in reply to an earlier Nepali communication informing about the appointment of M.P. Koirala as the Prime Minister, Dalai Lama sent his greetings and expressed the hopes that the relations between the two countries would continue as usual.[6] In Nepal King Tribhuwan and Prime Minister Koirala repeatedly affirmed that Nepal's relations with Tibet had not been affected by the Chinese action.[7] It is inconceivable that Peking authorities were unaware of all these happenings. Yet they kept silent. China did not make any overtures to Nepal and instead dealt with India in all the matters related to the Kingdom, in accordance with Indian advice.[8]

Besides India and Tibet, Nepal had diplomatic relations with Britain and the United States during King Tribhuwan's period. Following its withdrawal from the Indian sub-continent, Britain had virtually handed over its concern with Nepal to the United States. If any, there was little desire, and still less means on the part of the British to meddle in the "special relations" between India and Nepal. Their tacit, though reluctant, reconciliation with the position taken by the Government of India in the anti-Rana 'revolution', particularly on the question of King Tribhuwan's dethronement, may be recalled as an example.

The principal US interest in Nepal was to keep off communist influence. As such it had no basic conflict with India's objectives towards the Kingdom.[9] However, the United States wanted to have a foothold in Nepal and for that, it initiated the programme of economic aid which will be discussed later. India seems to have permitted the entry of US aid into Nepal but restricted its operation to the "carefully defined limits" so that it may not challenge its own position. India was cautious in tacitly permitting US aid into Nepal particularly because it strongly resented the US moves towards military alliances in the region. Nepal too had followed India in this respect as noted in the previous chapter. Notwithstanding this resentment, there was no serious attempt by the United States or Britain to undo the pattern of "special relations" between India and Nepal, except for some pinpricks.

Thus the Chinese silence, the tacit approval of Britain and United States, and the domestic factors of Nepal contributed to "very special and intimate" relationship with India.

MANIFESTATIONS OF "SPECIAL RELATIONS"

India, being the dominant partner in the "special" relationship, exercised immense and decisive influence over the affairs of Nepal. This influence was the characteristic feature of the pattern of "special relations" and was pronounced in Nepal's domestic politics, external relations and efforts towards economic progress and administrative stability.

Nepal's Domestic Politics and India

The Indian Government and leaders were often called on to resolve infights among the Nepali politicians. The Rana- Nepali Congress coalition installed under the "Delhi Settlement" of February 1951, had inbuilt dissensions. There was nothing in common between King Tribhuwan, the Ranas and the Nepali Congress. They were not only ideologically antagonistic but also each other's rivals for power.[10] The coalition had not worked even for two months when in early May 1951, the Nepali Congress members of the cabinet conveyed their inability to work with the Ranas to the King and asked him for a homogeneous cabinet.[11] Prime Minister Mohan Shumshere also complained that the "things have not developed the way as I expected them. He was, however, not in favour of referring the matter to the King, obviously fearing an un-favourable decision. He wanted the matter to be settled by the mediation of the Government of India since "it was in Delhi that the present basis of interim Government of Nepal was agreed".[12]

Accordingly, the leaders of the Rana and the Nepali Congress representatives in the cabinet visited New Delhi and held talks with the Indian leaders between 8 and 15 May 1951. As a result the cabinet crisis was resolved. The press note issued after the talks stated : "There was complete agreement that the Nepali cabinet should work in a cooperative and progressive spirit for the political development and economic prosperity of Nepal".[13] When asked about his reaction, B.P. Koirala said, "We have received some political education" in Delhi and added that the differences between the two groups were more psychological.[14] In accordance with the Indian advice, the cabinet was reshuffled on 9 June 1951, a week before Nehru visited Kathmandu, and Baber Shumshere Rana, Defence Minister and No. 2 in the cabinet, was dropped. However, the uneasy lull brought about in the Nepali cabinet proved short-lived ; the Ranas and the Nepali Congress leaders again clashed and ultimately the cabinet collapsed in November 1951.

Even after the fall of the Rana-Nepali Congress coalition, the practice of consultation with the Indian Government and leaders regarding the cabinet matters of Nepal continued. This is borne out by the following evidences. The appointment of M.P. Koirala as the new Prime Minister in November 1951 was said to have been manipulated by the Indian Ambassador in Kathmandu, C.P.N. Singh, against the wishes of the Nepali Congress which favoured B.P. Koirala.[15] The crisis in the Nepali Congress Cabinet in March-April 1952, resulting from the rift between B.P. Koirala and M.P. Koirala was resolved by the mediation of the Indian Sarvodaya leader Jaya Prakash Narayan in Calkata.[16] Establishment of the Advisory Regime under King Tribhuwan himself, after the fall of the Nepali Congress Cabinet in August 1952 was supported publicly by an ICS Officer, Govind Narain, placed as Personal Secretary to the King.[17] When opposition to the Advisory Regime became stronger, King Tribhuwan made a sudden and secret visit to Delhi in December 1952, believably to discuss with the Government of India, the issue of replacing his direct rule (Advisory Regime) with a government of political parties.[18]

The Advisory Regime was terminated in June 1953 and M.P. Koirala was appointed Prime Minister for the second time. Official circles in Delhi were reported to have welcome the change as it was alleged to have been in "conformity with Nehru's advice to King Tribhuwan".[19] Finally, in order to make the cabinet broad-based, Prime Minister M.P. Koirala visited India in October 1953, had talks with Nehru in Kolkata before he left for China and then rushed to Bombay to apprise King Tribhuwan who was on his way to Switzerland for medical treatment, with these talks.[20] Soon after his return from Switzerland, King Tribhuwan reshuffled the Cabinet in January 1954 and included D. R. Regmi of the Nepali National Congress and T.P. Acharya of Praja Parishad in it.

India's Role in Nepal's Administrative

Reorganization and Economic Development

The Nepali administration faced a serious problem of law and order soon after the "Delhi Settlement". Some of the Nepali Congress 'revolutionaries' under the leadership of Dr. K.I. Singh in western Nepal, refused to abide by the "Delhi Settlement" which they described as the "betrayal of the revolution". They indulged in terrorist activities which paralyzed economic life in the Terai and created panic among its inhabitants. These activities also effected the adjacent Indian villages since the border was open and unguarded. On the request of the Nepalese Government, the Indian troops of U.P. Armed Constabulary undertook joint operations with the Nepal State troops to counteract lawlessness in Nepal Terai.[21] A part of these troops remained in Nepal to stabilize peace in the area.[22] Similar operations were undertaken again in 1953.[23] Then to find a permanent solution of the border crossing by the criminals on either side, Nepal and India signed the Treaty of Extradition in October 1953.[24] Nepali police officers also received training in India.[25]

Law and order was only a part of the problem of the administration. The administrative structure of the Ranas, inherited by the new Government was anchronistic in relation to the political aspirations and economic expectations of post-Rana Nepal. It, therefore, needed complete reorganization for which the Government of India was approached. In response to that, a few Indian experts and advisers were immediately rushed to Kathmandu. An Indian study team visited Nepal in January 1952 with a view to systematically reorganize the administration.[26] On the recommendations of this team, the Government of India appointed a three member commission under N.M. Buch, an ICS officer. The Commission was to submit a report in consultation with the Nepali leaders and officers, on administrative reorganization, with special reference to the requirements in number and nature of the Indian personnel to help bring about that reorganization.[27] The Buch Commission started its work in May 1952 and submitted a report by the end of the year. This report formed the basis for administrative reorganization in Nepal and the loan of Indian experts and advisers to the Kingdom that followed.[28] The Government of India had also started giving economic assistance to Nepal in 1951, the details of which will be discussed later.

Coordination in Foreign Policies

Another important aspect of the "special relations" was India's guidance and leadership in Nepal's external relations. There was even a move between the two countries towards getting their foreign policies coordinated formally.

In May 1954, Nepal's Foreign Minister D.R. Regmi accompanied the King to India and discussed with the Indian leaders, besides other things, the matter of formally coordinating foreign policies of the two countries. The theme of the discussions in Delhi was incorporated into an *Aide Memoire* and presented by the Government of India to its Nepalese counterpart. The *Aide Memoire* stated that:

1. The Government of Nepal would consult the Government of India with regard to foreign policy and matters connected with foreign powers while India too would consult Nepal in all matters related to the latter.
2. In particular, Nepal would consult India in all matters affecting Sino-Nepalese relations.
3. The Indian missions would, if and where Nepal so desired, represent the interests of Nepal and all Indian foreign missions would be instructed to give all possible help and assistance to Nepali nationals.
4. The two governments would, from time to time, exchange information relating to foreign affairs and relations with foreign powers in so far as they affected each other.[29]

The matter was brought before the Nepalese Cabinet where some amendments were suggested in the draft to make the obligations of the two parties equal and just towards each other. The amendments related mostly to the first two aspects. It was suggested that India should take Nepal into confidence (a) with regard to its foreign policy and matters connected with foreign powers in all and not only with those relating to the Kingdom alone; and (b) in all matters affecting Sino- Indian relations as well.

Reciprocity to this extent was perhaps, not the kind of 'coordination', the Indian Government was looking for in foreign policy matters with Nepal.' Therefore, when suggestions of amendment in the draft were conveyed by Nepal to India, there was no response till the end of 1954. It seems that the Indian Government was waiting for a different Cabinet to take office in Nepal when the suggested amendments could either be mellowed down or dropped altogether. But in early 1955, King Tribhuwan died followed by a domestic political environment in Nepal which was not sympathetic to the revival of the foreign policy coordination move. There is no evidence to show that the matter was pursued subsequently.

Interestingly, the cabinet infights in Nepal at that time particularly between Prime Minister M.P. Koirala and Foreign Minister D.R. Regmi threw a sidelight on the *Aide Memoire* incident. The Nepali delegation's visit to India in May 1954, took place in the absence of Prime Minister Koirala. Therefore, Foreign Minister Regmi played an important role, next only to the King, in the negotiations leading to the conclusion of the *Aide Memoire.* It was said that by thus projecting himself as more friendly and amenable to the Indian leaders, the Nepali Foreign Minister tried to consolidate and improve his position in the cabinet *vis-a-vis* the Prime Minister, who for his allegedly growing pro-Western leanings in foreign policy matters had lost the hitherto enjoyed trust and goodwill of the Indian Government. It may be recalled in this context that the Indian Government and leaders were in a position as well as inclined to exercise considerable influence in adjusting Nepal's domestic power equilibrium.

M.P. Koirala on his return to Nepal, smelt D.R. Regmi's 'motives' and tried to thwart the *Aide Memoire* move. The amendments suggested into the original draft were believed to have been formulated by Prime Minister Koirala in consultation with the British Ambassador to Nepal. The amendments were in fact aimed at making the scheme unacceptable to the Indian side. And further, when the Indian Government learnt that the British Ambassador had something to do with the amendments, it pushed the 'coordination' move into freeze.

The matter of foreign policy coordination between India and Nepal was under consideration even when the Ranas were in power. At that time, however, India was not very enthusiastic about it for two reasons : First, India feared that its enthusiasm in the matter would provoke the British to put pressure to the contrary, on the Ranas. Secondly, the Ranas might demand an assurance from the Government of India that in return for coordinating their foreign policy, India would help them to remain in power in Nepal. Such a commitment could not have possibly been made by the Government of India in view of its sympathies for King Tribhuwan and the 'revolutionaries' well as its interests in having a democratic Nepal. Hence, it was not given a formal shape as such at that time. Nevertheless, the Treaty of Peace and Friendship between Nepal and India signed in July 1950 contained certain provisions for mutual consultations regarding the vital aspects of their foreign relations. The view that the foreign policy coordination was one of the objectives behind the Treaty of 1950 was confirmed by Nehru. Replying to a question in Parliament on 18 May 1954, he said:

> Rather for some time past—I forget now when we had our last Treaty with Nepal about four or five years ago and that was before the change took place in Nepal, even then we had that treaty—we had a treaty and it was stated in that treaty, I think in letters attached to that treaty, that the foreign policy of Nepal would be coordinated with that of India.

The question arises here as to why, if the Government of India was not enthusiastic in the matter during the Rana period and when the Treaty of Peace and Friendship already had some provision of that nature, the matter was revived in 1954? In answer to this question, a few points may be made. In the first place, the successors of the Ranas were friendly to the Government of India. Secondly, the provisions in the Treaty of Peace and Friendship were of a specific nature, namely, for consultation when either of the two parties had "any serious friction or misunderstanding with any neighbouring state" likely to rupture its relations with the other. As compared to this provision, the *Aide Memoire* was more broad based and covered almost every aspect of foreign policy and relations. Thirdly, it seems that the coordination move was aimed at reiterating and formally stabilizing the pattern of relationship between the two countries for the future. This was particularly so because anti-Indian sentiment was getting stronger in Nepal, foreign powers were becoming active, and the Opposition was demanding extension of Nepal's diplomatic contacts. This was evident in the context and content of Nehru's statement in the Parliament on 18 May 1954.

Lastly, in reviving the foreign policy coordination move, India was prompted by its Agreement with China regarding the status of Tibet. Since this Agreement formalized China's dominance over Tibet, India thought it necessary to clearly define and assert its own position in the Himalayan region. Towards that end, the move for the coordination of foreign policy with Nepal as stated in the *Aide Memoire* was an important step. It may be noted in this connection that there were indications that Nehru had secured an understanding from the Chinese leaders that Nepal was in India's sphere of influence.[112] A further indication in this regard was the time chosen for the high level discussion on the matter between India and Nepal. These discussions were held in early May 1954 soon after Nehru's return from Colombo after attending the S.E. Asian Prime Ministers Conference and after the signing of the *Panchsheela* agreement on Tibet.

Though the *Aide Memoire* did not take the formal shape of an Agreement as desired, the principles contained in it had been observed in practice between India and Nepal all through the Tribhuwan period. This was evident in Nehru's occasional statements. In February 1952 he said :

> On two occasions the Prime Minister was here and the King was also here once or twice. We naturally discussed various matters and gave advice, and in two matters more particularly we are closely associated, in matters of foreign policy and defence, not by any formal agreement but simply because both matters are common to us.[31]

Again after the *Aide Memoire* incident, Nehru told the Indian Parliament on 18 May 1954 :

> Now since these changes have taken place in Nepal, we have been brought in fairly close touch with developments there. We have often discussed these things and it has been very clearly agreed to between us, and only the other day—about less than a few weeks ago when His Majesty the King of Nepal and some Ministers of the

> Nepal Government were here—*it was again reiterated that the foreign policy of the Nepalese Government should be coordinated with the foreign policy of India. That is so : there is general agreement and even consultations with each other.*

Similarly, the Nepalese Foreign Minister D.R. Regmi said in a Press Conference in New Delhi on 8 May 1954 :

> Nepal's foreign policy is very similar with India's. We being very close to each other, have to face similar problems, difficulties and dangers and thus we will have to adopt a similar policy on many issues. *To discuss foreign policy matters and relations with friendly nations, the Foreign Ministers of India and Nepal will continue to have mutual consultations.*

Nepal's diplomatic contacts with the outside world were severely limited. Besides its embassy in New Delhi, it had only one mission stationed in London. Foreign missions stationed in Kathmandu were also only two : the Indian and the British. Therefore, if and when needed, Nepal conducted its diplomatic relations either through the foreign missions stationed in New Delhi or the Indian missions stationed abroad.

Nepal also depended upon India for its membership of, and participation in, the international organizations. The Kingdom hailed India's leadership in Asian affairs and commended its contribution to the cause of world peace, and its efforts towards securing a better recognition for the Asian voice in the international forum.[32] Nepal took India's side on issues like Goa where the latter was directly involved.[33] The question of Kashmir was, however, an exception in the sense that Nepal's support to the Indian stand was quiet and informal.

As regards the regularization of diplomatic relations with China, Nepal was guided by the Indian attitude towards it. The latter did not seem to have favoured the idea until May 1954. When asked in June 1951 to comment on a resolution of the Nepali Congress Working Committee demanding establishment of diplomatic relations with China, Nehru gave a cold response.[34] It is in this light that Nepal's reluctance to formally recognize the Communist Government of China and to have diplomatic relations with it, even when other countries of the region—India, Pakistan, Burma and Ceylon—had done so, as also to readjust its relations with Tibet in the new context, can be understood.

Unified Measures for Mutual Defence and Security

India had very high stakes in the security and defence of Nepal. The strategic considerations that formed the basis of India's policy towards Nepal in general, were repeatedly underlined by Prime Minister Nehru and other Indian leaders as have already been noted. These considerations led India to secure Nepal's cooperation and participation in certain measures which were common to defence and security of both the countries.

Thinking on these measures had started in early 1950 with the developments in China and Tibet. The Indian Government constituted two committees, one under the chairmanship of Deputy Minister of Defence, Maj. General Himmat Singhji and another headed by Maj. General Thorat on which fell the task of studying the problem and working out details of the measures.[35] While these committees were working, India and Nepal concluded the Treaty of Peace and Friendship in July 1950. The Treaty had adequate provisions for "mutual consultations" to "devise effective counter measures" in case of any threat to security of either, and thus the Treaty provided the basic and legal framework for the unified measures for mutual security and defence, between the two countries.

Soon after the conclusion of the Treaty of Peace and Friendship, India proposed to Nepal that for strategic and military intelligence purposes, checkposts should be established along the Kingdom's northern border.[36] The checkposts were accordingly established in September 1951. They were manned jointly by the Indian technicians and Nepali Army personnel. The Indians functioned as wireless operators and passed on coded messages about the 'movements' and 'activities' across the border, to the Governments of India and Nepal through the Indian Embassy in Kathmandu.[37] The checkposts were increased and strengthened in 1954 and subsequently.

The law and order situation created by the "terrorist activities" of Dr. K.I. Singh and his associates in February 1951 had exposed the "bad shape" in which the Nepali Army was at that time. Motivated by this, as also in pursuance of Himmat Singhji's and Thorat's committee recommendations to the Government of India, an Indian Military Mission arrived in Kathmandu in February 1952.[38] The Mission was sent after a formal request to that effect by the Government of Nepal and the task of the Mission was to assist the host Government in the "training and reorganisation of the Nepalese Army". The strength of the Mission was 20 officers and men initially but it rose to 197 officers and men by December 1953.[39] Among other things, the Mission proposed a reduction in the strength of "ill-trained" and "ill-equipped" 25,000 Nepali troops to "well trained" and "well equipped" 6,000 troops.[40]

These arrangements along with the Agreement on Gurkha recruitment and the Treaty of Peace and Friendship constituted the links that unified the policies and measures the two countries adopted in dealing with problems of their defence and security. The substance and form of these arrangements underwent various changes subsequently.

CLIMATE FOR THE CHANGE

India's influence in the internal as well as external affairs of Nepal was due to a particular set of factors. A change in them, therefore, was to change the nature of 'special' relationship between the two countries. The change in the domestic milieu resulted from the death of King Tribhuwan in March 1955, whereas the external milieu for Nepal had begun changing even a few months earlier. As the process of change in the domestic and the external milieu advanced in Nepal, the pattern of its "special relations" with India also changed. Instead, Nepal evolved the policy of balance of power in relation to the neighbouring region which will be discussed in the next chapter.

External Milieu

In the international context, the most important event for Nepal was the conclusion of an Agreement between China and India in April 1954, regarding the status of Tibet. The following was the sequence of events concerning Nepal, India and China after the signing of the Agreement.

Nehru returned to Delhi on 2 May 1954 after attending the Colombo Conference. The King of Nepal and some Ministers visited New Delhi at that time. During this visit, Nepal's willingness to regularize its relations with China was officially hinted at for the first time.[41] This willingness was expressed more explicitly in June when Chou En-lai visited India. It was reiterated thereafter.[42] China was reported to have welcomed and reciprocated Nepal's willingness to establish formal diplomatic relations.[43] Two months later, Chinese Premier Chou En-lai, stated in the first People's Congress in China that his Government was prepared to establish normal relations with Nepal.[44] In October, when Nehru was leaving for China, Nepal's Prime Minister M.P. Koirala conferred with him at Kolkata and conveyed his "good wishes" to the Chinese leaders.[45] M.P. Koirala met Nehru again at Darjeeling when the latter returned from China.[46] A month later he disclosed in the Advisory Assembly of Nepal that normalisation of relations with China was under consideration of the Government and decision on the subject was to be announced soon.[47] Again, within a month of this disclosure, Foreign Minister Regmi said in the same Assembly that an agreement with China on the basis of Five Principles of Peaceful Co-existence, agreed upon between India and China, was afoot and was to be finalized after negotiations with the Chinese Government.[48] However, due to the intra-cabinet dissensions, leading to the resignation, first, of three ministers and then of the whole cabinet, and the illness of King Tribhuwan leading to his death in March 1955, nothing could be done.

The important point which emerges from the above sequence of events is that the *Panchsheela* agreement between India and China opened the way for Nepal to normalize its relations with the latter. Towards this accord, the Government of India, in particular Prime Minister Nehru, played a key role.

Nepal itself was no less interested in regularizing these relations. The Nepali Congress resolution of May/June 1951 may be recalled in this context (n. 34). Nepal had cultural and historical ties with China and a 500-mile long common border with Tibet. Disturbances in Tibet had caused a fear of infiltration from the north. More so, because the transitional and unsettled state of politics and poverty, ignorance, and the ideological vacuum made the Kingdom vulnerable to such a threat. Above all, the Treaties of 1792 and 1856 concerning Nepal, Tibet and China, though in abeyance, had not been abrogated officially. These Treaties, it may be recalled, had provision which could be easily twisted to offer justification for China's imperialistic motives, if there were any.

Besides all these reasons, there was a historical logic for Nepal to have normal friendly relations with China. Before 1846, when China's position in Tibet was strong and its control there was effective, Nepal felt Chin;, close at the door and had remained friendly to it. After that, the Chinese grip over Tibet weakened, resulting in the break of relations with Nepal. Now again, China was asserting its position in Tibet, thereby coming closer to Nepal and, thus, it was necessary for the latter to be in friendship with its powerful northern neighbour.

Domestic Milieu

The process of regularizing diplomatic relations with China received further impetus in Nepal from the changes in the domestic milieu. In King Tribhuwan, the Government of India had a dependable friend and ally in Nepal, which his successor son, King Mahendra, could not be. The latter found the Indian influence come in the way of his strong urge for the exercise of authority and political participation. Besides his supreme position in the power structure of the Kingdom, what facilitated King Mahendra's task of weakening the hindrance was the presence of anti-Indian sentiment in Nepal.

Sentiment against India was expressed in the form of the charges that India was interfering in the domestic affairs of Nepal. Its targets, therefore, were the Government of India and the Indian Embassy in Kathmandu, the Indian teams present in Nepal to reorganise military and civil administration and to help in other developmental activities, the frequent visits of the Nepali King and Ministers to New Delhi as also the Agreements, like on the Koshi project, which involved sharing of the benefits both by India and Nepal.[49]

The anti-Indian feeling was given vent to in various public statements by the political leaders, party-resolutions, comments in the press and demonstrations and processions. Noteworthy of them were two black flag demonstrations. The first was staged against Nehru when he visited Kathmandu in June 1951. The second was staged three years later in Kathmandu against a visiting Parliamentary delegation from India.[50]

There were a number of factors behind the origin and growth of the anti-Indian sentiment in Nepal. In the first place, it was the outcome of Nepal's size-psychology—or the small power complex—*vis-a-vis* India which Randhir Suba of the Gorkha Parishad described as the "dark suspicion".[51] Primarily, India's Nepal policy with its builtin ambivalence, was responsible for aggravating this suspicion. The policy, as evident in the statements of the Indian leaders, particularly Nehru, was based on two contradictory premises, namely:

(a) Nepal was a fully independent and sovereign country and India should scrupulously observe non-interference in its affairs.

(b) Nepal being strategically important, India had a legitimate claim of "keen and personal" interest in the domestic as well as external affairs of the Kingdom.

It appears that the policy-makers in New Delhi failed to strike a proper balance between their ideological moorings and concept of international morality on the one hand, and vital national interests of India on the other. Further, in the implementation of the policy, the second aspect being operative it got precedence over the first and added to Nepal's psychological imponderables.

Prompted by the second aspect, the Government of India made their advice, good offices and help frequently available in Nepal to bring about changes in the governments and preserve domestic peace, as has been discussed above. One might wonder as to why in the process, India did not help Nepal to erect viable constitutional and political structures based upon the professed bias of the two in favour of democratic ideals and institutions. The Government of India's objective to allow no other country to interfere in Nepal or be more friendly to it as compared to India, in fact led them to prevent Nepal from taking initiative in extending its diplomatic contacts. This resulted in an apparent gap between the profession and practice in the policy and made the Government of India a suspect in Nepal. What further strengthened it was the extremist opinion of certain sections in India demanding that Nepal, along with Bhutan and Sikkim, should be integrated with their country.[52]

The basic contradiction in India's Nepal policy would have been saved, or at least delayed, from being exposed if the policy had been backed by a discreet and dexterous diplomacy. The Indian Ambassador, C.P.N. Singh, who was instrumental in securing the Government of India's help for the King and the 'revolutionaries' against the Ranas, was alleged to have participated in the cabinet meetings and Governors' (Bada Hakim) conferences, taken undue interest in the domestic affairs of Nepal and kept troops in the Embassy to "force his directives", if need be, on the Nepalese Government and people.[53] It is difficult to say whether, and to what extent, he was acting in these matters under instructions from New Delhi. While explaining his position, the Ambassador though refuted the motives attributed to his behaviour, defended some of his activities on "the basis of democratic practice", privileges of an Ambassador in a foreign land and the Treaties and Agreements entered into, between India and Nepal.[54] This open style of diplomacy only spurred his opposition and ultimately the Government of India had to withdraw him. It is very likely that his personal biases towards individuals and organizations—developed as a result of his participation in the anti-Rana movement—continued to be reflected in his behaviour even later and, thus, made him a controversial figure in the fluid condition of the Nepali politics.[55] The fact that the open style of diplomacy and personality factors displayed by C.P.N. Singh were considered undesirable, was evident from the conduct of his successors Balchandra K. Gokhale and Bhagwan Sahay who adopted a reverse course.

Ambivalence in India's policy followed by its unsophisticated diplomacy in Nepal gave rise to confusion in the Kingdom. Whereas the political and economic situation in Nepal prompted the Government to approach New Delhi frequently for consultations and help, the very awareness of this fact pricked the conscience of an emerging nation. Whereas geographical contiguity and socio-cultural affinity between the two countries called for a very close relationship between them, the closeness viewed against the historical background, was feared, would eclipse Nepal's entity as an independent sovereign nation and prove detrimental to the growth of its international personality. The arrangements that symbolised the cooperation between the two countries, like the Indian Military Mission, Indian Advisers, etc. were also the symbols of India's presence in the Kingdom and as such militated against the Nepali sense of identity and self-respect. Therefore, though everyone in Nepal realized that the Kingdom needed India's help, some or the other point was made to criticize the help that was forthcoming. The attitude of various political parties towards the Indian Military Mission in Nepal can be taken as an example to substantiate the point.

The Nepali Congress was responsible for calling the Military Mission during its partnership in the ruling coalition. Later the party demanded its withdrawal to "stabilize close relations between the two countries and defeat evil attempts of the opportunist elements aimed at damaging these relations".[56] The Gorkha Parishad agreed that the Mission did useful work but held that "because of the intolerable and discourteous words towards Nepal and the Nepali people it had become unpopular and should be withdrawn.[57] The Nepali National Congress Bulletin described the Mission as "foreign army" which had been brought to Nepal to deal with the domestic situation under a "secret pact" with the Government of India.[58] Later its working committee, on the one hand, thought that it was "not only desirable but even natural" for Nepal to expect help from India which the latter must provide, and on the other, warned India that its help should be "selfless" and should not lead to its "political influence".[59] Another leader, R.K. Shah, said that he had no objection to the continuation of the Mission, provided Nepali people were convincingly told of the progress made by it.[60] The nature of the criticism against other matters was also the same.[61]

All these factors of India's Nepal policy and Nepal's in shibitions and apprehensions towards it were exploited by the Nepali politicians in giving vent to their frustrations. The fall of the Ranas had created a power vacuum in Nepal which the new political order filled in only inadequately. The political parties were in disarray and none of them, for lack of ideological coherence and organizational and political experience, was capable of filling in the vacuum. The monarch, on the other hand, was reluctant to assert himself fully. In this situation, the political parties (most of them were groups of a handful of persons) tried to manipulate a share in power through seeking favour from the King and/or the Government of India. Whosoever failed in the manipulation became anti-Indian and anti-King. And whenever a party or a leader secured power, his attitude abruptly turned in favour of the Government of India. This is avident from the following examples:

(a) The Ranas who themselves insisted upon the mediation of the Government of India when their coalition with the Nepali Congress was in danger in April 1951, later vehemently criticized the practice of holding consultations about the cabinet in New Delhi.[62]

(b) The Nepali National Congress which had earlier joined the anti-Indian chorus, appealed for friend-ship and close relations with India when given a share in the Cabinet.[63] Its leader, D.R.Regmi who earlier criticized the Government of India for its role in the "Delhi Settlement" and for not taking the "true representatives of Nepalese people" into consideration at that time,[64] later, in the capacity of Nepal's Foreign Minister, said that anti-Indian feeling was the expression of "defeatism and frustration" among the Nepali politicians.[65]

(c) Tanka Prasad Acharya of the Praja Parishad, who earlier defended black flag demonstrations staged against Nehru in June 1951, and accused the Indian Government of giving importance to the "opportunist elements" in Nepal at the cost of patriots",[66] later as the Home Minister, warned those who were trying to drive a wedge between India and Nepal. He described them as "disgruntled politicians trying to gain power through political blackmail".[67]

(d) It has been noted that the Nepali Congress while in power, either along with the Ranas or independently was responsible for inviting the Military Mission and various other advisers from India. But later, when it no longer remained in power, it came out against all these advisers and the Mission and attacked the Government of India.

(e) The opinion of the Rastriya Praja Party of M.P. Koirala and the Communist Party need not be recorded here because whenever there was a cabinet of political parties during the period, it always included the former and always excluded the latter. Therefore, all the important statements of M.P. Koirala were pro-Indian and those of the leaders of the Communist Party, anti-Indian. There were apparent ideological reasons and political considerations behind the Communist Party's stand.

In the last it may be mentioned that some "external agents", particularly the Americans and the British, were believed to have been encouraging anti-Indian sentiment in Nepal. Reacting sharply to the black flag demonstration against the Indian Parliamentary Mission visiting Nepal, Prime Minister Koirala said in June 1954 :

> We almost believe now that some foreign agency is abetting and inciting Nepalese...Why are not Americans and European experts, now in Nepal, being criticized by these very people? Why are all the guns of the India baiters

> turned only against the Indian assistance to Nepal? (Then he added) : "There should be no mincing of matters. Our relations with India have been and will always be more intimate than any other country.

In response to these allegations, George Allen, the US Ambassador in India, who was also accredited to Nepal, visited Kathmandu. After his observations, he maintained that the United States only wants Nepal's progress and had no connection with Nepalese politics.[68]

This was, however, not the first time that the US sympathies were alleged to be with the anti-Indian sentiment in Nepal. Earlier, Foreign Minister D.R. Regmi, while referring to the US arms aid to Pakistan, observed that "certain forces" which created division between India and Pakistan were also trying to ferment bitterness and trouble between India and Nepal.[69] India's Prime Minister Nehru also said in the Parliament that his Government was aware of the "outside interference" in Nepal which was creating mischief against India there.[70] Former Nepali Congress Home Minister S.P. Upadhyaya in an article on "India and Nepal" said that the Government of India was unaware of the reasons, ways, and intensity of Americanism in Nepal.[71] Later in 1953, the Nepali Congress Working Committee held in a resolution that the superpowers were getting active in Nepal to achieve their selfish motives and were trying to eract a wall between India and Nepal.[72]

Thus the anti-Indian sentiment in Nepal was not the out-come of any single factor. It was mixed effect of Nepal's size-psychology and its nascent nationalism, India's policy and diplomacy in Nepal, frustration among Nepali politicians, and external influences, as discussed above. However, in spite of all its apparent intensity, the anti-Indian sentiment was only a surface phenomenon and remained confined to the Nepalese capital and its political circles. It was mostly used by the opposition to beat the party in power. The politicians in their anti-Indian campaign were joined by those who were retrenched or otherwise suffered owing to the administrative, police and military reorganisation schemes carried out in Nepal under the Indian guidance.[73] A political observer in Kathmandu commenting on anti-Indian sentiment said:

> Countries like Japan, Turkey, and Pakistan relied upon foreign aid and had a large number of British and foreign advisers. But none of these countries lost their independence. Even

> then we are afraid that we will lose our independence due to the presence of one Ambassador and three advisers (Indian). This is due to lack of self-confidence among us resulting from lack of development and progress. Political parties are responsible for this.[74]

Nevertheless, the synchronisation of the anti-Indian feeling with other domestic and external developments in the Kingdom strengthened the case for Nepal's "special relations" with India to be revised.

Notes

1. Stuart R. Schram, *The Political Thought of Mao Tse-tung,* New York, 1963, 257.
2. A Minister in the first Cabinet under M. P. Koirala, who prefers to remain unidentified, confided to the author that the Government of Nepal received a communication from China saying that the rights and privileges hitherto enjoyed by Britain, India and Nepal in Tibet were no longer valid. (Kathmandu, March 1968).
3. Dr. K. I. Singh, former Prime Minister of Nepal, who was in Tibet at that time under political refuge, told the author in an interview. It was further confirmed by the Bhikshus and Nepali traders who kept on travelling between Nepal and Tibet. (Interviews, Kathmandu, May and June 1968).

   A daily from Kathmandu also expressed its thankfulness early in 1952 to the Tibetan authorities for the facilities provided to the Nepali traders. *Awaz,* 2 *Magh* 2008 (January 1952), Vol. I, No. 315.
4. *The Statesman,* 10 March 1953 ; *The Times of India,* 14 March 1953.
5. The spokesman of the Chinese Foreign Ministry said in a statement on 20 January 1950:

   "Tibet is the territory of the People's Republic of China. This is a fact which is known to everybody in the world and which has never been denied by anybody. Since this is the case, the Lhasa authorities, of course, have no right to arbitrarily send out any missions and still more to prove Tibet's 'independence'.

   ...If the Lhasa authorities...send out illegal mission to engage in splitting and traitorous activities; the Central People's Government of China will not tolerate such traitorous activities of the Lhasa authorities. Any country receiving such illegal missions will be regarded as harbouring hostile intentions towards the People's Republic of China." *China Monthly Review*, Vol. 119, No. 2, October 1950. (Supplement: China's Foreign Relations), 11.

6. *Awaz*, 14 *Falgun* 2008 (February-March 1952), Vol. 2, No. 6, 1. Also *The Statesman*, 15 March 1952.

7. For example see, King Tribhuwan's speech to the Advisory Assembly in July 1952. *Goikhapatra*, 24 *Ashad* 2009 (7 July 1952), Yr. 53, No. 33. M. P. Koirala's speeches and statements: *Hamro Par Rastra Sampark* (Our Foreign Relations), Publicity Department, Government of Nepal, Kathmandu, n.d., 22, 50.

8. *K. M. Panikkar,* In Two Chinas: The Memoirs of a Diplomat, *London, 1955, 171.*

9. Chester Bowles, *Ambassador's Report*, London, 1954, 265, 280.

10. In the very first meeting of the Coalition Cabinet, the clash between the Ranas and the Nepali Congress seemed imminent when the two sides disagreed over the order of precedence among their respective representatives in the Cabinet.

    The Hindu, 20 February 1951.

11. *The Hindu*, 8 May 1951.

12. *The Hindu*, 9 May 1951.

13. Text of the Press Note, *The Hindu*, 17 May 1951.

14. *The Hindu*, 17 May 1951.

15. Bhuwan Lal Joshi and Leo E. Rose, *Democratic Innovations in Nepal*, Berkeley, Los Angeles, 1966, 96-100; Aniradha Gupta, *Politics in Nepal*, Allied Publishers, Bombay, 1964, 67, 171-74.

16. Grishma Bahadur Devkota, *Nepal ko Rajnitik Darpan* (Political Mirror of Nepal), Kathmandu, 1960, 169-71.

17. Ibid., 200.

18. The King was accompanied by his Counsellor for Home Affairs, Mahabir Shumshere J.B.R. *The Hindu*, 6 December 1952.

    Denying that the King had political consultation with the Indian leaders, a press note issued by the Nepalese Embassy in New Delhi said that the King visited India to consult throat specialists as he was not keeping well. *The Hindu*, 8 December 1952. The denial sounds incredible.

19. *The Hindu*, 6 June 1953.

20. *Gorkhapatra*, 26 Ashvin 2010 (12 October 1953), Yr. 53, No. 77; Devkota, n. 16, 223.

The move to broaden the cabinet was afoot for some time and the Prime Minister had had consultations with various political leaders including B.P. Koirala, D.R. Regmi and tanka Prasad Acharya. The objective could not be achieved because a common minimum programme was not forthcoming from the political parties. "Text of King Tribhuwan's Message before leaving for Switzerland", *Gorkhapatra,* 5 Ashvin 2010 (21 September 1953), Yr. 53, No. 68.

21. *The Hindu,* 23 February 1951.
22. India, *Parliamentary Debates,* Part I, Vol. VII, No. 35, 14 May 1951, Cols. 4236-38.
23. *Gorkhapatra,* 9 *Shravan* 2110 (24 July 1953); *The Hindu,* 20 July 1953 ; *The Statesman,* 20 July 1953.
24. For the text of the Treaty see *Foreign Policy of India: Text of Documents 1947-59,* 2nd edn., Lok Sabha Secretariat, New Delhi, 1959, 93-95.
25. Hamro Par Rastra Sampark, *n. 7, 35.*
26. The study team included Deputy Secretary in the Ministry of External Affairs and Commander Umrao Singh. *Gorkhapatra,* 16 *Magh* 2008 (30 January 1952), Yr. 52, No. 115.
27. Preface to the *Report of the Nepal Administrative Reorganization Committee,* Ministry of External Affairs, Government of India.

    The appointment of the Commission had been officially finalized during the visit of the Nepalese Ministerial delegation to New Delhi in April 1952.

    India, *Parliamentary Debates,* House of the People (16 to 28 May 1952), Press Note, Ministry of External Affairs, Appendix I, No. 27, 58.
28. *Ibid.* A copy of the Report was shown to the author by a former Prime Minister of Nepal. He was, however, not allowed to study it and was given to understand that it was a classified document.
29. *Jhyali,* 8 July 1958. Also see *Nepal Press Digest,* Regmi Research Project, Kathmandu, 16-31 July 1958, No. XXXI. Also see Joshi and Rose, n. 15, 246-48.
30. Nehru's Press Conference in New Delhi on his return from China. *The Tribune,* 14 November 1954. For similar views see also *The Statesman,* 16 April 1954.
31. *The Hindustan Times,* 16 February 1952.
32. Advisory Assembly resolution on the peace in Indo-China, *Gorklia- patra,* 32 *Shravan* 2011 (16 August 1954). Also see *The Hindustan Times,* 12 August 1954 ; *The Hindu,* 23 February 1954.
33. The Advisory Assembly of Nepal unanimously passed a resolution supporting the cause of Goan freedom fighters and

upholding India's claims on Goa in August 1954. *The Statesman,* 11 August 1954. This had been stated even earlier in the Assembly by the Nepalese Foreign Minister. *Gorkhapatra,* 4 *Ashad* 2011 (18 June 1954), Yr. 55, No. 29.

34. *The Hindu,* 12 June 1951. For the resolution of the Nepali Congress, see *Nepal Pukar,* 22 *Jaistha* 2008 (May-June 1951), Yr. 4, No. 4.

35. B. N. Mullik, *The Chinese Betrayal.* New Delhi, 1971, 122, 124.

36. *Ibid.,* 123.

37. Pradyuman P. Karan and William H. Jenkins Jr., *The Himalayan Kingdoms : Bhutan, Sikkim and Nepal,* Princeton, 1963, 117.

38. Gazette Notification of 27 *Falgun* 2008 (February-March 1952), Part 9 *Government Notifications,* Government of Nepal, Kathmandu. Also, *Gorkhapatra,* 16 *Vaishakh* 2009 (April-May 1952), Yr. 53, No. 7.

39. A. S. Bhasin, *Documents on Nepal's Relations with India and China,* New Delhi, 1970, 37.

40. Leo E. Rose, *Nepal: Strategy for Survival,* California, 1971, 197.

41. Foreign Minister D. R. Regmi commenting on the Sino-Indian agreement said: "We will face the same question. We have Treaty relations with Tibet. We stand for friendship with China", *The Statesman,* 6 May 1954, *Hamro Par Rastra Sampark,* n. 7, 54. Also. *The Hindu,* 4 May 1954.

42. Hamro Par Rastra Sampark, *n. 7, 55;* The Statesman, *30 June 1954.*

43. This was conveyed to the Nepalese Ambassador by the Chinese envoy in New Delhi. *The Times of India,* 1 July 1954.

44. *Gorkhapatra,* 13 *Ashvin* 2011 (29 September 1954) ; *Survey of China Mainland Press,* American Consulate General, Hongkong ("Summary of Premier Chou En-lai's report on Government's work in last five years"), No. 895, 24 September 1954, 6.

45. Evading specific questions about his talks with Nehru and Sino- Nepalese relations, M. P. Koirala said: "Anything might have come up during our meeting". When asked if Nehru would take anything from him to China, he replied: "No proposals, but certainly our good wishes". He, however, added that Nepal was ever eager to regularize its relations with China, provided there was a "suitable opportunity" for negotiations. *The Hindustan Times,* 15 October 1954. On reaching back to Kathmandu, the Prime Minister said that Nepal will have relations with all countries of South East Asia whose foreign policies were not in clash with that of Nepal. *Gorkhapatra, 2 Kartik* 2011 (18 October

1954).

46. *The Hindu*, 5 November 1954.

47. *The Hindu.*, 25 November 1954.

48. *The Statesman*, 18 December 1954.

49. These points had been framed after scanning available published material on the subject and various interviews the author had in Nepal. Our discussion on this subject is largely based upon this material unless otherwise specified. For few important references see :

    Nepal Pukar (Nepali Congress Official Organ): Surya Prasad Upadhyaya, "Nepal re Bharat" (Nepal and India), 12 *Kartik* 2009 (October-November 1952), Yr. 5, No. 9, 7 (Editorial); "Hath Zhik" (Hand Off), 19 *Jaistha* 2010 (June 1953), Yr. 6, Nos. 12 and 1% 2; *Rastravani* (Gorkha Parishad's Official Organ, Translation) Editorial, "Intimacy or Suspicion", Issue No. 6, 9 June 1953; Editorial, "Sovereign Independence", Issue No. 19, 16 August 1953; *Rastriya Congress Bulletin* (Nepali National Congress Official Organ): "Open letter to Nehru", 2 *Ashad 2008* (June 1951), No. 17; Editorial, 10 *Jaistha* 2009 (May-June 1952), No. 58. Devkota, n. 16, 143-50. (Collection of various statements on the subject); *Rastrihit*, Chanakya *(pseud)*, "Current Thoughts", 16 *Shravan* 2009 (July-August 1952), Yr. 1. No. 1.

50. The first demonstration was believed to have had the sympathies and support from the Praja Parishad and the Communist Party of Nepal. *The Hindu*, 17 and 18 June 1951; Devkota, n. 16, 96. Also see, Leo E. Rose, "Communism under High Atmospheric Conditions: The Party in Nepal", *The Communist Revolution in Asia*, Robert A. Scalpino (ed.), Prentice-Hall, Inc., New Jersey, 1965, 345.

    The Gorkha Parishad and the Nepali Congress were the suspects behind the second demonstration. Both justified the demonstration and none disowned it. *The Times of India*, 2 June 1954; *The Hindu*, 2 June 1954; *Rastravani*, 2 June 1954; *Nepal Pukar*, 24 *Jaistha* 2011 (June 1954), Yr. 7, No. 8. Also see Devkota, n. 16, 246; *Government Notifications*, 17 *Jaistha* 2011 (June 1954).

51. *Rastravani*, 2 June 1954; also *Nepal Pukar*, 12 *Kartik* 2009 (October-November 1952), Yr. 5, No. 9, 7.

52. A statement of this nature was made by Dy. Speaker of India's Lok Sabha, A. S. Ayangar in Bombay in April 1954. *Free Press Journal*, 5 April 1954. This raised a public controversy in Nepal. Rendering an explanation, the Indian Embassy in Kathmandu

said that the Dy. Speaker in a clarification issued later said that by "integration" he meant the integration of the foreign and defence policies only. It said that the Government of India considered it as a personal opinion which had nothing to do with the official policies. The Embassy explanation reiterated that the Government of India respected Nepal's independence and sovereignty and would continue to do so. *Rastravani,* 10 May 1954. For another example of such opinion see *The Organiser,* New Delhi, 18 October 1954.

53. These charges were systematically listed by B. P. Koirala in December 1951. Also see *Rastravani, 7 Bhadra* 2011 (August-September 1954); Devkota, n. 16, 123-24; *The Times of India,* 22 February 1952.

54. *The Hindustan Times,* 21 December 1951; *Gorkhapatra, 4 Paush* 2008 (19 December 1951), Yr. 52, No. 98, 14 *Magh* 2008 (January 1952); Devkota, n. 16, 131-33, 135-36.

55. C. P. N. Singh was quoted by a former Nepali Minister to have admitted that his support to the Nepali Congress leader brought him only discredit. Dharma Ratna Yami, *Nepal to Kura* (Talk of Nepal), Kathmandu, 1957.

56. *Nepal Pukar,* 13 *Chaitra* 2009 (March-April 1953), Yr. 53, No. 25. Also *Nepal Pukar,* Editorial, (Nepal's northern line of defence), 12 *Jaistha* 2011 (May-June 1954).

57. *Rastravani, 2* June 1953, Issue, 5.

58. *Rastriya Congress Bulletin,* No. 51, *Vaishakh* 2009. (It was officially contradicted by the Government of Nepal.) *Gorkhapatra,* 21 *Chaitra* 2008 (March-April 1952).

59. *Rastriya Congress Bulletin,* No. 58, 10 *Jaistha* 2009 (May-June 1953).

60. Amrit Bazar Patrika, *1 May 1953.*

61. For example *see Nepal Pukar,* 28 *Vaishakh* 2011 (April-May 1954), Yr. 7, No. 5 and *Rastravani,* 20 May 1954, on Koshi Project.

62. *Rastravani,* 26 October 1953.

63. *The Hindu,* 3 June 1954; *Rastriya Congress Bulletin,* No. 25, 22 *Shravan* 2008 (July-August 1951), No. 58, 10 *Jaistha* 2009 (May-June 1952).

64. *The Hindu,* 21 February 1951.

65. *Gorkhapatra,* 8 Magh 2011 (21 January 1955). Also see *The Times of India,* 21 June 1954.

66. Devkota, n. 16, 143.

67. Amrit Bazar Patrika, *9 June 1954. Also* see *The Statesman,* 17 September 1954; *The Times of India,* 13 September 1954.

68. *Nepal Pukar,* 31 *Jaistha* 2011 (June 1954).
69. *The Hindu,* 8 March 1954.
70. India, *Parliamentary Debates,* Council of States, Vol. VI, No. 49, 18 May 1954, cols. 6762-63.
71. *Nepal Pukar,* 12 *Kartik* 2009 (October-November 1952).
72. *Nepal Pukar,* 13 *Chaitra* 2009 (March-April 1953).
73. Leo E. Rose, n. 40, 197-98.
74. Charvak *(pseud),* "Nepal ma Samyavad, Ek Dhristikaun" (Communism in Nepal, A View-point), *Rastrahit,* Yr. 1, No. 5, 1 *Kartik* 2009 (October-November 1952). Also see *Awaz,* 21 *Falgun* 2008 (February-March 1952), Vol. 2, No. 12, "Nepal and India" (Editorial).

4

THE REGIONAL BALANCE OF POWER

King Mahendra's rise to power in March 1955 proved to be a land mark in Nepal's foreign policy. Nepal moved away from the policy of "special relations" with India and evolved a certain balance of power in relation to its neighbours. The factors, domestic and external, that were responsible for initiating the shift have been discussed in Chapter 3.

The balance of power policy pursued by Nepal was strikingly different from what is commonly understood as balance of power. It was not of the type pursued by Great Britain to expand its sphere of influence in Europe during the 19th and the early 20th centuries. Nepal is a very small power, a 'mini' power according to some scholars,[1] and its policy in the region, dominated by bigger powers like India and China, was primarily a strategy for defence and economic development, This policy resulted from Nepal's responses to the pulls and pressures exercised on it by its two great neighbours.

Nepal's regional balance of power had three dominant features. They were : (*i*) the extension and maintenance of friendship based on mutual respect and goodwill, with every one of the neighbours : *(ii)* the exploitation of regional differences—between the neighbours—to further self-interests; and *(iii)* the declared stand of neutrality in the disputes between the neighbours.

THE INITIAL PHASE 1955-58

The emergence of the policy of balance of power was marked

by two developments taking place simultaneously, namely, regularization of diplomatic and trade relations with China and revision of the pattern of "special relations" with India. While cultivating new relations with China, Nepal took care, not to weaken its basic friendship and understanding with India. The simultaneity of the two developments, coupled with the Nepali leaders, particularly Prime Minister Tanka Prasad Acharya's occasional references to the triangular friendship among Nepal, India and China, at times gave rise to the impression that Nepal was heading towards the policy of "equal friendship" with its neighbours. The subsequent developments, however, did not sustain the impression.

Regularization of Diplomatic Relations with China

In April 1955, Nepal and China had the first informal exchange of views on the question of regularization of their mutual diplomatic relations, at Bandung during the Conference of Afro-Asian countries.[2] It was followed by formal negotiations in 1955 at Kathmandu where the two countries agreed, on 31 July, to have friendly relations on the basis of *Panchsheela*—the five principles of peaceful co-existence. It implied Nepal's formal recognition of the Communist regime in China. It also served as a prelude to another Agreement on "Trade and Intercourse" between the two countries which was signed in Kathmandu on 20 September 1956.

This new Agreement of 1956 and the 'Notes' exchanged with it, had three main features.[3] One, it reaffirmed, and elaborately defined, the *Panchsheela* as the governing principles for the relations between Nepal and China. (Preamble, Art. I) Two, by implication, Nepal recognized China's new position in Tibet as India had done. Accordingly, the claims and rights enjoyed by Nepal in relation to Tibet in the past were surrendered and the Kingdom agreed to withdraw its military escorts from Tibet, "together with all their arms and ammunition" within six months (Notes: para 2). Three, it abrogated "all treaties and documents" that existed between Nepal and China, and between Nepal and Tibet (Article III). A new pattern of trade and intercourse was instead, established between them (Article IV and Notes).

After the conclusion of the "Trade and Intercourse" Agreement, Nepal's Prime Minister, Tanka Prasad Acharya, paid a goodwill visit to China from 25 September to 7 October 1956. This was reciprocated by the Chinese Prime Minister Chou En-lai who visited Nepal from 25 to 29 January 1957. A mood of warmth and friendly feeling prevailed during these visits.[4] Both the Prime Ministers recalled the traditional friendship between the two countries, reaffirmed their faith in the *Panchsheela* and expressed identity of views on the issues of world peace, anti-colonialism, anti-imperialism and Afro-Asian Solidarity.[5] Tanka Prasad Acharya's visit to China was marked by an Agreement on China's aid to Nepal amounting to sixty million rupees in Indian currency. (The details of this agreement are discussed later). With these visits, the process of regularization of relations between the two countries became complete. This also led to the revival and extension of cultural ties between Nepal and China.[6]

Maintaining Friendly Relations with India

While regularizing diplomatic relations with China, Nepal maintained its friendly ties with India. King Mahendra undertook a goodwill visit to India from 6 November to 8 December 1955. It was reciprocated by the President of India, Dr. Rajendra Prasad, in October 1956. Nepal's Prime Minister, Tanka Prasad Acharya's visit to India took place within two months of the Indian President's visit to Nepal, from 4 to 7 December 1956.

The Nepali side tried to impress two things upon India during these visits. One, Nepal's desire to "maintain and further consolidate" its traditional "bonds of friendship and goodwill" with India[7]; and two, a strong urge to assert its independence and sovereignty, particularly *vis-a-vis* India. The first aspect found expression in the speeches of King Mahendra and Tanka Prasad Acharya—it was particularly prominent in the former—during their respective visits to India.[8] The second aspect was discernible in Tanka Prasad Acharya's speeches and statements. Soon after assuming office on 27 January 1956, he stated that he would revise Nepal's "special relations" with India even in matters pertaining to aid and trade.[9] In a press conference in May 1956, he hinted at Nepal's desire to change the existing basis and terms of facility given to India and Britain to recruit Gurkha troops.[10] Then during his visit to India in December 1956, Acharya told the Indian leaders that Nepal's wish and efforts to remain friendly with other countries including China, should not be misunderstood.[11]

The Indian leaders seem to have sensed Nepal's new mood.

Accordingly, they showed sympathy and accommodation towards its assertive tone. Prime Minister Nehru told Acharya in December 1956, that India was interested in the independence and progress of Nepal. He then talked of "temporary mistakes which might be made" regarding the Indo-Nepalese relations and said : "We will try to learn something from your experience and advice". Dr. Rajendra Prasad also assured the Nepali leaders in Kathmandu : "We do not threaten the sovereignty or integrity of any other state, nor do we wish to interfere in the internal affairs of other countries."[12] Further, the informality which marked the exchange of visits between leaders of the two countries earlier was replaced by the observance of diplomatic decorum and etiquette. Tanka Prasad Acharya was the first Nepali Prime Minister to be accorded a formal civic reception in New Delhi. As for King Mahendra, wherever he went during his visit, formal receptions were arranged in his honour. Unlike his father, he addressed farewell messages to Prime Minister Nehru and President Rajendra Prasad on the conclusion of the visit (n. 8).

While accommodating the demands of Nepal's 'status' motive, the Indian leaders kept reminding Nepal of the intimate ties and mutual interests subsisting between the two countries. Dr. Rajendra Prasad told his hosts in Kathmandu :

> We are parts of the same subcontinent, standing together in perpetual amity and friendship. India is vitally interested in the peace and prosperity of your great country and I am sure, you are equally interested in ours....We are faced with common problems and we cherish common ideals. India and Nepal are inseparably linked together by strong ties since time immemorial.... Any threat to the peace and security of Nepal is as much a threat to the peace and security of India. During these visits, King Mahendra was urged to bring about the establishment of a representative government in the Kingdom and until that was to be done, to ensure a "clean and vigorous administration".[13] The King's response was favourable. He promised to work "for giving a permanent shape to the democratic institutions in Nepal".[14]

Relations between India and Nepal operating within the pattern initiated during the preceding years remained restricted in 1957 and 1958. In 1957, the new Prime Minister of Nepal, Dr. K.I. Singh shelved all suggestions for the expansion of diplomatic relations and advocated "special ties" with India.[15] But Dr. Singh's Prime Ministership failed to make any lasting impact on Nepal's policy towards India. In January 1958, a Nepalese political delegation visited India, reportedly at the latter's initiative without permission of the Nepalese Government. A protest was lodged by Nepal in this connection and the Government of India, in turn, apologised.[16] Later during the same year, King Mahendra announced gradual withdrawal of the Indian Military Mission from Nepal,[17]—an issue which was often referred to in support of the allegations of Indian interference, by various political parties and leaders during King Tribhuwan's period.

MEETING THE PRESSURE FROM CHINA 1959-60

The years 1959-60 constituted the next stage of evolution in Nepal's regional balance of power policy. The popularly elected Government of the Nepali Congress was in power during this period. Nepal's relations with its neighbours during the period were dominated by two factors: (*i*) the disturbances in Tibet, resulting from the Chinese military action against the "Tibetan revolt" and their repercussions on Sino-Nepalese relations; and (*ii*) the growing tension between India and China on the question of territorial demarcation of boundaries and of Tibet.

The main burden of Nepal's policy in the region during this period was, however, to meet the situation created by the first factor which had become a matter of anxiety and concern in the Kingdom. Nepal adopted a two-pronged policy. In the first place, it made serious efforts, marked with success, to settle outstanding issues with China through peaceful and friendly negotiations. Secondly, and simultaneously, it mobilized the already existing close understanding with India in order to meet any probable threat or pressure from China. The developments in Nepal's relations with India and China during this period should be seen as the elaboration of these two aspects.

Settlement of Outstanding Issues with China

The disturbances "in the Tibet Region of China" in 1959 gave rise to certain issues between China and Nepal. The issues were mostly related to the difficulties of the Nepali traders in Tibet and the demarcation of boundary between Nepal and China. The question of boundary demarcation had a long history.[18] It was raised for settlement by Tanka Prasad Acharya with the

Chinese leaders in 1956, but without any outcome.[19] The flow of the Tibetan refugees into the Kingdom and violations of the Nepali border resulting from the movement of Chinese troops in their action against the Tibetan 'rebels' called for an immediate settlement of the boundary issue.

On assuming office in May 1959, the Nepali Congress Government headed by B.P. Koirala took up the matter with the Chinese Government. The latter was ready to hold a joint meeting of the two sides to discuss the issues.[20] Accordingly, Nepal's Village Development Minister, Dr. Tulsi Giri visited China in October.[21] However, nothing significant emerged from this visit and Dr. Giri was quoted as having said on his return from China that he "did not believe that the Chinese would be ready to solve their border problem with Nepal".[22]

The failure of Dr. Giri's mission made Kathmandu anxious. Public pressure in favour of a firm policy towards China, which had been mounting on the Government since the beginning of disturbances in Tibet, further increased. In view of this, Prime Minister Koirala himself visited China from III to 22 March 1960. There he had "free and frank discussion on matters of common interest" with the Chinese leaders. As a result, the two sides reiterated their faith in *Panchsheela* and "agreed to establish embassies mutually in Peking and Kathmandu".[23] The most important outcome of this visit was the signing of two Agreements. The first was on the "question of the boundary between the two countries". It included the following features:[24]

1. The boundary was to be scientifically delineated and formally demarcated...on the basis of the existing traditional customary line. (Art. I)
2. The task of delineation and demarcation was to be performed by "a joint committee composed of an equal number of delegates from each side". (Art. II) Broad guidelines for the committee were also laid down in the Agreement. (Art. Ill)
3. "In order to ensure tranquillity and friendliness on the border", the two sides agreed to demilitarize an area of twenty kilometres from the border on their respective sides. (Art. IV)

Thus the Agreement achieved the twin objectives of delineating, formally and finally, the boundary between the two countries;

and of reducing tension along the border. Under the second Agreement, China gave economic aid to Nepal amounting to 14 crores of rupees.

B.P. Koirala's visit was returned by the Chinese Prime Minister Chou En-lai between 26 to 28 April 1960. Chou En-lai came to Kathmandu on his way back from New Delhi where he had futile discussions on the Sino-Indian boundary question with India's Prime-Minister Nehru. The Nepalese and the Chinese Prime Ministers reiterated their faith in the principles of peaceful co-existence and assured goodwill and understanding to each other.[25] They concluded a Treaty of Peace and Friendship. This Treaty was first proposed to B.P. Koirala during his visit to China, in place of the initial offer of a unilateral non-aggression pact. Neither the non-aggression pact nor the Treaty could find favour with the Nepalese Prime Minister at that time. He turned down the idea of the pact and deferred the signing of the Treaty in Peking.[26]

The Treaty of Peace and Friendship between Nepal and China was far less comprehensive and significant as compared to the Treaty Nepal had with India under the same title. The former was a simple reiteration, of the recognition and respect of the one party in the other's independence, sovereignty and territorial integrity". (Art. I[27]) Under the Treaty, the two sides undertook to settle their mutual differences through peaceful negotiations. (Art. II). They also expressed their desire to "develop and further strengthen" economic and cultural ties between them "in accordance with the principles of equality and mutual benefit and of non-interference in each other's internal affairs." (Art. III). The Treaty was subject to ratification and was valid initially for a period of ten years. (Art. V). The only importance of the Treaty lay in Chou En-lai's comment that it was political in nature and had a greater scope than the agreement on *Panchsheela* concluded between the two countries in 1956.[28]

Intimately connected with the boundary question was another issue of importance—the ownership of Mount Everest. In the maps exchanged along with the Boundary Agreement in March 1960, the conflicting claims of Nepal and China in this context were recorded formally for the first time. Whereas the mountain belonged to China according to the Chinese maps, it was shown on the boundary line in the Nepalese maps.[29] Both the countries had drawn the maps on the basis of their respective historical documents. However, B.P. Koirala claimed that the Everst belonged to Nepal. Chairman Mao Tse-tung, on the other hand, expressed his readiness to follow the Nepalese maps, *i.e.* to accept the position that the northern half of the Everest belonged to China and the southern half to Nepal. This was disclosed by Chou En-lai in Kathmandu. The Chinese Premier also cited the delineation in the Indian and the British maps in support of his country's stand.[30] Since the evidences were exceedingly in favour of this position that the Everest lay on the boundary line and, so its southern slope belonged to Nepal and northern slope to China, the Nepalese side appeared to be adjusting its position accordingly.[31] The issue was, however, left open in April 1960 for further discussion between the Prime Ministers of the two countries.[32]

While controversy over the Everest was still fresh, another dispute arose involving violation by China of Nepal's border and thus of the recently concluded Boundary Agreement. On 28 June 1960, the Chinese troops crossed over to the Mustang region of the north-west Nepal, killing one Nepali border guard and capturing a few others.[33] Only two days before this incident, China had informed Nepal that its troops in order to deal with the "Tibetan rebels" were to enter into the 20 kilometre zone on the Chinese side, demilitarized under the Boundary Agreement. Nevertheless, the Chinese Note had promised that the troops were not to violate the Nepalese border.[34] Therefore, the incident, which almost followed this Note, took the Nepalese side by surprise.

The Government of Nepal made a strong protest to the Chinese Government and followed it by rejoinders. The Chinese promptly confessed that the Mustang incident took place due to "the carelessness of certain low ranking personnel". Accordingly, Prime Minister Chou En-lai apologised on behalf of his Government and agreed to pay compensation for the life of the Nepali guard, as desired by the Nepalese side.[35] The dispute regarding location of the incident was left to be resolved by a Joint Committee of China and Nepal constituted to demarcate the border under the Boundary Agreement. And the matter was regarded as closed.[36]

Thus, the issues that had arisen between Nepal and China during this period were brought nearer to their final settlement by the end of the period. An important factor that made it possible was the spirit of accommodation and understanding displayed by China towards Nepal. By peacefully settling the boundary question with Nepal and other neighbours like Burma,

China tried to demonstrate that it was open to mutual adjustment and indirectly suggested that in its border dispute with India, the latter was to be blamed. This was, in fact, a part of China's strategy in South Asia to extend its influence and isolate India. The settlement of the issues proved to be a major achievement towards the stabilization of relations between China and Nepal. These relations were further consolidated by King Mahendra in the following years.

Closer Understanding with India

Soon after the establishment of the Nepali Congress Government, India's Prime Minister Nehru paid a goodwill visit to Nepal in June (12 to 14) 1959. It was returned by the Nepalese Prime Minister B.P. Koirala in January (17 to 31) 1960. The two Prime Ministers highlighted the "invincible, in-destructible and everlasting" nature of the "age-old brotherly" relations between India and Nepal. They held that these relations based on mutual respect for sovereignty, independence and dignity on common interests, and on identical approaches to the fundamental issues of international politics.[37]

Nepal and India had identical understanding of the disturbances in Tibet and their repercussions. Therefore, their approaches to China in this context were described as basically similar.[38] B.P. Koirala during his visit to India in January 1960, described Nepal-India friendship as indispensable and the Himalayas as the symbol of "friendship and cooperation" between them.[39] He stressed that the two countries had vital stakes in each other's security and so would stand together in facing problems of present and future and added, "what is good for you is good for us and what is bad for you is bad for us."[40] Prime Minister Nehru also expressed similar sentiments. In April 1960, B.P. Koirala did not allow the visiting Chinese Prime Minister Chou En-lai to criticise India in a Press Conference in Kathmandu.[41]

The Government of Nepal was in close touch with the Indian Government while negotiating with China. Soon after Dr. Tulsi Giri's return from China in October 1959, Nepal's Deputy Prime Minister Subarna Shumshere Rana made a quiet and quick visit to India, where he met Nehru, presumably to acquaint him with the outcome of Dr. Giri's mission.[42] Prime Minister Koirala also discussed various aspects of the Sino-Indian and the Sino-Nepalese boundary issues with the Indian leaders on his way to China. During the negotiations that preceded the Boundary Agreement, the Nepalese side insisted on the inclusion of the phrase "on the basis of the traditional boundary line" in the Agreement to lend support to India's case *vis-a-vis* China's, in the settlement of the border dispute between them.[43] Further soon after the Mustang incident, King Mahendra had talks with India's Prime Minister, Home Minister and the Defence Minister, in New Delhi.[44] It was followed by B.P. Koirala's discussions with Nehru on the developments across the Himalayan border in August 1960, when he made a brief stopover in New Delhi on his way to Isreal.[45]

There existed close understanding and arrangement between India and Nepal in matters pertaining to their mutual defence and security. The Agreement on the recruitment of the Gurkhas in the Indian Army and the Treaty of Peace and Friendship between the two countries have already been discussed. Military intelligence of the two countries was coordinated by the presence of the "Indian technicians" at Nepal's military checkposts along its border with China. These "technicians" kept a watch on the activities across the border and passed on the relevant information to the Government of Nepal through the Indian Embassy in Kathmandu. An Indian military advisory group, the composition and functions of which underwent substantial changes from time to time, had also been stationed in Kathmandu since 1952.

In view of these arrangements, and the situation in the region, Nehru declared in the Lok Sabha on 27 November 1959 that any aggression on Nepal and Bhutan will be treated as an aggression on India and will be accordingly dealt with.[46] B.P. Koirala welcomed the statement as a gesture of friendship.[47] However, since Nehru in his statement had bracketed Nepal with Bhutan, an Indian protectorate, there was a furore in Kathmandu. To assuage popular sentiment, B.P. Koirala asserted Nepal's independent and sovereign status and held that the discretion to ask for India's help in any eventuality of an aggression lay entirely with Nepal. He said that if sought, Nepal would also readily help India in case of an aggression. But he refused to term Nehru's statement as "uncalled for":[48] Explaining his position, Nehru referred to the provisions of the Peace and Friendship Treaty of 1950 between the two countries and made it clear that he neither meant any unilateral action on India's part nor made any reflection on Nepal's independence and sovereignty.[49] Again, it was in view of this already existing understanding that B.P. Koirala termed as "unnecessary" any move for a joint India-Nepal defence arrangement, suggested at a press conference during his visit to India.[50]

While activising its understanding in political and security matters with India, Nepal played cool towards Chinese overtures which, in effect, sought to belittle this understanding and strengthen China's position in the Kingdom. China's offer to Nepal of a unilateral non-aggression pact and the latter's cold response to it may be recalled here. The non-aggression pact, if signed, would have turned the "mutual understanding in defence matters" between India and Nepal as redundant since the understanding was based on the perception that China posed a threat to them. The Nepali leaders also rejected another Chinese offer to construct the Kathmandu-Kodari (Tibet) highway which in effect aimed at changing the geo-political context of the Kingdom and to undermine the strategic advantage enjoyed by India in Nepal *vis-a-vis* China, through the Tribhuwan Rajpath.

The burden of the foregoing facts is to underline the degree of understanding and the identity of interests displayed by Nepal and India towards each other during 1959-60. This, however, brought the Nepali Congress Government under attack at home from the opposition. The Government was attacked for toeing India's line and having compromised Nepal's independence and sovereignty. This does not appear to be true. Prime Minister B.P. Koirala's forthright stand on Nehru's statement has been noted above. Further, in economic matters, while signing the Gandak Project Agreement and revising the tenyear old trade Treaty with India, the Government had taken adequate care to protect Nepal's interests and its independent and sovereign status.

MEETING THE PRESSURE FROM INDIA 1961-62

By the end of 1960, the issues that had cropped up between Nepal and China were almost settled and the factors that caused immediate anxiety and a sense of insecurity in the Kingdom from the Chinese side were, by and large, removed. But then suddenly, there arose a situation which brought in pressures on Nepal from the Indian side. This sudden change resulted from the dismissal of the Parliamentary system by King Mahendra on 15 December 1960 and the establishment of his personal rule. These developments had far-reaching repercussions on Nepal-India relations.

With the King's "takeover", a number of leaders and workers of the erstwhile ruling party, the Nepali Congress, crossed over to India in order to escape arrests. From there, they conducted activities against the new regime. In this situation the Government of India's approval of the change in Nepal and its consequent support to the King's regime were vital for the latter's legitimacy and stability. The implications of India's sympathy with the anti-Ranas revolution in 1950, which ultimately led to the fall of the Ranas were not very old to be forgotten by the King.

The Indian Government's immediate reaction went against the interest of the new regime in Nepal. This reaction was characterised by Prime Minister Nehru's statement in the Lok Sabha on 16 December 1960, in which he regretted that the "experiment of democracy should have suffered a setback". Later, he deplored the anti-Indian attitude of the Nepalese Press (which was a reaction to the Indian attitude towards the King's action) and expressed sympathies for the deposed Prime Minister, B.P. Koirala.[51] The Indian public opinion also joined the Government in disapproving the King's action and expressing sympathy for the dismissed government.

The Government of India's disapproval of the King's action acted as a morale booster to the Nepali Congress and gave a fillip to its activities. This created a difficult situation for the new regime in Nepal which tried to deal with it in three ways. First, by employing all its resources and strength to counteract the activities of the Nepali Congress. Secondly, by making efforts to secure support from the Government of India. Third, by mobilizing support from other countries, particularly China and Pakistan, to create counter-pressures on India. The first aspect concerned wholly with Nepal's domestic affairs and so is out of the scope of this study. The second and the third aspects are discussed below.

Towards Securing India's help

Nepal's new government adopted a soft policy towards India during the year 1961. King Mahendra was reported to have sent a letter to Prime Minister Nehru immediately after his "takeover", explaining the circumstances which impelled him to do so and assuring that it would not affect the friendly relations subsisting between India and Nepal.[52] These points were further elucidated to, and help sought to curb the activities of the Nepali Congress from the Government of India by Nepali Ministers

Dr. Tulsi Giri and R.K. Shah, who visited India in January and December 1961, respectively.[53] King Mahendra also had talks with Prime Minister Nehru in New Delhi in August 1961 with the same objectives.[54] On several occasions, the Nepali leaders discounted any possibility of Nepal going against India and instead, highlighted the intimate times between the two countries. The Government of Nepal appealed to the Indian press and public opinion to desist from prejudicing, through comments, "ancient and indispensable" friendship between the two countries.[55] Above all, at one time, it was also indicated that the release of B.P. Koirala and other political detenus would be considered if the Indian Government only approved the change brought over by King Mahendra in Nepal.[56]

This approach of the King's regime, however, did not seem to produce a desirable impact on India. Meanwhile, King Mahendra had also initiated the third dimension of his policy, of cultivating support of China and Pakistan. This, in fact, hardened India's attitude towards the King's regime. Simultaneously, the activities of the Nepali Congress against the new regime increased—an attempt on King Mahendra's life in January 1962 was followed by numerous instances of gun- running and raids, mostly in the Terai. These developments created tension in Indo-Nepalese relations during 1962.

The Nepalese Government, therefore, shifted to a firm posture towards India. King Mahendra impliedly and his Ministers led by Dr. Tulsi Giri and Viswa Bandhu Thapa, openly held the Government of India responsible for the anti-regime activities.[57] The Government of Nepal produced and published 'evidences' in support of this contention. A communique issued by the Home Ministry said that the arms and ammunition seized from the rebels were manufactured in India and the 'paybook' recovered from them further confirmed that they had their base in India.[58] Accordingly, a strong protest was lodged with the Government of India and the recovered articles were exhibited in Kathmandu.[59] The charges were, however, denied by the Government of India which claimed that it was keen to prevent the smuggling of arms into Nepal and the violent activities of the Nepali exiles from the Indian side.[60]

Notable in the propaganda war on India were two publications: *Friendship on Trial* and *Hostile Expeditions and International Law.* These publications were released in Kathmandu in March and April 1962 respectively by the HMG's Department of Publicity.

The first booklet contested the Indian Government's argument that the law of the land did not provide for anything to restrain the activities of the Nepalis. By quoting the Indian Penal Code and the Indian Extradition Act of 1903, it argued that the Government of India was competent to take action against the Nepali outlaws and/or deport them to Nepal. The second pamphlet was released on the eve of King Mahendra's visit to India. It tried to establish that the lack of action against the anti-regime activities of the Nepali Congress in India constituted a breach of International Law by the Indian Government.

In continuation of the attempts to bring the Indian Government round to his views, King Mahendra visited India from 18 to 22 April 1962. In a "heart to heart" talk, the King and the Indian leaders reiterated their respective stand towards the activities of the Nepali Congress exiles in India. However, they agreed that an informal Joint Inquiry Committee should go into the details of particular incidents resulting from such activities and remove the difference of opinion. They also agreed to stop propagandistic publications against each other. As usual, close ties and common interest between Nepal and India were underlined. The Indian side, on its part, requested the King to broaden the scope of the Panchayat System in order to ensure popular participation in it.[61] The King told the Indian leaders not to misunderstand Nepal's relations with China and Pakistan.[62]

The decisions arrived at this visit were not implemented satisfactorily. Soon after the visit, the Government of India registered a protest to their Nepalese counterpart for unauthorised intrusions into Indian territory by Nepalese police.[63] It was denied by the Nepalese Government which, in turn, resented that the lack of cooperation from the Indian police thwarted Nepali Police operations against the 'rebels'.[64] The informal Joint Committees were also not functioning satisfactorily. But the two sides appeared to be moving cautiously.

R.K. Shah was appointed Nepal's Foreign Minister in July. He believed that the successful implementation of the Nehru-Mahendra joint communique of April, could improve the relations between the two countries. He advocated "quiet diplomacy" towards that end.[65] R.K. Shah visited India in September 1962 where he discussed the then existing arrangements for informal Joint Inquiry Committees with the view of improving them. Prime Minister Nehru and the Bihar Chief Minister B. N. Jha reassured him that strict vigilance would be observed on the

Indian side to prevent "gun-running" by the Nepali outlaws across the border. R.K. Shah also tried to dispel, what he called an "erroneous impression" in India that Nepal was playing China and Pakistan against it. Nehru, on his part, repeated the advice that the King should burden the Panchayat system and have friendly negotiations with the Nepali Congress leaders.[66]

The outcome of R.K. Shah's September visit in particular, and his "quiet diplomacy" approach in general, did not satisfy King Mahendra because it failed to bring about the desired change in the Government of India's attitude. Therefore, R.K. Shah was relieved of his ministerial portfolio on 22 September 1962. The communique issued on the occasion repeated the charges against India which indicated a further hardening in the Nepalese approach. Reacting to the Indian suggestion for negotiations with the Nepali Congress leaders, the communique said :

> Nepalese are capable of sacrificing themselves in the cause of their sovereignty and independence. The gallant Nepalese race has always held its head erected and never learnt to bend it. Nepal is not prepared to enter into any kind of compromise on the basis of the threats of evil actions engineered by fifth columnists and anti-national elements.

Immediately after the release of the communique, a clash between the Indian intelligence officials and armed Nepalis took place at the Indian border town Raxaul on 29 September 1962. It led to anti-Nepalese demonstrations in Raxaul and anti- Indian rallies and processions in Birganj, Kathmandu and other parts of the Kingdom. The commercial traffic between the two countries came to a standstill resulting in a sudden price rise and panic in Kathmandu, particularly because it coincided with one of Nepal's biggest festivals, *Dashiu*. The armed Nepalis involved in the clash were described as Nepali Congress 'rebels' by the Government of Nepal and the "Nepali policemen" by the Government of India. Charges and counter-charges were exchanged between the two Governments through official communiques and statements. The Government of India offered to inquire jointly with Nepal into the incident but the Nepalese Government did not agree.[67] An annoyed King Mahendra repeated the charges against India in his message to the nation on the occasion of *Vijaya Dashmi* and hinted at the "possibility of Nepal's age-old friendly relations with friendly country India being spoiled."[68] Thanks to the armed conflict between India and China of October 1962, this possibility was averted.

Cordial Relations with China

Unlike the Indian reaction, China acquiesced with the termination of the Nepali Congress Government and the Parliamentary system by King Mahendra. The Chinese Vice-Premier Chen-Yi acclaimed King Mahendra's leadership while welcoming the Nepalese delegation to the Joint Committee on Boundary in Peking in early February 1961. To further consolidate this moral support for his political innovations at home, King Mahendra visited China from 26 September to 19 October 1961.[69] On landing in China, the King hoped that from the Chinese side "there will be no chance for any unfriendly behaviour calculated to spoil our good relations".[70]

During this visit, King Mahendra and Liu Shao-chi signed the Boundary Treaty which defined border alignments in accordance with the findings of the Joint Committee constituted for the purpose under the previous Agreement on the subject.[71] The task of fixing permanent boundary markers and of drafting the final protocol, were left to the same Joint Committee (Art/ III). As a result of the new alignments, Nepal gained some 300 sq. miles of the territory.[72] Regarding Mount Everest—called *Sagarmatha* in Nepali and *Jol-mo Lungma* in Tibetan—the Treaty confirmed the earlier position, accepted by the Chinese that the boundary line passed through it. The Treaty stated:

> *...The boundary line...runs generally southwards along the mountain ridge passing through Cho-Oyu Mountain, Conire Langur (Pumoli Mountain), Sagarmatha (Mountain-Jol-mo Lungma)* and Lhosta to Makalu mountain... (Art. I, para 12).

King Mahendra on his return to Kathmandu, however, maintained that *Sagarmatha* "continues to be, as it has been, ours and within our territory."[73] It seems that the King had the southern slope and/or the peak, and not whole of the mountain, in his mind while saying so.[74] The Treaty did not clarify the position of the two tri-junctions, of China, Nepal and Sikkim on the east and of China, Nepal and India on the west, of the Sino-Nepalese boundary. It involved India's approval which could not be obtained due to Sino-Indian differences on the question of their boundary. But the position of China and Nepal regarding these two tri-junctions was in conformity with that of India's.[75]

Besides the Boundary Treaty, an Agreement on the construction of a highway was also signed between Nepal and China during the visit. The idea of the highway originated on 1957 when the Nepali traders asked the visiting Chinese Premier, Chou En-lai, in Kathmandu to get the old trade routes between the two countries improved and reactivised.[76] Chou En-lai proposed the construction of the highway to the Nepalese Government during his second visit to Kathmandu in April 1960. The latter did not find the project economically beneficial and politically sound and hence declined the offer.[77]

King Mahendra also did not seem to have thought of it before his visit. He was urged by the Chinese leaders in the course of talks to accept the proposal.[78] The ostensible purpose of the highway was to facilitate trade and intercourse between the two countries as well as within the Kingdom.[79] However, for China the political and strategic implications of the highway to improve the Chinese position in Nepal *vis-a-vis* India's were of important concern.[80]

King Mahendra returned from China with the assurances of support for his regime.[81] Since then the Chinese leaders continued to reiterate their sympathy and support for the Nepalese Government. Vice-Premier Chen Yi stated on 4 October 1962 :

> On behalf of the Government and People of China, I assure His Majesty King Mahendra, His Majesty's Government and the Nepalese people that if any foreign forces attack Nepal, we (the) Chinese people will stand on your side.

The timings of Chen Yi's statement added to its significance. It was issued when India-Nepal relations had touched their lowest point. It also preceded the Sino-Indian conflict by two weeks. Nepal's reaction to the statement was all favourable. The Kingdom heaved a sigh of relief.[82]

Thus King Mahendra's Government was found to be receptive to China's overtures towards Nepal, which the previous government discouraged for political and strategic considerations. A small but weighty rider of understanding in defence matters against, what was called, "the threat from the south", appeared to be emerging in Nepal-China friendship. This led to China's demands for the withdrawal of Indian technicians from Nepal's northern military check-posts, and for stopping the use of Gurkhas by India against China during 1961-62 and even later.[83]

Activization of Relations with Pakistan

Nepal established diplomatic relations with Pakistan on 19 March 1960.[84] These relations were activized by King Mahendra when he paid a state visit to Pakistan from 10 to 16 September 1961. During the visit King Mahendra and President Ayub exchanged personal adulations,[85] and expressed keen interest in, and support for, each other's political systems— Basic Democracy of Pakistan and the infant Panchayat System of Nepal.[86]

Indirectly referring to India's disapproval of King Mahendra's "takeover" President Ayub resented the behaviour of such "friendly countries" which "instead of being helpful, have become a nuisance" and asked the King to go ahead in establishing the Panchayat System in Nepal without caring for "what anybody else from outside says about it".[87] He also commended King Mahendra's efforts to preserve Nepal's in-dependence and sovereignty, and offered all possible help from Pakistan towards that end.[88] King Mahendra, on his part, indicated the desire to have cultural and commercial relations with Pakistan.[89] Later, while accepting Pakistan's new Ambassador to his court on 14 February 1962, the King high-lighted Nepal's "newly acquired friendship" with Pakistan and declared: "Nepalis, like Pakistanis, shall not deter in the defence and preservation of sovereign rights."

Thus Nepal's relations with China and Pakistan during 1961-62 were largely to demonstrate that it was determined to stand and face Indian pressures. As such, it was an exercise in creating counter-pressures. However, these counter-pressures made the Government of India's attitude towards King Mahendra's regime more stiff instead of softening it. To what extent Nepal would have carried this policy in the region in the face of Indian displeasure could not be seen because the Sino-Indian conflict of October 1962 abruptly changed the entire situation.

MAINTAINING FRIENDSHIP AND UNDERSTANDING WITH ALL NEIGHBOURS

The Sino-Indian conflict marked the peak of tension in the

region; the ensuing years saw conditions gradually settling down. Nepal also adjusted its policy in the region accordingly. With India its concern was to restore the damaged cordiality and understanding; with China and Pakistan, to maintain existing friendly relations. Moreovere, it had to manoeuvre these relations to further its interests, as best as possible, steering clear of prejudices amongst its neighbours.

Restoration of Cordiality and Understanding with India

The Sino-Indian conflict had immediate repercussions on India-Nepal relations. The Nepali Congress suspended its activities against the King's regime. The Party's President, Subarna Shumshere Rana, explaining the stand, said in a statement in Calcutta on 24 October 1962 :

> Nepal is very much in the area of conflict and a wrong step at this juncture might jeopardise the future of our country. We do not want the people's democratic movement in Nepal to be an excuse for the King to compromise our country's independence, the sovereignty or territorial integrity.

In November, the Government of India sent its former Ambassador in Nepal, Bhagwan Sahai, to discuss the Sino-Indian developments with the Nepalese Government and leaders.[90] This visit was returned by Nepal's Foreign Minister Dr. Tulsi Giri between 8 to 11 December. In India Dr. Giri met Prime Minister Nehru, Home Minister Lai Bahadur Shastri and Defence Minister Y. B. Chavan. During these meetings, steps to restore understanding between India and Nepal were discussed in the light of the situation arising after the Sino- Indian conflict. Dr. Giri on his return to Kathmandu declared that there was no basic difference between India and Nepal and whatever "misunderstandings had cropped up" between them, were also "in the process of being removed".[91]

The process of removing misunderstandings was streamlined and carried further through several visits exchanged between the two countries by their respective leaders. The visits can be listed as follows:

S. No.	The Visit	When it was undertaken
1.	Home Minister Lai Bahadur	Shastri to Nepal 4-6 March 1963.
2.	King Mahendra to India	27-31 August 1963.
3.	President Dr. S. Radha-Krishnan to Nepal	4-8 November 1963.
4.	Foreign Minister S. Swaran Singh to Nepal	23-25 August 1964.
5.	Chairman of the Council of Ministers Dr. Tulsi Giri to India—on way to visit to Yugoslavia	26 October 1964.
6.	Foreign Minister K.N. Bisht to India	24 January to 6 February 1965.
7.	Minister of State for External Aifairs Mrs. Laxmi Menon to Nepal	15-18 February 1965.
8.	Prime Minister Lal Bahadur Shastri to Nepal	23-25 April 1965.
9.	King Mahendra to India	25 November- 20 December 1965.
10.	Chairman of the Council of the Ministers Surya Bahadur Thapa to India	11-28 April 1966.
11.	Prime Minister Mrs. Indira Gandhi to Nepal	4-7 October 1966.
12.	Defence Minister Burathoki to India	3-17 November 1966.

Besides these visits, King Mahendra informally visited India from 17 to 27 January 1963.[92] India's Minister Manubhai Shah made two visits to Nepal in February 1964 and January 1965 and Dr. K.L. Rao visited Nepal from 22 to 25 February 1964. Since these visits were largely concerned with economic matters, they have not been included in the above list.[93]

During these visits, an attempt to appease Nepal was clearly discernible on India's part. Contrary to the earlier stand, the Indian leaders quickly got reconciled to the establishment of the Panchayat System and the King's supremacy in Nepal. King Mahendra's "poetic and philosophic bent of mind" and other personal qualities were highlighted. Mrs. Gandhi described him in October 1966 as the incarnation of Plato's ideal : "The Philosopher King". Indian leaders repeatedly stressed during these visits that the Government of India neither did, nor will encourage unlawful activities of the

Nepali Congress outlaws.[94] This change in India's attitude was viewed by King Mahendra as a vindication of the strength and viability of his policy towards India.[95] Nevertheless, there were reports that the Indian Government quietly dropped hints to their Nepalese counterpart to adopt a sympathetic attitude towards the Nepali Congress rebels.[96]

To dispel Nepal's apprehensions, the Indian side reiterated its respect for the latter's independence, sovereignty and territorial integrity, assuring that it will never interfere in the Kingdom's internal affairs. But it highlighted the close ties and natural interests of the two countries in each other's security and stability, and thus emphasized the need for mutual understanding and cooperation. The two sides discussed the international situation and declared that they had similar approaches in this context. It is notable that the Sino-Indian and the Indo-Pakistan relations (the latter after 1965) invariably figured during these visits—mostly at India's initiative — wherein the emergence of Sino-Pak collusion in the region and its implications on the security of India and Nepal were underlined. In October 1964 Dr. Tulsi Giri's talks with Nehru in New Delhi were held in the background of China's first nuclear blast.

The matters related to mutual cooperation in the economic field gradually acquired an increasing importance in the discussions between the two sides. India offered assistance for Nepal's economic development while accommodating the latter's psychological impulses. Mrs. Gandhi during her visit, renamed the "Indian Aid Mission" in Kathmandu as the "Indian Cooperation Mission".

The Nepali leaders were particular in asserting the "in-dependent and distinct personality" of Nepal. Along with this assertion, however, they reciprocated the views expressed by the Indian leaders regarding close ties and common interests. They appreciated India's economic assistance and desired its un-interrupted continuation.

In the environment of understanding and goodwill, developed during these years, India and Nepal also took up the issues awaiting mutual adjustment. These included : the transfer to His Majesty's Government, of a Post and Telegraph Office run by the Indian Embassy; the movement of one country's vehicles into the territory of the other; the transfer of foreign exchange to Nepal earned as a result of the Gurkha recruitment in the British Army but deposited with the Government of India; Nepal's demand for an increase in the number of Nepalese checkposts along the border for the entry of foreigners coming via India; the reorganization of the Indian Military Advisory Group stationed in Kathmandu; the issues pertaining to trade, transit and economic cooperation and the border dispute in the Susta region and Narshani forests in the Lumbini Zone of Nepal adjoining U.P. and Bihar provinces of India. The initiative in most of the cases came from Nepal which, looking at the nature of the issues, manifested its urge for the assertion of independent identity *vis-a-vis* India. These matters were discussed at the level of joint secretaries as well as high dignitaries. Slowly and gradually, the Government of India accommodated most of these demands.[97] Thus by the end of 1966, the understanding and goodwill, damaged during 1961-62, was restored. This was evident in King Mahendra's comments, made while being interviewed by the *Indian Express* on 29 November 1966. He said :

> The misunderstandings that had appeared some years ago in Nepal-India relations are being gradually dispelled. Mutual understanding is developing between the two countries in a satisfactory manner. I welcome any opportunity that is available to extend cooperation in any matter that will benefit both nations in the right manner....! do not think there are any serious differences between Nepal and India at present. If there is any, we can solve it in an amicable manner.

Maintenance of Friendship with China

China's image as a dependable friendly neighbour facilitated its contacts with Nepal in the years following 1962, until this image suffered a serious jolt in 1967 owing to the consequences of the Cultural Revolution in China. Friendly contacts between the two countries were evident in a number of state visits to China undertaken by the Nepali dignitaries. The visits were:

1.	Rishi Kesh Shah, Nepal's Permanent Representative at the UN (Ministerial level)	November-December 1962.
		and former Foreign Minister
2.	Dr. Tulsi Giri, Foreign Minister	January 1963.
3.	Surya Bahadur Thapa, Vice-Chairman of the Council of Ministers	September-October 1964.
4.	Kirti Nidhi Bista, Vice-Chairman of the Council of Ministers	August-September 1965.
5.	Birendra Bikram Shah Dev, Crown Prince	June-July 1966.

Rishi Kesh Shah visited China as a special envoy of King Mahendra. The armed conflict between China and India in October 1962 created a situation which was both grave and embarrassing for Nepal. Shah's mission was, therefore, to impress upon the Chinese Government that Nepal wished to remain, and so be left, aloof from the conflict. He met the Chinese leaders, including Liu Shao-Chi and Chou En-lai, and told them that Nepal was interested only in the friendship, understanding and peace between its neighbours.[98]

This was also emphasized by Dr. Tulsi Giri during his visit, since the tension continued to exist between India and China even after the ceasefire.[99] Besides, Dr. Giri signed the protocol on the Boundary Treaty between Nepal and China on 20 January 1963. It may be noted here that Notes on trans-frontier cultivation, pasturing and citizenship pertaining to the inhabitants of the border areas to be transferred from one country to the other under the provision of Article I of the Treaty, had been exchanged between the two countries earlier in August 1962.[100] Dr. Giri also explored possibilities of further economic cooperation between the two countries and had preliminary discussions with the Chinese leaders regarding the conclusion of a trade treaty. This Treaty was signed later on 19 May 1964.[101]

The emphasis during the visits of S.B. Thapa, K.N. Bista and Prince Birendra was largely on matters of economic cooperation between the two countries.[102] Prince Birendra's visit was marked by an additional Chinese grant of 150 million Rupees in aid.[103]

From the Chinese side, Vice-Premier Marshal Chen Yi visited Nepal from 30 March to 3 April 1965. Earlier, Premier Chou En-lai had planned to visit Nepal, but the visit did not materialise due to various reasons.[104] During Chen Yi's visit also, economic matters of mutual interest figured prominently. Besides, it was underlined during this visit that Nepal and China had similar views on issues like the Vietnam question and Afro-Asian solidarity.[105] This identity in outlook was reiterated when K.N. Bista visited China after four months. Touching upon international issues during his visit, Prince Birendra reiterated Nepal's stand that China's participation in the efforts towards disarmament and world peace was necessary for the success of these efforts.

Thus between 1963 and 1966 Nepal was found to be more keen and active, as compared to China, in maintaining its friendly relations with the latter, as evident from the number of visits exchanged between the two countries. China's response was favourable and the relations between them remained cordial, though restricted and formal, particularly, as compared to Nepal-India relations. The emphasis in the Sino-Nepalese relations was largely on matters of economic cooperation. In that context, we shall see later, that with regard to both trade and aid, China's responses were casual, punctuated by only occasional enthusiasm.

Normal Friendly Relations with Pakistan

King Mahendra's September 1961 visit to Pakistan was returned by President Ayub in May (9 to 12) 1963. The visit was initially scheduled for October 1962, but due to the out-break of the Sino-Indian conflict, it could not take place. Meanwhile, the two countries worked out details for economic cooperation between them. A Trade Agreement was signed in Karachi on 19 October 1962, which provided for "the most favoured nation" treatment to each other in commercial matters.[106] In March 1963, Air Services between Dacca and Kathmandu were inaugurated and an agreement was reached in principle on having a tele-communication link between them.[107]

During his visit, President Ayub underlined the common features between Nepal and Pakistan and stated that both the countries were determined to preserve their independent sovereign status. He hoped that the "leaders of this region and the world" will adopt a sympathetic attitude and dispel the apprehensions of the two countries in this context.[108] The President discussed with King Mahendra the "tensions and problems of the region" including the Kashmir dispute,[109] as also presumably, the Sino-Indian conflict and Western arms aid to India.[110] The King, however, did not take sides on these issues. The Joint Communique, issued at the end of the visit, stated :

> Keeping in view the tensions and problems of the area, they (the King and the President) reiterated their belief that the settlement of all problems as well as the elimination of the causes of friction by peaceful means would be in the highest interest of the countries and peoples of this region, as of the world at large.[111]

The Nepalese side was largely concerned with the bilateral ties, particularly economic.[112] Besides, the usual exchange of personal adulations, and expression of mutual interests in each other's political systems by the two leaders, it was also agreed that residential embassies on a reciprocal basis would be established in both the countries.[113]

Relations between Nepal and Pakistan remained casual after this visit. Except for the inauguration of the long proposed tele-communication link between Dacca and Kathmandu and Pakistan's agreement in August 1965 to allow Nepal the use of Chittagong port for transit of goods to and from a third country, and the offer of a few Pakistani Scholarships to the Nepali[114] even the economic intercourse between the two countries was restricted. This was in spite of King Mahendra's unofficial visit in June (15 to 17) 1964, Foreign Minister K.N. Bista's official visit in January (25 to 31) 1966, and the exchange of a number of trade, industrial and other delegations between them.[115]

FUNCTIONAL PRE-REQUISITES OF THE REGIONAL BALANCE OF POWER

It is evident from the foregoing discussion that Nepal's policy of regional balance of power was evolved in the background of the clash of interests between its neighbours—India on the one hand, and China and Pakistan on the other. The conflict and competition that characterized the behaviour of the two sides towards each other, placed Nepal in a vantage position and made it an object to be wooed by each of them against the other. This position enabled Nepal to ward off pressures from one side by mobilizing support from the other; as also to secure benefits, economic and otherwise, from one side by playing the other against it. And all this without much of commitments and liabilities. But to exercise discretion and extend the scope of its manoeuvrability in the region, Nepal adopted a posture of neutrality and non-alignment between its neighbours as an essential condition.

If we examine the propositions negatively, Nepal's policy of regional balance of power would be dusfunctional under the following conditions :

1. When the relations between China and India are cordial and their behaviour towards each other is characterized by convergence and cooperation instead of conflict and competition in the region.
2. When Nepal allys itself with either of the two neighbours.

Conditions almost identical to those mentioned above, existed during the Tribhuwan period (1951-54). Nepal both in the military and the political sense, was virtually an ally of India. India and China had very cordial relations and the convergence in their policies in the region was evident in India's recognition of China's suzerain status in Tibet and China's recognition of India's special interests and position in Nepal. As a result, the balance of power policy was non-existent. Even the establishment of diplomatic relations with China, which was imperative in the situation, could not materialise.

Neutrality in the Sino-Indian Dispute

There was a third condition under which the balance of power policy though in existence, became dysfunctional. This was in 1962 when tension between India and China turned into an armed conflict.

During the period of tension (1959-62), Nepal took a neutral stand *vis-a-vis* the Sino-Indian dispute. Prime Minister Koirala maintained a non-committal stand regarding the validity of the McMahon line between India and China and advocated silence for Nepal in their mutual differences.[116] The growth of tension between Nepal's two neighbours posed a threat to its neutrality and resulted into an embarrassing situation for the Government.[117] During 1961-62, even at the height of the Nepal-India differences, King Mahendra did not take China's side in the Sino-Indian dispute. His Government scrupulously observed silence on the subject and it was denied that Nepal was playing off one neighbour against the other.

As soon as the conflict broke out on 20 October 1962, the balance of power policy of Nepal which was hitherto operating vigorously came to a standstill and remained so, as long as the fighting continued. But after the ceasefire between India and China, since the hot war had again regressed into a situation of tension, Nepal could reassert its neutrality. Accordingly, King Mahendra sent his emissaries, R.K. Shah and Dr. Tulsi Giri, to China and India in November and December 1962, respectively, to impress upon the two neighbours that Nepal desired to be left alone in the conflict. The King stated : "Nepal sees no reason why she should become a victim of the struggle between her two neighbours, nor in fact does she want to be in that position."[118] Though the King also expressed the desire that Nepal would work for easing the tension between India and

China,[119] it did not have enough potential to do that.[120]

However, behind Nepal's declared neutrality in the dispute, there was a veiled attitude of sympathy and support for India. It was evident in the quickness and sincerity, after the conflict, with which Nepal buried all its complaints against India and responded to the latter's initiatives for the restoration of mutual goodwill and understanding. King Mahendra went to the extent of saying that Nepal had sympathies for a "friend in distress"—which implicitly meant India. Chairman of the National Panchayat, Vishwa Bandhu Thapa, who was one of the foremost critics of India, stated on the occasion of India's Independence Day, 15 August 1963 :

> We felt anxious when India's northern borders were encroached upon....Our brave Gurkha soldiers then shed their blood for India on many fronts. Everybody can imagine what every Nepali mother, wife or brother felt at that time... (in future it would be only after) trampling over the dead bodies of the Nepalese people that any invader would be able to enter India through our territory.

Besides, heavy recruitment of the Gurkhas for the Indian Army was reported in Nepal.[121] Later, Nepal and India negotiated an Agreement under which the former agreed to purchase all its arms and ammunition requirements from the latter.[122] As against this, the reports of Nepal receiving any military assistance from China were firmly denied.[123]

Nepal and the Kashmir Dispute

Nepal's role in the Kashmir dispute between India and Pakistan, and the war between them resulting from the dispute in September 1965 was basically the same as during the Sino- Indian dispute. Officially, Nepal kept silence on the Kashmir question upto 1956. In 1957, Nepal's Prime Minister Dr. K.I. Singh stated that Kashmir belonged to India.[124] However, in view of Dr. Singh's short-lived Prime Ministership and the subsequent developments, his statement does not merit serious consideration. King Mahendra's refusal to take sides on the Kashmir question when it was raised by President Ayub in 1963, can be recalled here. When the Indo-Pakistan war broke out in September 1965 Nepal expressed its concern and urged for peace. King Mahendra addressed identical letters to the Presidents of India and Pakistan on that occasion, wherein he explained that Nepal had "taken no sides on the question of Kashmir".[125]

Nevertheless, under this overt neutrality of Nepal, there was a discreet stand in favour of India, particularly in the context of the war. In his identical letters, King Mahendra favoured the bilateral settlement of the differences "without interference or counsel from any third party" and also asked both the sides to accept the UN Security Council Resolution for a ceasefire, in the interest of peace. Both these points were in conformity with India's stand in the matter. Then, the Foreign Ministry in Kathmandu promptly denied Radio Pakistan's reports which said that Nepal had sided with Pakistan in the war and had asked India not to use Gurkha troops in the war against it.[126] It was further promised that Nepal would not allow Pakistan to indulge in such false propaganda against India any more.[127] The fact of Nepal's sympathy for India's cause became further evident when King Mahendra, during his state visit to India in November-December 1965, along with the Indian President maintained : "that the principle of self-determination can apply only to dependent and trust territories and cannot be extended to integral parts of sovereign states."[128] By implication, the declaration dismissed Pakistan's demand for a plebiscite in Kashmir.

This made Pakistan unhappy. To avoid any damage to their relations, Nepal's Foreign Minister K.N. Bista visited Pakistan from 25 to 31 January 1966. He explained to the Pakistani leaders that Nepal's Treaty obligations towards India rendered the Kingdom helpless regarding the use of Gurkha troops by India against a third country. Bista was reported to have stated in this context that Nepal was seriously considering a change in the existing agreement on the use of Gurkha troops by India and Britain.[129] It seems that this statement was only to appease Pakistan, because on his return to Kathmandu, Bista ruled out the possibility of revising the Gurkha Agreement "for the present".[130] He also delivered a personal communication from King Mahendra to President Ayub Khan in which the former was said to have expressed his desire to meet the President.[131] Bista's main concern during this visit, however, appeared to be with the economic matters between the two countries.[132]

Military Protection from India

Nepal's tacit leaning towards India in the latter's conflicts with China and Pakistan was in conformity with the socio-cultural identity and economic interests between the two. More concretely, it was dictated by mutual understanding and arrangements relating to matters of defence and security. This involved commitments on the part of Nepal but, in turn, also ensured India's military protection for the Kingdom. The protection, instead of being a hurdle, facilitated its *political manipulations* in the region. Its absence, in view of Nepal's power potential and geopolitical situation, would have enhanced its vulnerability in the region and thus have adversely affected the evolution and functioning of the policy of balance of power.

There can be another plausible explanation also. The Sino-Indian conflict had upset the power balance in the region to China's advantage. It was a step in the direction of one power (China's) hegemony in the region. If the hegemony could be established, Nepal's balance of power would not work, since India would have ceased to be an effective counter-weight against China. Similar threat was inherent in the emergence of Sino-Pak collusion against India during the 1965 Indo-Pak conflict. Nepal's action of throwing its weight, *militarily,* in favour of India was, therefore, a clear step towards the pre-servation of the desirable power equilibrium in the region.

To sum up, Nepal's regional balance of power policy operated within the framework constituted by its three dominant features spelt out in the beginning of this chapter. The functional pre-requisites of this policy were : that. Nepal, while enjoying *military protection* from one of its big neighbours, took a *politically neutral* stand in the regional disputes; that there was tension and not war, nor cordiality, between the major powers of the region who competed with each other for allies and influence and lastly, that the power equilibrium between them was not seriously jeopardised.

Notes

1. Leo E. Rose and Roger Dial, "Can a ministate find the true happiness in a world dominated by Protagonist Powers—The Nepal Case", *The Annals*, Vol. 386, November 1969, 89-101.
2. *New Developments in Friendly Relations between China and Nepal,* Chinese People's Institute of Foreign Affairs, Peking, 1960, 55 (Hereafter referred as *New Developments).*

   The return of Dr. K. I. Singh to Nepal from China, where he

had been under political asylum since 1952, also figured at this informal contact, *Keeping's Contemporary Archives,* 17-24 September 1955.

3. Text of the Agreement and the Notes, *New Developments* n 21-14.
4. See the Speeches and Statements of the two leaders, *Survey of China Mainland Press* (Translation of Chinese Press reports by American Consulate, Hongkong) (Hereafter referred as *SCMP)* No. 1318, 1 October 1956, 19-21 ; No. 1382, 3 October 1956 48-49 57 ; No. 1461, 30 January 1957, 22, 24-26.
5. Text of the Joint Communiques issued at the end of these visits. *SCMP,* No. 1387, 10 October 1958, 30; *Gorkhapatra,* 1 February 1957 (19 *Magh* 2013).
6. Leo E. Rose, *Nepal: Strategy for Survival,* University of California, Berkeley, 1971, 210-213.
7. King Mahendra's speeches in Kathmandu before and after his visit to India. H.M. King Mahendra, *Proclamations, Speeches and Messages,* Department of Publicity, Ministry of Information & Broadcasting, HMG, Nepal, Kathmandu, 1967 (Hereafter referred as *Speeches),* Vol. I, 19, 31-33.
8. *Ibid.,* 21-30; *Foreign Affairs Record,* Publication Division, Ministry of External Affairs, Government of India, New Delhi (Hereafter referred as *FAR),* Vol. II, No. 12, December 1956, 212-13. Also see, King Mahendra's farewell messages to Prime Minister Nehru and President Dr. Rajendra Prasad at the conclusion of his visit to India. Text in *The Hindu,* 20 December 1956.
9. *Gorkhapatra,* 30 January 1956.
10. *The Asian Recorder,* 2-8 June 1956, 873.
11. For the speeches of Nehru and Acharya, see *FAR,* Vol. II, No. 12, 212-13. Also, *The Hindu,* 5 and 7 December 1956.
12. Text of the President's Speech, *FAR,* Vol. II, No. 10, October 1956, 157.
13. Text of the welcome addresses presented to the King in New Delhi and elsewhere in India, *The Hindu,* 16 and 28 November 1955. It maybe recalled here that the Governance of the Kingdom was directly under King Mahendra's control since March 1955.
14. Reply to the civic address in New Delhi, *Speeches,* Vol. 1,21,29, 30. Also see *The Hindu,* 22 October 1956.
15. The Hindustan Times, *4 August 1957.*
16. *Nepal Samachar,* 20 January 1958.

17. The concerned declaration described the withdrawal of the Mission as such. However, a number of officers of the Mission were retained in Nepal to form an Indian Military Training Advisory Group to advise the Nepalese Government on matters related to the Army. *Tritiya Varsh: Shri 5, Maharajadhiraj Mahendra Bir Vikram Shah Dev Ko Chattrachhaya ma* (Third year of King Mahendra's rule), Publicity Department, HMG, Nepal, Kathmandu, n.d., 29.
18. For historical background of discrepancies in the boundary line see, Chittaranjan Nepali, *Nepal-Cheen Seemana Sandhi* (Nepal-China Boundary Treaty), HMG, Dept. of Publicity, Kathmandu, 1965, 6-15.
19. Tanka Prasad Acharya, "Nepal-Cheen ko Sambandh: Ek Naya Adhyaya" (Nepal-China relations: A New Chapter), *Miteri-Gantho* (Friendly Ties), Nepal-China Friendship Association, Kathmandu, 1968.
20. Prime Minister's disclosure in the Parliament, *Kalpana* 5 and 7 September 1959; also see, *Nepal Press Digest*, 1-7 September 1959.
21. *Samaj*, 23 September 1959; *The Statesman*, 2 October 1959.
22. *Swatantra Samachar*, 24 November 1959; *Halkhabar*, 24 November 1959.
23. Joint Communique signed at the end of Koirala's visit, *New Developments*, 17-20.
24. Text of the Agreement, *Ibid.*, 21-24.
25. Joint Communique signed at the end of the visit, *Ibid.*, 32-34.
26. Kalpana, 4 *April 1960;* Swatantra Samachar, 4 *April 1960;* The Hindustan Times, *5 April 1960.*

    The Joint Communique issued at the end of B. P. Koirala's visit to China mentioned that he had appreciated the proposal of the Treaty. No reason, however, was given as to why the Treaty was not signed.
27. Text of the Treaty, *New Developments*, 29-31.
28. New Developments, *72.*
29. Chou En-lai in a Press Conference in Kathmandu on 28 April 1960, where B. P. Koirala was also present. *New Developments*, 69-70.

    It is noteworthy that B. P. Koirala was received in China as a guest from "the south of the Himalayas" and Chou En-lai, while welcoming him at the Peking airport .said: "The towering Himalayas lay between our two countries", *ibid.*, 35; *SCMP*, No. 2218, 17 March 1960, 39, 42.

    The dispute was revealed to the public in Nepal by B. P. Koirala in a Press Conference in Kathmandu after his return from China. *Kalpana,* 4 April 1960. The Government, however, did not produce the maps exchanged with the Boundary Agreement. *Halkhabar,* 7 April 1960.

30. Chou En-lai's Press Conference in Kathmandu, *New Developments,* 69-71. A spokesman of the British Foreign Ministry also stated that Britain had always regarded the southern part of the mountain as Nepali and its northern part as Tibetan. *Nepal Samachar,* 8 April 1960.
31. B. P. Koirala in Nepal's House of Representatives, *Kalpana,* 30 April 1960. Also in a Press Conference on 2 May 1960, *Kalpana,* 3 May 1960.
32. Chou En-lai's Press Conference in Kathmandu, *New Developments.* 72-73.
33. Nepal's Home Minister S. P. Upadhyaya's statement on the incident in the House of Representatives, *The Commoner,* 1 July 1960.
34. Nepal's Foreign Office Press Release in Kathmandu, *The Hindu,* 29 June 1960. Earlier the Government of Nepal repeatedly refused to protest to the Chinese Government against the movement of troops along the border. It seems that the former had some prior official information about such movements, *The Commoner,* 6 and 14 June 1960.
35. Text of the letters exchanged between B. P. Koirala and Chou En-lai on the Mustang incident, *Gorkhapatra,* 27 July 1960. Also see, *The Times of India,* 1 July 1960; *The Hindu,* 4 July 1960; *The Statesman,* 3 and 5 July 1960; *The Hindustan Times,* 7 July 1960.
36. B. P. Koirala's statement in the House of Representatives, *The Hindustan Times,* 28 August 1960.
37. Speeches of Nehru and B. P. Koirala during these visits, *FAR,* Vol. V, No. 6, June 1959, and Vol. VI, No. 1, January 1960, 9-14. Also, *The Hindustan Times,* 13, 14 and 15 June 1959; *Gorkhapatra,* 15 June 1959; *The Statesman,* 21 June 1959; *The Commoner,* 23,25, 28 and 29 January 1960, 1 February 1960; *The Hindustan Times,* 25, 28 and 29 January 1960; *The Statesman,* 30 and 31 January 1960.
38. *Ibid.* Joint Communiques issued at the end of Nehru's and B. P. Koirala's visits to Nepal and India respectively. Text in, *Foreign Policy of India', Text of Documents 1947-64,* Lok Sabha Secretariat, Government of India, New Delhi, 1966, 341-4. Also see, B. P. Koirala's Press Conference in Kathmandu after the conclusion of Nehru's visit, *The Statesman,* 21 June 1959.

39. *Nepali,* 25 January 1960.
40. *The Commoner,* 29 January 1960.
41. New Developments, *76-77.*

    The moment Chou En-lai started criticising Nehru and the Government of India for their stand in the Sino-Indian border dispute, B. P. Koirala, who was present at the Press Conference, closed it. *The Times of India,* 30 April 1960.
42. *Kalpana,* 19 and 20 October 1959; *Halkhabar,* 22 October 1959.
43. *The Statesman,* 14 March 1960.
44. The Hindustan Times, *24 July 1960.*
45. *The Hindustan Times,* 10 August 1960. Officially, this meeting was described as private and the nature of the talks was not revealed.
46. India, *Parliament Debates* (Lok Sabha), II Series, Vol. XXXV, 1959, 16-27 November 1959, col. 2211. Similar statement by Dr. Sushila Nayyar, *ibid.,* col. 1773.
47. *The Hindustan Times,* 30 November 1959.
48. *Ibid.*
49. *The Times of India,* 28 November 1959; *The Commoner,* 4 and 9 December 1959.
50. Doirala's Press Conference, *The Commoner,* 1 February 1960. Koirala also said that even nehru did not like such an idea. It can be inferred from this that the subject of mutual defence of India and Nepal and had been discussed by the two Prime Ministers. *The Statesman,* 31 January 1960. It may be noted that Koirala had talks with India's Defence Minister during this visit, *Kalpana,* 26 January 1960.
51. *The Hindustan Times,* 7 January 1961. Nehru's statement in Parliament while speaking on budget demands. India, *Parliamentary Debates,* II Series, Vol. Ill, No. 35, 3 April 1961, Cols. 8901-8903.

    The leaders of Nepali Congress and Deputy Prime Minister in the dismissed government, Subarna Shumshere Rana from Calcutta, claimed support of the Government of India, *Swatantra Samachar,* 29 January 1961. His speeches against King Mahendra's "takeover" were broadcast by the All India Radio, *Halkhabar,* 29 January 1961.
52. *The Hindustan Times,* 16 December 1960; *The Indian Express,* 20 December 1960.
53. For details see, Dr. Giri's visit, *Kalpana,* 20, 21 and 23 January 1961; *The Indian Express,* 20 January 1961 ; *The Statesman,* 23

January 1961 ; R. K. Shah's visit, *The Hindustan Times,* 29 December 1961.

54. *The Hindu,* 30 August 1961; *Nepal Press Digest,* 26 August 1 September 1961. Dr. Giri's statement on these talks, *Gorkhapatra,* 22 September 1961.

55. *Kalpana,* 13 January 1961; *Naya Samaj,* 16 January 1961; *The Times of India,* 16 January 1961.

56. The Finance Minister R. K. Shah, while he was passing through New Delhi, stated that the Government was contemplating to release B. P. Koirala and others and that Nepal-India friendship was "too valuable to be sacrificed for temporary difference of opinion", *The Indian Express,* 23 February 1961.

57. *Speeches,* n. 7, Vol. II, 89, 92-93, 97 and 100. Also *Dainik Nepal,* 11 January 1962; *The Commoner,* 25 and 27 January 1962; *Naya Samaj,* 13 February 1962; *The Hindustan Times,* 13 February and 1 September 1962; *The Indian Express,* 16 February 1962; *Gorkhapatra,* 16 February 1962 ; *The Indian Express,* 8 January and 1 October 1962 ; *The Statesman,* 27 February and 15 May 1962; *Gorkhapatra,* 15, 16 and 17 October 1962.

58. *Gorkhapatra,* 28 February 1962; *The Hindustan Times,* 28 February 1962.

59. *Gorkhapatra,* 2 March 1962. The Director of Publicity invited the Indian Press Correspondents in Kathmandu to his office to show these articles. In answer to a question, the Director admitted that the Nepalese Army also had the ammunition of similar make, but he held that it was not of the same period of manufacture, *The Statesman,* 8 March 1962.

60. *The Indian Express,* 2 March 1962. Nehru and Mrs. Laxmi Menon in the Indian Parliament on 13 March and 16 March 1962, respectively. India, *Parliamentary Debates,* Series II, Vol. LXI, No. 2, 13 March 1962, Cols. 61-64; *Ibid.,* No. 5, 16 March 1962, Cols. 689-91.

    Earlier in an interview to *Hindustan Samachar* (Hindi) on 7 February 1962, King Mahendra admitted that he had the knowledge of the Government of India's instructions to the Indian States bordering Nepal, to prevent smuggling of arms and also to Subarna Shumshere Rana and other Nepali Congress leaders to desist from doing anything against the law of the land. *Speeches,* n. 7, Vol. II, 97.

61. Joint communique issued at the end of the visit, *Foreign Policy of India,* n. 38, 345-46; *Speeches,* n. 7, Vol. II, 117-31, 345; *Gorkhapatra,* 25 April 1962.

62. King Mahendra told a Press Conference after the visit that he

had convinced Nehru about the economic rationale of the proposed Kathmandu-Kodari Road to be constructed in Nepal by China. *Gorkhapatra,* 24 and 25 April 1962.

63. Details about the intrusion were disclosed by Nehru and his junior colleagues in the Indian Parliament. India, *Parliamentary Debates* (Rajya Sabha), Vol. XXXVIII, No. 12, 3 May 1962, Starred Question No. 226, Cols. 1655-56; *Ibid.* (Lok Sabha), Series III, Vol. VIII, 4 September 1962, Cols. 5749-51. Another such intrusion was reported to have occurred on 24 August 1962.

64. Dr. Giri in a Press Conference in Kathmandu, *Gorkhapatra,* 15 May 1962; *The Statesman,* 15 May 1962; also *The Hindustan Times,* 1 September 1962.

65. *Gorkhapatra,* 18 July 1962; *The Statesman,* 27 July 1962. R. K. Shah had all along favoured a conciliatory and moderate approach towards India, *The Statesman,* 8 January 1961 ; *Navabharat Times* (Hindi), 17 August 1961; *The Hindustan Times,* 29 December 1961; *The Times of India,* 28 March 1962; *Dainik Nepal,* 23 January and 27 March 1962; *The Indian Express,* 9 April 1962.

66. For the speeches and statements of R. K. Shah and the Indian leaders see, *The Indian Express,* 7 and 11 September 1962; *The Statesman,* 7 September 1962; *Swatantra Samachar, 1* September 1962; *Naya Samaj,* 10 September 1062. R. K. Shah's Press Conference in New Delhi, *The Hindustan Times,* 12 September 1962.

67. For details of the incident see, *Gorkhapatra,* 1, 2, 6, 8, 15, 16 and 17 October 1962; *Halkhabar,* 12 and 16 October 1962; *Nepali,* 11 and 14 October 1962; *The Hindustan Times,* 10 and 14 October 1962.

68. *Speeches,* n. 7, Vol. II, 142-43.

69. King Mahendra's message to the Nation while leaving for China visit, *Speeches,* n. 7, Vol. II, 45-46.

70. *Ibid.,* 41

71. Text of the Treaty, *SCMP,* No. 2601, 19 October 1961, 26-30. Here the quotes and references have been taken from the original Text made available to the author in Kathmandu.

72. This was disclosed by King Mahendra in Kathmandu on his return from China, *Speeches,* n. 7, Vol. II, 56.

73. Ibid., 58.

74. It is a hindsight assumption based on the statements of Nepal's succeeding foreign ministers on the subject who from time to time have been confirming this position:

    (a) R. K. Shah, *The Times of India,* 10 September 1962.

    (b) Dr. Tulsi, Giri, *The Hindustan Times,* 25 January 1963; *The*

Commoner, 29 September 1964.

75. This was stated by India's Dy. Minister for External Affairs Mrs. Lakshmi Menon in answer to a question in the Lok Sabha, India, *Parliamentary Debates,* Series II, Vol. LXI, No. 5, 16 March 1962, Starred Question No. 75, COl. 667; also *The Times of India,* 19 October 1961.

76. The Commoner, 28 January 1957. SCMP, No. 1464, 7 February 1957, 33.

77. B.P. Koirala in a Press Conference on 30 August 1960, *The Times of India,* 3 September 1960.

78. *Speeches,* n. 7, Vol. II, 98. Notable in this context was the absence of any indications regarding the highway project during the visit of a Chinese economic delegation which concluded its deliberations in Kathmandu on 5 Septmber 1961.

79. *Speeches,* n. 7, Vol. II, 57, 288. Also Preamble of the Agreement, Text in *SCMP,* No, 2611, 2 November 1961.

80. The keen interest shown by China and the concern expressed by India regarding the Highway Project, support the contention. *The Times of India,* 2 November 1961; *The Hindu,* 25 November 1961. For details see author's Kathmandu-Kodari Road: Justification and Anxiety", *Mainstream,* Vol. VI, No. 7, 14 October 1967, 22-25.

81. *Speeches,* n. 7, Vol. II, 42-52, 56-58.

82. This inference is based on the author's interview in Kathmandu with the Nepalese officials and leaders who were dealing with China at that time. In fact it was given to understand that the Chinese statement was in response to a Nepalese demand to that effect.

83. *Ibid.* China had been unhappy about the use of Gurkhas by India in minor Sino-Indian skirmishes. In reply to a Peking Radio's comment, Foreign Minister R. K. Shah stated that India had a right to use Gurkhas in its defence, *Janata,* 31 July 1962.

84. For details, see author's "Nepal-Pakistan Relations: Partnership in Expediency", *South Asian Studies,* Vol. V, No. l, January 1970, 63-78.

85. They decorated each other with the highest civic titles of their respective countries, *Gorkhapatra,* 12 September 1961; *The Statesman,* 12 September 1961.

86. Joint communique issued at the end of the visit, *Gorkhapatra,* 17 September 1961.

87. *Gorkhapatra,* 14 September 1961; *The Hindu,* 14 September 1961.

88. *Gorkhapatra,* 12 September 1961.

89. *Speeches,* n. 7, Vol. II, 43. Dr. Tulsi Giri's statement in Kathmandu, *Gorkhapatra,* 22 September 1961.
90. *Nepal Samachar,* 22 November 1962; *Motherland,* 23 November 1962; *Dainik Nepal,* 24 November 1962; *Gorkhapatra,* 25 November 1962.
91. *The Hindustan Times,* 13 December 1962; *Gorkhapatra,* 13 December 1962.
92. The purpose of the visit was ostensibly to see his ailing Queen Mothers at Calcutta. He made a stop over in Lucknow where he met Chief Minister C. B. Gupta and participated in the Republic Day Celebrations on 26 January 1963, *Gorkhapatra,* 28, 30 and 31 January 1963 ; *The Hindustan Times,* 28 January 1963.
93. The purpose of Manubhai Shah's visit was confined to the discussion and settlement of issues between the two countries related to trade and transit, *Gorkhapatra,* 20, 21, 22 and 23 February 1964, and 7, 8 and 9 January 1965.

    Dr. Rao participated in the inaugural function of Tadi and Trishuli bridges, and discussed draft amendment on the Gandak Agreement, *Gorkhapatra,* 19, 23, 25 and 26 February 1964.
94. The Government of India proscribed under the Defence of India Rules, 1962, a pamphlet entitled *The Indian Nepali Congress and King Mahendra,* written by J. B. Singh and printed at Lucknow in 1964, *The Motherland,* 29 December 1964. The pamphlet contained 'slanders' against King Mahendra.
95. *The Motherland,* 2 September 1963.
96. *The Times,* 24 November 1964; *The Hindustan Times,* 26 April 1965.
97. *(a)* For P&T Office transfer, movement of vehicles and Gorkha earned foreign exchange transfer, see: *Gorkhapatra,* 16, 17, 18 and 24 October and 9 November 1963; *The Statesman,* 24 October 1963 ; *Rashtriya Panchayat: Kariyavahi ko Samkshipt Viveran* (Hereafter referred as *Summary Records),* IV Session, 1 and 2 *Shravan* 2021 (July 1964).

    (b) Checkpost for the foreigners' entry into Nepal: Mrs Laxmi Menon in the Indian Lok Sabha, *Nepal Samachar,* 19 November 1963; *Gorkhapatra,* 29 January and 21 April 1964.

    (c) Indian Military Advisory Group's reorganization, *Naya Sandesh,* 28 December 1963.

    (d) Border dispute in Susta and Narsha, *Mother land,* 29 January 1964; *Naya Samaj,* 31 january 1964; *Gorkhapatra,* 4 and 15 February and 16 April 1964, 2, 3, 4 June 1965; *Dainik Nepal,* 20 April 1964; *Summary Records,* II Session, 3 *Bhadra* 2020 (August 1963); III Session, 20 *Magh* 2020 9January 1964); IV Session, 14, 19 and

21 *Shravan* 2021 (July 1964). The settlement of the problem is still under negotiation.

(e) Issues pertaining to economic cooperation and trade and transit matters will be discussed in Chapter 6.

98. R. K. Shah's speeches in Peking, *SCMP,* No. 2868 and 2869, 28-29 November 1962, 36-38, 39-40. respectively. Press Conference in Hongkong on his way back home, *Nepal Samachar,* 13 December 1962. In Kathmandu, on return, *Gorkhapatra,* 23 December 1962.

99. Dr. Giri's speeches in China, *SCMP,* No. 2906 to 2908, 28 to 30 January 1963; *Gorkhapatra,* 20, 21, 24 and 25 January 1963; *The Times of India,* 21 January 1963.

100. Text of the Notes, *Gorkhapatra,* 17 August 1963; *SCMP,* No. 28C4, 22 August 1962, 28-30.

101. *Nepal Press Digest,* Vol. VII. No. 19, 16 to 22 May 1964; *SCMP,* No. 3226, 26 May 1964, 34.

102. S. B. Thapa's visit, *Gorkhapatra,* 6 and 12 October 1964; *SCMP,* No. 3314, 4 October 1964. K. N. Bista's visit and Joint Communique, *Gorkhapatra,* 8 September 1965; *SCMP,* No. 3536, 14 September 1965. Prince Birendra's visit, *Gorkhapatra,* 26 to 28 June and 4, 8, 12 and 15 July 1966; *SCMP,* No. 3729, 30 June 1966, 36-40 and No. 3734, July 1966.

103. *Samaya,* 8 July 1966. A formal Agreement to this effect was signed on 21 December 1966, *Gorkhapatra,* 22 December 1966.

104. Chinese Premier disclosed this in Peking to the leader of a visiting Nepal's National Panchayat Delegation, Vishwa Bandhu Thapa in November 1963. He was reported to have said to the latter that he planned to visit Nepal when he had offered to visit India. But due to "Nehru's reluctance", the latter visit did not come up and, therefore, he could not visit Nepal, *Gorkhapatra,* 13 November 1963; *Motherland,* 13 November 1963.

105. Joint Communique issued at the end of Chen Yi's visit, *SCMP,* No. 3433, 7 April 1965, 37-38.

106. *Gorkhapatra,* 20 and 27 October 1962.

107. National News Agency Report, *12 and 13 March 1963.*

108. *National News Agency Report,* 10 and 11 May 1963. Ayub's address to the National Panchayat, *Summary Records,* 1 Session, 10 May 1963 (*Vaishakh* 2020).

109. It was disclosed by Dr. Tulsi Giri after his talks with President Ayub on 10 May 1963, *The Statesman,* 11 May 1963. Significantly, the Pakistan Embassy was reported to have distributed a special issue of its bulletin *Pakistan News* to the guests at the State banquet given by King Mahendra in honour of President Ayub Khan on 9 May 1963. The brochure gave population statistics of Kashmir and argued for a plebiscite there, *The Times of India,*

10 May 1963.

110. This presumption is based upon Ayub's speeches in Kathmandu which contained oblique references to India. His condemnation of the Western military aid to India on the eve of leaving Pakistan for the visit was another indication to that effect. *Naya Samaj,* 5 May 1963.

111. Text of the Communique, *The Pakistan Times,* 13 May 1963.

112. *Ibid., Speeches,* n. 7, Vol. II, 182-84.

113. *Gorkhapatra,* 6, 11 and 13 August 1965.

114. *Gorkhapatra,* 6, 11 and 13 August 1965.

In august 1966, Foreign Minister K.N. sta disclosed in Nepal's National Panchayat that out of a total of 1,137 foreign scholarships received by Nepal during the last five years Pakistan gave 38. *Gorkhapatra,* 23 August 1966.

115. For details see, author's "Nepal-Pakistan Relations", n. 84.

116. *Kalpana,* 5 September 1959; *The Commoner,* 12 September 1959.

117. Reports of the ruling party Nepali Congress's General Secretaries, *The Commoner,* 10 November 1959; *The Hindustan Times,* 9 May 1960.

118. *Speeches,* n. 7, Vol. II, 147-8.

119. *Ibid.* Prime Minister Tanka Prasad Acharya had also expressed similar views in 1956, *The Hindu,* 7 December 1956; *The Times of India,* 5 December 1956.

120. Nepal was out of even the group of non-aligned Asian countries which jointly put forth the 'Colombo Proposals' for the settlement of differences between India and China.

Earlier, Dr. Tulsi Giri's statement in October 1959, offering Nepal's mediation in the Sino-Indian dispute did not find favour with other leaders of the ruling party, *Nepali,* 4 November 1959; *Nepal Samachar,* 10 November 1959; *Janata,* 11 November 1959; *Samaj,* 13 November 1959. Prime Minister B. P. Koirala later declined that Nepal wanted to make any offer of mediation between India and China, *The Commoner,* 1 February I960.

In April 1966, Chairman Surya Bahadur Thapa, when asked during his state visit to India whether Nepal would help India and China in solving their boundary dispute, said, "We are a small nation and have good relations with both India and China. I do not think it is proper for us to interfere in this matter",. *The Commoner,* 15 April 1966.

121. *Samaj, 25* September 1963; *Lumbini,* 20 October 1963.

122. Commander-in-Chief of the Nepalese Army Surendra Bahadur Shah visited India in January 1966 where he was believed to

have further discussed the Agreement signed in 1965. *Gorkhapatra,* 4 and 5 January 1966; *Motherland,* 4 January and 15 February 1966. Also *Samaj,* 4 September 1964.

123. The denial was issued in a statement by Foreign Minister K. N. Bista contradicting the US Defence Secretary Robert MacNamara's statement, saying that China had provided military assistance to Nepal, *Gorkhapatra,* 31 January 1964.

124. *The Hindustan Times,* 4 August 1957.

125. *Speeches,* n. 7, Vol. II, 348-9 (Text of the letters). Also see *Samiksha,* 7 September 1965; *Gorkhapatra,* 6 September 1965.

126. *Gorkhapatra,* 13 and 17 September 1965.

127. *Samiksha,* 16 September 1965.

128. Joint Communique, issued at the end of the visit, *FAR,* Vol. XI, No. 11 and 12, November and December 1965.

129. *Mother land,* 26 January 1966.

130. *Gorkhapatra,* 2 February 1966.

131. *Gorkhapatra,* 30 and 31 January 1966.

132. Bista's speeches in Pakistan, *Gorkhapatra, 26,* 28, 30 and 31 January, and 2 February 1966; *The Dawn,* 26 and 30 January 1966.

5

THE GLOBAL NON-ALIGNMENT

Successors of the Ranas opted for non-alignment to be Nepal's policy in the global context. They were inspired and guided by India's leadership in this respect. The policy of non-alignment was outlined during 1951-54 by King Tribhuwan, Prime Minister M.P. Koirala, Foreign Minister D.R. Regmi and other Nepali leaders in their various statements. Accordingly, the cold war between super powers and military alliances forged by them were strongly criticized; colonialism, imperialism and racialism were condemned; dedication to peace, progress and cooperation based on the principles of peaceful co-existence was stressed and the significance and necessity of the UN was lauded.[1]

Upto 1954, Nepal's adherence to these principles of non-alignment remained only vocal. This was largely owing to Nepal's "special relations" with India and severely limited diplomatic contacts with Britain, the United States and France. In 1955, a breakthrough in the regional dimension of Nepal's foreign policy also coincided with a shift, from theory to practice, in its policy of global non-alignment.

The factors that accounted for the change in regional dimension of Nepal's foreign policy were also responsible for the shift in its global non-alignment. The change in the Soviet Union's approach towards South Asia as a whole, from hostile indifference to active interest following the crystallisation of SEATO and CENTO proved to be an additional factor. Nepal's way for admission to the UN was declared as a result of this change in the Soviet approach.[2] Nepal was finally admitted to the UN in December 1955. Earlier in April the same year, Nepal had participated in the Bundung Conference. These two events opened the way for Nepal's exposure to the world community and facilitated its active participation in international affairs. As a result, the policy of non-alignment became active.

Nepal's policy of non-alignment in the global context operated in three directions : towards the super powers and their allies, towards small uncommitted nations, and in the UN and other international forums. In general, the pursuance of non-alignment by Nepal was in conformity with its broad framework enunciated by India and followed by various Afro-Asian nations. The dominant features of Nepal's global non-alignment are discussed below.

NEPAL AND THE SUPER POWERS

Nepal's policy towards the super powers in general, was one of friendship and peaceful co-existence. Conscious of its strategic position in South Asia and of the fact that this position was duly recognized by the super powers, Nepal was found to be mainly interested in encashing its strategic location for as much benefits, political and economic, as possible. In the cold war and clash of interest between the super powers, Nepal's stand was one of declared neutrality and aloofness. Against the backdrop of these guiding principles, Nepal developed its relations with the super powers.

(A) Relations with the USA

It has been noted that till 1954, Nepal, though it willingly received American aid, was averse to US political and strategic motives in the region. This aversion continued during 1956- 58 and was expressed mostly through the criticism of American aid.[3] Its intensity was evident in the press reaction on an incident reported in April 1958 pertaining to the alleged smuggling of American arms into Tibet to help the local people fight against the Chinese Communist authorities there.[4] The US had also become somewhat suspicious of Nepal's growing cordiality with China and the USSR during this period.[5]

Growing Understanding

Towards clearing the mutual misunderstanding between the two countries, Nepal decided in November 1958 to establish a residential diplomatic mission in Washington. The process of clearing misunderstanding received an impetus from the popular government installed in the Kingdom in May 1959. The US Charged' Affairs, Douglas Heck met Prime Minister Koirala and discussed the repurcussion of disturbances in Tibet on Nepal that almost coincided with the new government's assumption of office. On this occasion Heck also congratulated the Nepalese Government for having successfully conducted the first General Elections in the Kingdom.[6] A few months after Heck's meeting with Prime Minister Koirala, the US Ambassador designate to Nepal, Henry E. Stebbins declared that Nepal was a militarily strategic area and, therefore, should be protected from communist imperialism.[7]

With the tone set for mutual understanding between the two countries, King Mahendra undertook a state visit to the United States, beginning from 27 April 1960.[8] During this visit, the King highlighted Nepal's firm belief in the efficacy of the democratic system and its independent and non- aligned foreign policy.[9] President Eisenhower assured King Mahendra of US readiness to assist Nepal "in its high objective of developing the resources of the country for the welfare of its people".[10] Recalling the long standing relations between their two countries, both the President and the King expressed their concern with the vital world problems of achieving "lasting peace" and "international justice". They underlined their "profound belief" in "the sovereignty and independence of nations and in genuine non-interference in the affairs of others".[11] The visit was marked by the signing of the Nepal-US Investment Guarantee Agreement on 17 May 1960 which provided for the security of US capital to be invested in Nepal.[12]

King Mahendra seems to have discussed Nepal's border problem with China with the US leaders quietly, while reviewing the international situation. In an oblique reference to the situation along Nepal's northern border he stated :

> In matters of self-defence of the country, we are confident that our human and material resources are sufficient to meet any eventuality but that should not mean that we rule out all extraneous help in times of real need.[13] This statement can be interpreted to mean that Nepal did not envisage any immediate danger from China but was willing to seek US or other help in times of real danger. In this context, King Mahendra further explained in his press conferences during this visit that there were no differences

> between Nepal and China, that China did not violate Nepal's border and that the relations between the two were *"strictly formal and cordial"*.[14] (italics added)

Three months after the King's visit, Prime Minister B.P. Koirala met President Eisenhower at New York while attending the UN General Assembly session. The main purpose behind this meeting seems to have been to acquaint the US President with the developments pertaining to the Sino-Nepalese relations in general and the settlement of border disputes between them in particular.[15]

After King Mahendra's "Takeover"

King Mahendra's "takeover" was viewed by the United States as an internal matter of Nepal.[16] Further probings by the King to secure US support and recognition for his action were favourably responded to. The newly elected US President John F. Kennedy in his reply to King Mahendra's "goodwill" message in February 1961 assured him that the friendly relations between the two countries will be preserved.

In May 1961, Nepal's new Finance Minister R.K. Shah met the US President at New York and secured his continued sympathy and cooperation.[17] Towards the same end, King Mahendra also granted an audience in the same month to the US Ambassador in Kathmandu Henry E. Stebbins and the USOM Director John L. Roch.[18] In the following few months Nepal's growing cordiality with China caused a little anxiety in the United States which Nepal tried to remove through normal diplomatic channels.[19] The Nepali Ambassador to the United States M.P. Koirala stated in July 1962 in this context :

> When the new political system was introduced in Nepal, there had been some misunderstanding in the United States. This misunderstanding has been dispelled now. The Americans do not want to interfere in Nepal's internal affairs and there was no plan to curtail American aid to Nepal.

Military Aid

In the following years, Nepal sought US help, particularly in strengthening its armed forces and the newly established Panchayat System. The need for the first was felt after the Sino-Indian conflict of October 1962. Towards securing military assistance, Nepal's Chairman of the Council of Ministers and

Foreign Minister, Dr. Tulsi Giri paid a state visit to the United States in September 1963. Dr. Giri carried a personal message from King Mahendra for President Kennedy. He discussed Nepal's "great concern" about the Sino-Indian conflict with the President and the US Secretary of State, Dean Rusk. The American leaders appeared quite willing to help Nepal, as well as India, in their defence against the threat of Chinese aggression.[20]

The agreement on the US military help seems to have been signed sometime in March-April 1964. The terms of the agreement were kept secret. However, the following points emerged from Dr. Tulsi Giri's statements on the subject :[21]

(a) The United States was to supply modern light weapons, military equipments and medical supplies to Nepal. It included technical advice and practical training in handling the modern equipments supplied.

(b) The weapons and equipments to be supplied were given as "military aid". It did not involve any "purchase of arms" by Nepal.

(c) No US military mission was to be stationed in Nepal in this context.

Britain also joined the US in this "arms aid' .

Nepal's request for western arms aimed at reducing the undue burden on its traditional supplier, India who was hard- pressed since the October 1962 conflict. Nepal also disclosed that it had no plans to buy arms from "any other source". Both the United States and Britain also consulted and secured approval of the Government of India in this matter before finalizing the proposals. They stated that the "arms aid" to Nepal was only to supplement what was already given by India and that it was to improve the Kingdom's "internal security capacity".[22]

The first instalment of supplies under the western arms aid from US was received by Nepal on 17 October 1964. Following that, another round of negotiations started between the two countries. Nepal's Ambassador to the United States Maj. Gen. Padma Bahadur Khatri met the US Secretary as well as the Deputy Secretary of State on 23 October and 2 November 1964 respectively. On 4 December 1964, Foreign Minister K.N. Bista had talks with the US Secretary of State Dean Rusk, Ambassador Adlai Stevenson and senior US officials on "matters of mutual interests" and found them friendly and sympathetic. William J. Handley, Dy. Assistant Secretary in the US Department of State visited Kathmandu in January 1965 and had talks with Dr. Tulsi Giri and K.N. Bista on the same subject.[23] It seems, further details of the "arms aid" agreement were worked out during these meetings.

Following these negotiations a team of US military experts consisting of 9 Signal Corps and 8 Vehicle Maintenance Corps persons arrived in Kathmandu on 20 January 1965. This team was scheduled to stay in Nepal for a few months to demonstrate the use, repair and maintenance of the equipments received under the "arms aid". The next instalment of the equipments was received in December 1966.[24]

Strengthening the Panchayat System

The most important role in strengthening the Panchayat System in Nepal was played by US economic aid. On the ideological front—in propagating the "democratic values" of the system—the role of the US Peace Corps Volunteers and the Embassy officials was noteworthy.

Nepal signed an agreement with the United States in June 1962 under which the Peace Corps Volunteers were to be sent to the Kingdom.[25] The number of these Volunteers who visited Nepal under this agreement by December 1963 was officially given as 101. In January 1964 Sargent Shriver, the US Peace Corps Director visited Kathmandu to discuss the volunteers' programme with King Mahendra and his government. As a result, it was decided to raise the number from 100 to 160. This number underwent further increase and by the end of 1966 there were more than 200 volunteers scattered in Nepal's villages and districts.[26] The volunteers' fields of activities included the training of villagers in Panchayat philosophy and institutions, Nepali language, agricultural extension, forest development, and other economic and social matters.[27]

The activities of the Peace Corps Volunteers were objected to by the members of the National Panchayat and a section of the Nepalese press. The volunteers were accused of collecting economic and military information, propagating American values and way of life and indulging in local politics.[28] But the Nepali official circles continued to patronise the Peace Corps Volunteers. Minister Khadga Bahadur at a reception in Kathmandu arranged for the volunteers hoped that they would render "satisfactory cooperation in the implementation and development of the Panchayat System".[29] Both King Mahendra and Crown Prince

Birendra granted special audiences to these volunteers at the residence of the US Ambassador in May 1964 and June 1966 respectively. The Economic Planning Ministry promptly contradicted reports about government's decision to stop the services of the volunteers.[30]

Besides the Peace Corps Volunteers, the US diplomatic staff also indulged openly in strengthening the ideological base of the Panchayat System. The emphasis in their approach was on the anti-communist features of the system. In this connection the US Consular and other Embassy and USAID/Nepal staff directly approached the students, peasants, panchas and villagers. The role of Ambassador Henry E. Stebbins merits special attention. He visited various districts and villages in the Kingdom and highlighted the US objectives to strengthen the political and economic base of the Panchayat System and the role played by US aid in it.[31] He disclosed that King Mahendra had asked him to arrange for US assistance, both financial and technical, for the Panchayat Programme. Such assistance, he said, was assured "until the Panchayat System produced results". He also claimed that the US advice in the land reform measures was sought by, and given to the Nepalese Government.[32] On Panchayat Democracy, the Ambassador was quoted as having said :

> Democracy takes different forms and Nepal is experimenting with its own type...H. M. King Mahendra and I have often spoken of the need to give the people of Nepal adequate opportunities, leadership and encouragement to help them realise that they too can be participants in decisions effecting them.[33] The fact that the Government of Nepal fully connived with the US diplomats is evidently clear from the above statement.

Nepal and the Vietnam Issue

The cooperation between the United States and Nepal in Nepal's domestic field naturally led to a better rapport between them on international issues. Vietnam can be taken as an example. The United States kept Nepal informed about some of the major steps it took in Vietnam. President Johnson sent letters to King Mahendra and his government in that context.[34] Nepal on its part did not go beyond denouncing "all possible external intervention" in Vietnam and did not brand the United States as an aggressor.

Nepal's Vietnam policy appears to have been guided by two factors : first, that Nepal in real terms was incapable of influencing the course of developments,[35] and second, the powers involved in Vietnam—the USA, China and the USSR—being Nepal's friends, a non-committal attitude was considered most situable.[36] Accordingly, it pleaded for a peaceful, negotiated settlement in Vietnam based on the Geneva Agreement of 1954. The Kingdom also joined 16 non-aligned countries in appealing to the concerned parties for peace and welcomed the Conference called by Malaysia, Thailand and the Philippines in that context.[37] Besides, Nepal criticized the escalation of tension in Vietnam resulting from the US bombing of first, the Gulf of Tonkin then Hanoi and Haiphong as well as from the use of gas.[38] The criticism was, however, mild and the expressions used were 'regrets' and 'serious concern' and not condemn. Perhaps, considerations of US economic and military assistance and support for the Panchayat System mellowed down Nepal's otherwise strong stand against big powers pressurisation and intimidation of small states.

(B) Relations with Britain

Nepal's relations with Britain remained mainly centred around the recruitment of the Gurkhas in the British Army.[39] The intercourse between the two countries increased after 1959. King Mahendra accompanied by Deputy Prime Minister Subrana Shumshere Rana paid a state visit to Britain in October 1960. He was the first Nepali Monarch to visit Britain. There both he and Queen Elizabeth recalled the longstanding friendship between the two countries and their comradeship in the "defence of peace and freedom" during the two world wars. King Mahendra expressed his desire that the British cooperation in Nepal's economic development be increased.[40] Queen Elizabeth bestowed the honorary rank of Field Marshal in the British Army upon King Mahendra, who, in turn, conferred Nepali honours upon the distinguished personalities of Britain including Sir Winston Churchill and Professor Arnold Toynbee.

After King Mahendra's "Takeover"

Queen Elizabeth's return visit to Nepal which was scheduled for February 1961, raised a controversy as a result of King Mahendra's action against democratic government and the parliamentary system. The British Labour Party disapproved of the King's "takeover" and asked for the postponement of the

Queen's forthcoming visit.[41] In order to make a firsthand assessment of the situation, the British Minister of War paid a short visit to Kathmandu in January 1961. In Nepal also, members of the erstwhile ruling party Nepali Congress, circulated pamphlets calling upon the Queen to cancel her visit, but the visit took place as scheduled from 26 to 28 February 1961.

During the visit, Queen Elizabeth and King Mahendra reiterated the traditional bonds of friendship and understanding between the two countries and spoke of the need to further extend and strengthen these bonds.[42] Both the Heads of the States bestowed their respective country's highest honours upon each other. King Mahendra in an attempt to explain his action against the parliamentary system which he had lauded during his visit to Britain, told the Queen in a banquet speech :

> Although on account of many and diverse errors and shortcomings, my desire to work out a strong and un-alloyed form of parliamentary democracy for the betterment of my Kingdom could not be a success at the moment, I am still firm in my earlier belief that your experiences in the development and working of your institutions can be and are of great value to us. At the same time it is but natural for any good and successful system to take time to strike roots.

Undertaken in the face of a controversy, the Queen's visit could be taken as an approval of the King's action. However, it was slightly diluted by a lastminute small change introduced in the Queen's banquet speech on 26 February 1961, which raised doubts about such approval. In the original draft of the speech, the Queen was to state :

I wish to tell your Majesty that you are not alone in your concern. Around Your Majesty are many friends who are watching with sympathy your Majesty's efforts to organise the Nepalese Nation in a manner that would lead Nepal firmly to progress and a happy future on lines in keeping with Nepal's national traditions and human dignity.

But in the changed version, she instead said :

I want you to know that you have many friends both near and far who wish your people well and pray for a happy and prosperous future.[43] The Queen's support for King Mahendra's action being more clear in the original version, the change was resented in Nepal.[44] The British Government was reported to have expressed regrets for the confusion caused by the change in the Queen's speech.[45] The episode, however, showed that the British Government did not want to take a clear stand in Nepal's domestic conflict and did not want to displease either the King or the ousted Nepali Congress—as also the Government of India who had sided with the latter.[46] The British desire to mediate in this context was evident from its Ambassador's readiness to meet the deposed Prime Minister B. P. Koirala in prison and persuade him on King Mahendra's behalf to accept the new system.

Military Aid

The next significant development in Anglo-Nepalese relations was Dr. Tulsi Giri's, Nepal's Chairman of the Council of Ministers, visit to Britain in October 1963. During this visit, Dr. Giri expressed Nepal's concern about the Sino-Indian conflict of October 1962 and its consequences in South Asia.[47] In his talks with the British leaders, Dr. Giri made a specific request for military aid which was accordingly accepted.[48]

The Gurkha Recruitment in the British Army

The provisions of the Gurkha recruitment for the British Army constituted an anomaly in Nepal's foreign policy. It impinged upon its independent status and prestige in the inter-national field and was contrary to its non-aligned, anti-imperial and anti-colonial stand since the Gurkha troops had been stationed in South-East Asia to protect Britain's commitments as a colonial and imperial power. It did not contribute any-thing to Nepal's defence policy as was the case with similar arrangements with India.

The Nepalese Government, though aware of the evident contradiction in the recruitment of the Gurkhas for the British Army, was found to be interested in perpetrating rather than scrapping the arrangement for the economic benefits resulting from it. Britain bad eight battalions of the Gurkha troops, with a total strength of about 18,000 persons. Nepal earned about £800,000 (Rs. 2.4 million) in hard currency in the form of pensions and remittances of the troops as well as the expenditure made on the recruiting depots. The stoppage of the recruitment was to deprive Nepal of this important source of foreign exchange. Besides, the return of the troops was bound to create problems of rehabilitation and re-employment in the Kingdom. And in the absence of adequate facilities for rehabilitation, these well-trained well-paid fighters would have constituted a potent and explosive source of danger for internal political stability. In view of these factors, the Nepalese Government justified the arrangement on economic grounds. Commenting on it King Mahendra said in a press conference : "Not only I, but every Nepali feels unhappy over this matter. But we cannot say what can be done unless we find some alternative."[49]

Nepal extended the Gurkha recruiting facilities to Britain for ten more years in April 1958. The British Government on its own decided to curtail the strength of the Gurkha troops after 1962. This made the Nepalese Government worried. The British decision was a part of its plan to reorganise its overseas army and reduce defence expenditure. Field Marshal Slim visited Kathmandu in March 1963 to seek Nepal's approval for the British plan to reduce the strength of Gurkha troops. He had an audience with King Mahendra in this context.

As a result, the British proposal was accepted and His Majesty's Government of Nepal described the proposed reduction as "proper and timely".[50] However, this decision of reducing Gurkhas in the British Army could not be implemented owing to the fresh trouble in Malaysia and the deteriorating situation in South-East Asia. Britain now wanted to raise the number of Gurkhas. This aspect figured during Dr. Giri's visit to Britain in October 1963.[51] The HMG, Nepal agreed to the British proposal to raise the strength of Gurkha troops in the Royal Army from 14,000 to 20,000. The agreement was disclosed in November 1963.[52]

With the improvement of the situation in South-East Asia, the issue of reducing the Gurkhas' strength in the Royal Army was again opened by Britain. It was discussed by the two countries during the exchange of visits which took place between them in 1966. The decision was announced by the British Minister for Defence in Kathmandu at the end of his 4 day visit to Nepal on 7 December 1966. The terms of the retrenchment process were largely the same as agreed to in 1963. The British Government also agreed to help Nepal in the resettlement of the retrenched soldiers.[53]

(C) Relations with the USSR

Diplomatic relations at Embassy level between Nepal and the USSR were established on 20 July 1956. For "promoting goodwill" and "strengthening the newly established relations", King Mahendra paid a state visit to the Soviet Union in June 1958. Soviet President Voroshilov hailed the visit as a "new and important" step and he welcomed Nepal's policy of expanding diplomatic relations.[54] King Mahendra expressed his admiration for the economic progress made by the USSR and its 'endeavours' towards establishing universal peace. He also underlined that Nepal was committed to the democratic and parliamentary way of progress.[55] Both the sides affirmed their faith in the principles of peaceful co-existence and denounced war as a policy. China's right to be admitted to the UN was also upheld.[56] King Mahendra discussed the possibilities of Soviet economic aid for Nepal with his hosts who responded favourably.[57]

Problems and Progress in USSR-Nepali Relations during Nepali Congress Rule

King Mahendra while in Moscow in 1958 had invited Soviet President Voroshilov to visit Nepal. During his visit in February 1960, the Soviet President highlighted his country's unilateral decision to reduce the strength of the armed forces and the proposal to suspend nuclear tests. He also lauded Nepal's foreign policy in general and its role in the UN which, he said, had helped the cause of world peace.[58] King Mahendra hailed the Soviet initiatives in the causes of world peace and pledged Nepal's full cooperation in that direction. The King also praised the scientific and technological progress achieved by the Soviet Union and described it as a source of inspiration for others.[59] The two leaders reiterated their faith in peaceful co-existence and underlined that they had "common views on many international issues."[60]

During this visit, the two sides might have discussed China's border disputes with Nepal and India but they scrupulously avoided making any reference in this context.[61] This question was discussed at length by Prime Minister B.P. Koirala and Premier Khrushchev who met in October I960 at New York while attending the UN General Assembly Session. B.P. Koirala later told the press that the Soviet Premier was happy about the amicable settlement of the Sino-Nepalese border dispute. The two leaders also had identical approaches to issues like China's admission to the UN and the liquidation of colonialism. However, B.P. Koirala disagreed with Khrushchev's proposal to replace the UN Secretary General with a triumverate.[62]

Apart from this understanding and closer contacts, there

emerged a few minor irritants in Nepal-Soviet relations during 1959-60. First, the Russian maps were reported to have shown parts of Nepal's territory as Chinese which was resented.[63] Second, the Nepalese Government strongly objected to the Soviet Embassy's direct selection of Nepali students for the Russian Scholarship scheme.[64] Third, about the same time, the First Secretary in the Soviet Embassy in Kathmandu was alleged to have indulged in undesirable activities and encourged Communist demonstrations against the Nepalese Government.[65]

Yet another unpleasant incident took place between the two countries in the UN General Assembly in October 1960. The chief Nepali delegate R.K. Shah disapproved of Khrushchev's historic thumping of the table with his shoe in the UN General Assembly. In retaliation, Khrushchev made uncomplimentary remarks about Nepal and its Parliament. This was taken as an affront to Nepal's independence and prestige. To voice its protest as also to correct the Soviet Premier, a fact sheet about Nepal's Parliament was circulated by the Nepali delegation in the UN Assembly. It drew the Soviet Premier's attention towards the fact that at the time when he questioned the existence of the Nepali Parliament, a parliamentary delegation of Nepal was in the Soviet Union on a goodwill visit.[66]

After King Mahendra's "Takeover"

There was no adverse reaction from the USSR to the King's "takeover" in Nepal. The economic and cultural inter-course between the two countries continued uninterrupted for the first half of 1961. Later, however, the Soviet Union did not seem to have been happy with King Mahendra's efforts to woo China. The cancellation of Dr. Giri's earlier publicised plan to visit Moscow,[67] and the Soviet Union's indifference towards the aid projects in Nepal in which it had shown keen interest earlier may be taken as evidences in this context.[68]

Whatever misunderstanding had arisen between the two countries, was removed by October 1963 when Nepal's Chairman of the Council of Ministers Dr. Tulsi Giri paid a visit to the Soviet Union. A "wide and useful" exchange of views on "international problems of mutual interest" and on issues of "further development and strengthening" of their relations took place between the two sides during this visit. The discussions included the implication of China's emergence in South Asia following the Sino-Indian conflict and also the Sino-Soviet rift.[69]

More cooperation and mutual understanding between Nepal and the USSR on international issues followed Dr. Giri's visit. In January 1964, Soviet Premier Khrushchev sent a communication to King Mahendra, sounding his views on having an international agreement for the settlement of territorial disputes through peaceful means. King Mahendra endorsing it in principle, held that instead of concluding a formal agreement, the matter should be discussed in the UN and adopted as a general guideline of policy.[70] Nepal was also kept in touch by the Soviet Union on the question of its relations with West Germany.[71]

Bilaterally also, the cultural exchanges between Nepal and the Soviet Union increased markedly. Since 1961, yearly plans for cultural and scientific exchanges had been signed by them. In June 1964, Foreign Minister K.N. Bista visited the USSR. He had talks with the Soviet Foreign Minister Andrei Gromyko and on behalf of his Government, he signed a cultural exchange Agreement with the Soviet Union. The next year's Agreement was signed during Sergei K. Rouranvosky's visit to Nepal in May-June 196 5.[72] A similar Agreement for 1966 between the two countries was signed in Moscow.[73] Nepal and the Soviet Union also signed an Agreement on 3 June 1966 for the exchange of News Services between them.

Nepal and the Uncommitted Nations

By the end of 1966 Nepal's diplomatic relations had extended to more than 15 such countries which did not belong to "power blocs" and most of which were proclaimed non-aligned. Nepal cooperated and identified itself with these countries in the UN and other international forums. However, its bilateral relations with them individually, though cordial, were formal and restricted. Nepal's relations with Yugoslavia, one of the leaders of the non-aligned countries, are discussed below as an example.

Relations with Yugoslavia

Nepal established diplomatic relations with Yugoslavia in November 1959. Since then, except for King Mahenda's visit to Belgrade to participate in the First Non-aligned Summit Conference in September 1961 and his talks with the Yugoslav leaders at that time, bilateral ties between the two countries remained severely limited. Closer contacts between them were initiated with Nepal's Chairman of the Council of Ministers, Dr. Tulsi Giri's goodwill visit to Yugoslavia in October 1964.

Dr. Tulsi Giri discussed the international situation and matters of mutual interest with the Yugoslav leaders. The two sides expressed satisfaction at the international recognition won by the policy of non-alignment and "active and peaceful co-existence". In this context, they hailed the contribution of the Belgrade and the Cairo Non-aligned Summit Conferences. They also condemned colonialism and asked for general and complete disarmament. Underlining the significance of the UN in preserving peace, Dr. Giri and the Yugoslav leaders pleaded for the strict application of the principle of universality in its organisation. They further called upon the world body to engage itself in the task of economic development of the underdeveloped and the developing countries.[74]

During this visit, Dr. Tulsi Giri received an encouraging response to his request for economic assistance.[75] Yugoslavia agreed to send a mission to Nepal to explore "the possibilities as well as steps to be undertaken" for the promotion of economic cooperation. In order to facilitate such cooperation, the two countries also agreed to raise their diplomatic relations to the ambassadorial level.[76]

To enhance mutual cooperation, an economic and political delegation from Yugoslavia visited Kathmandu from 29 August to 5 September 1965. The delegation concluded a Trade Agreement between the two countries.[77] Besides, Yugoslavia provided scholarships, technicians and a long-term loan of $1 million to Nepal as a result of the negotiations held by the delegation.

The leader of the Yugoslav delegation Radivoj Uvalic delivered a letter from the Yugoslav Prims Minister to his Nepali counterpart S.B. Thapa, containing "the general hope that the two countries would come closer through development of economic and cultural contacts." Later, he also disclosed that the two countries shared identical views on the Vietnam problem and agreed to evolve a mutually coordinated approach towards it in the UN.

The signing of the Trade Agreement and commitment for increased cooperation was followed by the Yugoslav Premier Peter Stambolic's visit to Nepal in March 1966. The Yugoslav Premier strongly criticised the US intervention in Vietnam and called for an end to foreign intervention in Africa.[78] In a joint communique, issued at the end of Peter Stambolic's visit, the two sides reiterated their stand on colonialism, disarmament and non-alignment and asked for the codification of the principles of peaceful co-existence. They expressed anxiety over the prolonged conflict in Vietnam and pleaded for its solution on the basis of the Geneva Agreement of 1954. United States' intervention in Vietnam was, however, not mentioned. They felt concerned over the widening economic gap between the developed and the underdeveloped nations and decided to further increase their mutual economic cooperation.[79]

NEPAL IN THE UNITED NATIONS

Nepal's application for admission to the UN was sponsored by India, the United Kingdom, the United States and other Western countries. Owing to the cold war politics, Nepal could not secure admisson to the world body easily. The Soviet Union repeatedly vetoed its admission. In the Soviet perception, Nepal's independence was also questionable during to its very close relations with the UK and the USA since the Second World War, and with India since 1947. Later, however, the Soviet Union stated that it had nothing particularly against Nepal's admission.[80] The deadlock between the two power blocs on the question of new members' admission was resolved on 14 December 1955 when under the "package deal" all the countries supported and sponsored by either side were admitted.[81]

Thus admitted, Nepal participated enthusiastically in the UN and since 1956, used it as an important platform for the implementation of its policy of global non-alignment. Nepal's behaviour in the UN had two dimensions. First, Nepal pursued its self-interests, emanating from *security, stability* and *status* motives. Secondly, it projected its view of the world.

Pursuance of Self-interests

Being a small and weak nation, Nepal viewed the UN as a "bulwark" of its independence and security and the protector of its "rights and freedom".[82] Nepal underlined its status as an independent and sovereign nation and its distinct socio-cultural composition in order to undo any doubts in this respect.[83] Conscious of its limitations as a small and weak nation and guided by the considerations of security, the Kingdom strongly argued in favour of non-interference by one country in the domestic affairs of another and fully supported the UN declaration of 1965 on the subject.[84] Nepal also took pains in drawing the world body's attention towards the regional conflicts in its neighbourhood—Sino-Indian of 1962 and Indo-Pak of 1965—

which directly threatened its security and peace.[85] It took a great deal of interest in the peace-keeping operations of the UN and consistently pleaded for a small but effective force to be kept at the disposal of the world body. This, the Kingdom considered as a great step toward "perfecting the world body" and described it as a source of comfort and strength to the smaller countries.[86]

Nepal's desire to involve the UN in the task of its economic development was first expressed in 1958 when the Nepali delegation made a call in the General Assembly for increased economic and techinal cooperation between the "rich-advanced" and the "poor-developing" nations and the UN was asked to direct its efforts in this direction.[87] Nepal welcomed the initiatives taken in this context in the form of the adoption of the "UN Development Decade" and the United Nations Conference on Trade and Development (UNCTAD). However, it was sore that in concrete terms, the outcome of these initiatives was far less than the expectation aroused.[88] Nepal stood for the rights of land-locked countries and repeatedly raised this question at UNCTAD and other international forums.

Nepal also used the UN to secure international recognition for its domestic institutions and policies. In this respect, the significance of the monarchy, with particular reference to the roles of King Tribhuwan and King Mahendra, in bringing democracy were highlighted.[89] In 1959 Nepal informed the world through the UN that for the economic and political progress of its people, liberal political institution had been brought into being. Similarly, the characteristics of the Panchayat System, and the progress made under it in the field of law and land reforms were subsequently outlined.[90] The basic features of its foreign policy—non-alignment and peaceful co-existence—were invariably explained to the world body every year.

Projection and Pursuance of the World View

Nepal looked upon the UN as a very useful institution where it could identify its national interests with the varied and complex global issues and thus project and pursue its own view of the world. As a small Asian nation, it had a longing for world peace, a firm commitment to resist all forms of intimidation and exploitation of small nations by the bigger and powerful ones, and a deep faith in the utility and efficacy of the UN. This was evident in the position taken by Nepal on various issues that came up before the world body. Nepal took an uncompromising stand against colonialism, imperialism and racial discrimination. It was reflected in its regular condemnation of the colonial and imperial powers, mainly France, Portugal and South Africa; and in the un-equival support for the freedom struggles in Asia and Africa. The Kingdom lent support to the Organisation of African Unity, as well as to the decisions taken by the Summit Conference of Independent African States at Addis Ababa in May 1963, and by the African Heads of State and Government at Cairo in July 1964.[91] Nepal condemned the *apartheid* policies pursued by the white minority regime of South Africa and South Rhodesia.[92] The Kingdom took active interest in the UN Special Committee on *apartheid* which had recommended the severance of relations with and economic boycott of South Africa by the members of the UN.[93]

Nepal was equally emphatic in demanding general and complete disarmament and nuclear non-proliferation. It reflected fluctuations between hopes and dismay, resulting from the chequered progress of the efforts in this direction, both within and outside the UN. It was evident in its views on the disarmament negotiations between big powers and the work of the 18-Nation UN Committee on the subject.[94] As a way out from the rigid positions taken at times by the super powers, Nepal asked for placing the disarmament issues before public opinion and for convening a world disarmament conference.[95] In view of the complexities of issues involved, a progressive disarmament towards the ultimate objective of general and complete disarmament was favoured.[96] It was argued that the issue of disarmament need not necessarily be coupled with the question of ban on nuclear tests.[97] Led by these considerations, the Kingdom welcomed the Moscow Partial Test Ban Treaty, pleading that it should be extended to cover ban on underground tests also.[98]

For the preservation and consolidation of peace in the world, Nepal had great hope in the UN. Proclaiming un-wavering faith in the UN Charter, Nepal considered that through it, a process of adjustment and conciliation can be carried out for resolving conflicts and lessening tensions in the world.[99] However, Nepal felt that a lot needed to be done on the organisational side of the UN in realizing such expectations and hopes.

The major powers, particularly the super powers, due to the clash in their interests, were held responsible for the ineffectiveness of the organisation. It was evident in the failure of the Security Council to take any decision on the Korean issue in 1950. This led to the new role of the General Assembly in crucial political and security issues exemplified in its "Uniting for Peace" resolution of 1950. Nepal highlighted this new and significant role of the General Assembly by taking the position that the new role was more of a compulsion and that the Assembly was structurally ill-equipped to discharge such functions.[100]

Nepal also pointed out that the role and functions of the Secretary General were undergoing drastic changes.[101] In the midst of the controversy about the Secretary General's Office, when the Soviet Union proposed a triumverate in place of the existing provision, Nepal opposed it. Its contention was that a triumverate in a delicate and complex situation would not only make the UN ineffective and slow, but by preserving the concept of power blocs, would drag it into a clash of interests and prejudices at a time when quick and positive action would be needed.[102]

Another organisational aspect of the UN that received Nepal's attention was the question of representation and membership. It called for the principle of universality to be observed in this regard and welcomed every new member. The People's Republic of China's admission to the UN was strongly and consistently advocated. It was argued that politically it was unwise and unrealistic to keep such a great mass of people unrepresented in the world body, especially when China had acquired nuclear status. With China's absence in the world body all efforts towards disarmament and nuclear non-proliferation were incomplete. Legally, Nepal held that China had a stable and legitimate Government functioning in the mainland since 1949.[103] Nepal also supported China's right to control its offshore island, though it disapproved of the use of force in acquiring this right.[104]

Nepal saw the international situation as dominated by the "Big Power complex" where the smaller and weaker nations were not taken into confidence in the solution of world problems. Therefore, it made strong attacks on the big powers particularly the western, for their lack of faith in the small powers and their move to deprive them of equal voting rights in the UN.[105] The Kingdom asserted that the small, uncommitted powers could play a useful and positive role in realising UN ideals, since their uncommitted positions could help them steer away from power conflicts. In this context Nepal called upon all the uncommitted, small nations to demonstrate unity and understanding amongst themseleves and give positive responses to questions facing the world body.[106] Though conscious of the small nations limited power-potential, Nepal was confident of their "moral influence" on the big powers, exercised through their collective action.[107]

Voting Behaviour

Nepal's participation in the UN can also be studied by analysing its voting behaviour on some of the important questions. The voting pattern on 10 important issues related to political and security matters May be looked in to The issues taken are the Hungarian question, the Suez crisis, the Algerian question, the Cyprus question, the Cuban question, the Tibetan question and the issue of the People's Republic of China's admission to the UN, the Korean question, the Congo crisis and the issue of disarmament.

Nepal did not consistently follow a pattern or side with any single country while voting on these issues. Therefore, it can be inferred that it took an independent stand in the UN. Nepal's sympathy and support mostly lay with the small and non-aligned countries and to the extent possible, it avoided taking sides with the super powers. In some cases, Nepal even displayed initiative by sponsoring moves and introducing amendments either alone or in collaboration with others preferably with the members of the non-aligned group of countries.[108] Nepal's stand on the issues directly affecting it like the Tibetan question and Communist China's admission was cautious and calculated. Even care was taken to avoid a situation which could harm its larger national interests.

PARTICIPATION IN AFRO-ASIAN AND NON - ALIGNED NATIONS' CONFERENCES

Afro-Asian Conference

The first Afro-Asian Conference took place in Bandung in April 1956. At that time, Nepal had diplomatic relations with very few countries and was new to the complexities of international politics. Therefore, in spite of great interest and enthusiasm, its participation in the Conference was modest. Its delegation was headed by the Foreign Secretary as against the Heads of States and Foreign Ministers in the case of other countries.

At the Conference, Nepal traced the history of intra-Asian relations and underlined the role of Lord Buddha—a Nepali Prince—in that context. It welcomed the revival of Afro-Asian unity and co-operation in the changed international environment. Making a special reference to the Five Principles of Peaceful Co-existence, *Panchsheela,* evolved by India and China, Nepal stressed that international understanding and collaboration can be, and should be, built on these principles. Nepal emphasized its strong desire for economic development and pleaded for UN membership for all "peace-loving, sovereign and independent" nations. It also advocated that small nations be placed on "unassailable foundations".[109]

More important than the views expressed by the Nepali delegation in the Conference session was the informal contacts established with other delegates at Bandung. The informal talks with the Chinese delegation regarding the establishment of diplomatic relations between Nepal and China can be recalled here.

The Second Afro-Asian Conference scheduled to be held at Algiers in 1966 fizzled out on the question of Soviet Union's participation. In the preparatory meeting for the Conference, China strongly opposed the Soviet Union's participation and India staunchly supported it. This created a difficult situation for Nepal since two of its great neighbours had made it a prestige issue against each other. Besides, Nepal had friendly relations with the USSR and received Soviet aid. It, therefore, refused to take sides on this question and decided to abstain when it was put to vote. Explaining Nepal's stand, Foreign Minister K.N. Bista explained at Algiers that though the Soviet Union was an Asian power geographically, it was not so politically. The Bandung Conference regarded the Soviet Union as a European power and it had never been a member of the Afro- Asian group in the UN.[110] Later Bista denied that Nepal's decision was influenced by China.[111]

Non-aligned Summit Conferences

Upto 1966, there had been two Non-aligned Nations' Summit Conferences, at Belgrade in 1961 and at Cairo in 1964. Nepal described these Conferences as "a moral movement dedicated to the creation of world opinion in favour of peace."[112] It raised "some of the more important issues like colonialism, imperialism, racialism, disarmament, world peace and economic co-operation at the Conferences. There was consistency in Nepal's stand on these issues at these Conferences and its stand on these issues in the UN.

The significane of non-alignment and peaceful co-existence in a tension and fear-ridden world, was emphasized by Nepal at these Conferences. The Kingdom was, however, not in favour of forging a neutralist bloc. Stressing the necessity of the observance of "non-interference", Nepal drew the attention of its non-aligned colleagues towards the "direct and subtle ways" of "Big Power interference" in the internal affairs of small countries.

Nepal did not go into the details of controversial international issues having a direct bearing on world peace. It referred to the Berlin and Congo questions in the first conference and the Vietnam and Cuba in the second, but without going deep into them and taking sides, pleaded for their settlement through peaceful negotiations. It made only passing references to other areas of tension and specific questions.

Vagueness and an element of escapism in Nepal's stand on these specific issues emanated from its consciousness of being a small and weak country; it was also because of its friendly ties with all the countries concerned. Therefore, it wanted to keep away from the controversies. Nepal was also opposed to the discussion of bilateral disputes and the use of the Conferences as a forum for propaganda by one member-country against the other.[113] Accordingly, Nepal dissociated itself from unfavourable references to Israel in the Joint Communique of the Second Conference.[114] Except for indirect references, Nepal did not criticise either of the super powers by name on any specific issue. It was evident in its silence in the First Conference over the resumption of nuclear tests by the USSR,[115] and in the Second Conference over the US intervention in Vietnam and Cambodia. Unlike India, Burma and others, it also did not express any concern at the Second Conference about the expected Chinese first nuclear explosion.

The participation in these Conferences gave Nepal a sense of international protection and identification. The Kingdom stressed the need for economic development of poor countries and strongly urged the non-aligned nations to co-operate amongst themselves. Its leaders also underlined the need for developing "positive points of contact" amongst them. In the Second Conference, Nepal asked for a "useful code of conduct" to be evolved, not only to guide the relations between the Big Powers and the small non-aligned nations but also amongst the latter themselves. King Mahendra, who led Nepal's delegation in both the Conferences established "personal contacts with the leading personalities in the international world". A clear mention by him of this objective in the First Conference was significant in view of the disturbed situation at home and Nepal's deteriorating relations with India following the King's "takeover".

MAJOR CHARACTERISTICS OF THE GLOBAL NON-ALIGNMENT

The discussion of Nepal's policies in relation to the super powers and their allies", the small uncommitted nations and the UN as well as Afro-Asian and Non-aligned Nations' Conferences, reveals some important characteristics of its policy of global non-alignment.

Active and Independent Policy

It has been seen in the Second Chapter that Nepal's non-alignment had three broad characteristics: it was dynamic and positive; it was independent in operation and the elements of morality and idealism were important ingredients in it. We have noted many facts above which support the assumption made in the Second Chapter. The year 1956 was of particular significance in the emergence of these characteristics as practical features of this policy. Nepal's stand on the two incidents of immense international significance, that took place in that year, amply demonstrated the independent and active nature of its non-alignment.

The first incident was the aggression of the UK, France and Israel on Egypt to control the Suez Canal. In spite of close relations with the UK, Nepal condemned the aggression. It sided with Egypt when the question came up for discussion in the First Special Emergency Session of the UN and asked for the immediate withdrawal of the Western forces from Egypt before the political settlement of Suez Canal could be taken up.[116] The second incident was the Soviet Union's armed intervention in Hungary. Notwithstanding its newly established diplomatic relations with the USSR, Nepal deplored "the armed intervention" and pleaded for the restoration of Hungary's independence and sovereignty.[117] Nepal's vote in the Second Emergency Special Session of the UN General Assembly on the Hungarian question demonstrated that it could behave independently of India, its immediate big neighbour.

This indication in the very first year of its participation in the world body was significant as an emerging trend. It may be recalled that around that time, Nepal had initiated the policy of shift from the "special relations" with India. It is important to note that in both the incideiits on the one hand .Nepal sided with the countries—Egypt and Hungary—with which it did not have any diplomatic relations and on the other, opposed the big powers with which it was to have long-term ties and interests. These incidents showed that Nepal was capable of an independent decision *vis-a-vis* the super powers as well as *vis-a-vis* the major power in its neighbourhood. This also demonstrated Nepal's sympathy and support for the small nations against big power pressurisation.

However, Nepal's expanding diplomatic contacts and its increasing participation in international affairs brought in certain constraints on the active and independent pursuance of non-alignment. Unlike on Hungary and the Suez issues in 1956, Nepal largely took a passive and non-committal stand on controversial issues. Without going deep and taking any side, it pleaded for a peaceful settlement of the German question, Cyprus problem and the Cuban question. On Vietnam, it neither directly blamed the USA for intervention nor justified the US stand there. It may be recalled that the friendly relations of Nepal with China and the USA were referred to while explaining its stand on the Vietnam issue. On the confrontation between Malaysia and Indonesia, Nepal kept silence. Its position on this issue, however, was prejudiced due to the presence of Gurkha troops in Malaysia under the British command. This led to Indonesian President Soekarno's sharp reaction against King Mahendra's statement that the dispute be settled peacefully. President Soekarno, in this context, denounced co-existence with the imperialists and added :

> If the King of Nepal advocates a peaceful settlement of this dispute, why does he let his subjects, the Gurkha mercenaries, fight with the north Kalimton freedom fighters and the Indonesian volunteers.[118]

President Soekarno's statement was taken as "a breach of

diplomatic etiquette" in Nepal and it was explained that Gurkha's presence in Malaysia under the British command was the result of longstanding Treaty obligations between Nepal and Britain.[119]

Similarly, after the establishment of diplomatic relations with Israel in 1959, Nepal's stand on the Arab-Israel conflict also underwent change. Unlike its earlier stand in favour of the UAR, Nepal pleaded for a "realistic and practical" solution of the problem in 1960 and thereafter, without taking sides.[120] Its refusal to be associated with the criticism of Israel in the final communique issued at the end of the Cairo Non-aligned Conference in 1964, has already been noted.

In all the cases cited above, Nepal had friendly relations with both the parties in the conflict. Taking one side would have adversely affected its relations with the other. To remain aloof and non-committal and plead for peaceful settlement of these issues were, therefore, in Nepal's best interests. Again, it was in view of its larger interests that in contrast to the stand on Hungary, Nepal fully supported China's action in Tibet in 1959 and even refused to accept that the question of human rights was involved there in any manner.[121]

Exercise in Balance of Power

The whole concept of non-alignment has been viewed by some scholars as a balance of power policy through which the non-aligned countries aimed, on the one hand, at maximising their power and influence *vis-a-vis* the super powers by forging closer ties amongst themselves and thus evolving united response to international issues and, on the other, to try to make the best of both the power blocs by having friendly and cordial bilateral relations with each and keeping aloof from their mutual conflicts. Nepal's non-alignment was also in conformity with this.

As an exercise in the balance of power, Nepal's policy in the global context had two major components. Its ties with (a) the uncommitted nations along with its membership of the UN and participation in the Afro-Asian and the non-aligned conferences; and (b) the super powers and power-bloc countries.

The first component of the policy helped Nepal to work towards the maximisation of its power and influence and the minimisation of its 'vulnerabilities' *vis-a-vis* the super powers. Left to itself, Nepal was too small and weak to be of any consequence in international politics. It, therefore, threw its weight with the countries similarly placed in the international system. In this context, Nepal's participation in the UN where it identified its interests with the 'Afro-Asian group' as well as in the Non-aligned and Afro-Asian Nations Summit Conferences, where it raised its voice against the action of super powers and evolved a common approach towards them along with others, stand as clear evidences. Its call for solidarity among the smaller nations and its fight for equal voting rights in, and adequate protection through the world body, were of particular significance.

The second component of Nepal's non-alignment secured the involvement of both the power blocs in its economic development. Its strategic location in a region of vital interests to the super powers led the latter to focus their attention on the Kingdom. In view of it, through the policy of encouraging involvement of both the sides, Nepal neutralised the influence and pressure from one side with that of the other. The establishment of diplomatic relations with the USSR in 1956 and quickness with which Nepal expanded these relations later can be recalled as an example.

Leaning towards the Western Powers

However, if we take a comparative look at Nepal's attitude towards the super powers, we find that its policy had a leaning towards the West. It was evident in more than one ways. The number of countries belonging to the Communist bloc with which Nepal had diplomatic relations, was only four including the USSR as against more than 15 of those belonging to the Western bloc dominated by the USA. (See Appendix I) Besides the number, the amount of intercourse was also greater with the Western bloc. Nepal accepted arms from the USA and the UK and allowed the latter to employ Gurkhas. But nothing of this sort existed between Nepal and the USSR or any of the latter's allies. In the economic and political matters also, Nepal's dependence upon the Western bloc was greater.

Two factors explain this leaning. First, Nepal found the Western bloc more powerful and resourceful to fulfill its needs as also, more keen to take interest in its affairs. This was evident from the fact that whereas Nepal figured in the US global strategy since 1945, for historical and strategic considerations, the Soviet Union moved to cultivate the Kingdom only in the late fifties. The second factor was largely ideological. Whether it was the Parliamentary or the Panchayat Systems of democracy, it had a strong anti-communist bias and for the protection and consolidation of democracy, the USA and its allies were the countries to be relied upon.

The leaning towards the Western bloc did not seriously obstruct the pursuance of the non-aligned policy. This was primarily so because, owing to smallness, this posture did not have any larger consequences in international politics as such. Besides, since the emergence of the Sino-Soviet rift in 1959-60 Nepal gradually became an area of agreement between the two super powers, who seem to have then decided to neutralise the Chinese influence in the Kingdom. The displeasure with Nepal's growing cordiality with China during 1961-62, shown both by the USA and the USSR can be recalled as an example. The convergence in the objectives of the US and the Soviet polices in Nepal—against China—became more clear since the emergence of China in the South Asian region after 1962. This was clearly evident in the economic matters which will be discussed in the next chapter.

To sum up, it was the small and weak stature of Nepal that made its global non-alignment little different from the one followed by India and others. This stature introduced subtle nuances in the framework as well as in the practical application of the policy and gave it a distinct Nepali look. Nepal's concern, accordingly, was not restricted to the super and major powers. It was equally, and at times even more, pre-occupied with the 'regional' and non-aligned powers. This further led to its greater reliance upon the collective approach and upon international bodies and forums, in the solution of the problems facing the world', as also in the achievement of its objectives.

Notes

1. For the speeches of King Tribhuwan, M. P. Koirala, D. R. Regmi and others, see *Hamro Par-Rastra Sampark,* Department of Publicity, Kathmandu, n.d.
2. The change in the Soviet approach was welcomed in Nepal by Foreign Minister D. R. Regmi, *Gorkhapatra,* 1 October 1954; also *The Statesman,* 6 November 1954.
3. Replying to such criticism, the US Ambassador Ellsworth Bunker stated that the American assistance was without any strings attached and had "no ulterior motives", *Gorkhapatra,* 26 August 1957; *The Statesman,* 26 August 1957. This argument was repeated by the Ambassador on other occasions also. See, *Halkhabar,* 29 April 1958; *Naya Samaj,* 18 December 1958.
4. *Kalpana,* 25 April 1958; *Nepal Times,* 28 April 1958; *Naya Samaj,*

2 May 1958; *Samyukt Prayas*, 10 May 1958; *Nepal Samachar*, 29 May 1958.

5. The fact of the US suspicion was impliedly evident in Prime Minister Tanka Prasad Acharya's attempt to explain to the US Ambassador that there were no "sinister motives" behind Nepal's relations with the communist countries, *The Statesman*, 11 March 1957.
6. *Halkhabar*, 30 June 1959.
7. *Samaj*, 13 September 1959.
8. The invitation to this visit from the US seems to have been prompted by the King's visit to the USSR in June 1958. E. B. Mihaly, *Foreign Aid and Folilics in Nepal: A case study*, Oxford University Press, 1965, 59-60.
9. King Mahendra, H.M., *Proclamations, Speeches and Messages*, Department of Publicity, HMG, Nepal, Kathmandu, 1967 (Hereafter referred as *Speeches)*, Vol. I, Part Two, 181-88.
10. *The New York Times*, 28 April 1960.
11. Text of the Joint Communique issued at the end of the visit, *The Statesman*, 30 April 1960. Also see, *The Commoner*, 28 April I960.
12. *Gorkhapatra*, 20 May 1960; *The Commoner*, 17 May 1960.
13. *Speeches*, n. 9, Vol. I, 184.
14. *The Commoner*, 20 April 1960. Also *Asian Recorder*, Vol. VI, No. 35, 27 August-2 September 1960, 3508.
15. A joint statement was issued after the talks, *The Commoner*, 23 September 1960; *Naya Samaj*, 23 September 1960. White House Press Secretary refused to answer a specific question whether the two leaders had discussed "China's infringement of Nepal's border". He did not say no.
16. The US Department of State said that the "takeover" had nothing to do either with the Soviet Union or Communist China. That being so, there was nothing to worry about. *The Hindu*, 17 December 1960.
17. *Gorkhapatra*, 2 and 3 May 1961.
18. *Gorkhapatra*, 30 May 1961.
19. Interview with the US diplomats in Kathmandu (May-June 1962). The coldness between the two at that time was also reflected in the implementation of the US aid programmes in Nepal. Mihaly, n. 8, 120-23.
20. It was disclosed by Dr. Tulsi Giri after his meetings with the Amercian leaders, *Gorkhapatra*, 20 and 27 September 1963; *Samaj*, 25 September 1963. Also see *Samiksha*, 5 February 1964, which quoted Robert MacNamara, US Defence Secretary as saying that Nepal faced danger from China.

21. *Gorkhapatra,* 25 April 1964; *Nepal Samachar,* 28 September 1964.
22. The Statesman, *14 March 1964;* The Hindustan Times, *14 March 1964;* The Indian Express, *19 March 1964.*
23. *Gorkhapatra,* 17, 18 and 19 January 1965.
24. *Naya Samaj,* 15 December 1966. This instalment included 22 M-601 multipurpose military trucks each weighing 1 ton. The Royal Army had previously received 13 Jeeps, 12 trucks weighing 3/4 ton each, one 20 ton truck and 4 ambulance cars under the arms aid programme.
25. *Nepal Samachar,* 15 June 1962; *Samaj,* 8 June 1962.
26. *Gorkhapatra,* 6 July and 7 November 1965, and of 13 February 1966; *Motherland,* 5 February and 20 October 1966.
27. *Gorkhapatra,* 31 March 1964 and 13 February 1966; *The Rising Nepal,* 7 October 1966; *Motherland,* 20 October 1966.
28. *Gorkhapatra,* 6 July 1964; *Samiksha,* 5 and 14 October 1962, 5 February 1964 and 12 December 1966.
29. *The Commoner,* 12 October 1963.
30. *Gorkhapatra,* 9 January 1964.
31. *Nepal Samachar,* 3 February 1964; *Nay a Samaj,* 5 March 1964; *Gorkhapatra,* 13 March 1964; *Janavrata,* 21 March 1965.
32. *Janavrata,* 21 November 1965.
33. *The Rising Nepal,* 31 December 1965.
34. *Gorkhapatra,*7 August 1964 and 11 February 1965. Also *Metherland,* 9 February 1965. D
35. In a Press Conference, King Mahendra stated in response to a demand for Nepal's strong protest against the US bombing of North Vietnam : "I think our Government has already expressed its views on this question but in a situation where despite the functioning of the UNO, bombing of one country by another is possible, I see no good merely in voicing loud protests. Nor can we admire any action of that type", *Speeches,* n. 9, Vol. II, 330
36. Minister of Publicity and Broadcasting, Vedanand Jha told Nepali journalists : "We do not want that there should be outside interference in Vietnam. Both China and the USA are our friends and we should not, therefore, indulge in one-sided propaganda against the other", *Swatantra Samachar,* 2 October 1965.
37. *Speeches,* n. 9, Vol. II, 339; *Gorkhapatra,* 11 August 1966.
38. *Gorkhapatra,* 27 August 1964, 30 March 1965, and 5 July 1966; *Swatantra Samachar,* 30 June 1966.
39. The cooperation between them in other fields was limited, signified by a couple of British survey experts working in Nepal,

The Hindu, 20 November 1955. The British constitutional expert, Ivor Jennings helped in the framing of the *"Constitution of the Kingdom of Nepal (1959)"*.

40. *The Daily Telegraph,* 18 October 1960; *Speeches,* n. 9, Vol. I, Part Two, 190-92.

41. *The Statesman,* 7 and 13 January 1961, also of 16 March 1961.

42. *Gorkhapatra,* 27 and 28 February 1961; *The Commoner,* 27 February and 2 March 1961; *Speeches,* n. 9, Vol. II, 14-15.

43. *The Times of India,* 28 February 1961.

44. Samiksha, *1 March 1961;* Dainik Nepal, *2 March 1961;* Motherland, 2 March 1961; *Halkhabar,* 3 March 1961.

45. The Hindustan Times, *7 March 1961;* The Indian Express, *6 March 1961;* Halkhabar, *22 March 1961.*

46. The Nepalese Press attributed the change in the Queen's speech to the British Foreign Secretary Earl Home's talks with Prime Minister Nehru in New Delhi before the former joined the Queen in Kathmandu, *The Times of India,* 28 February 1961; *The Statesman,* 5 March 1961; *Swatantra Samachar,* 5 March 1961 ; *Halkhabar.* 6 March 1961; *Nepal Samachar,* 6 March 1961.

47. *Gorkhapatra,* 20 October 1963.

48. It was later disclosed by the British Foreign Secretary Mr. Butler in the British House of Commons in answer to a written question. Britain, *Parliamentary Debates* (Hansard) (House of Commons), Series V, Vol. 691,13 March 1964, Cols. 97-99.

49. *Gorkhapatra,* 25 May 1965. See also *Motherland,* 28 January 1965; *The Hindu,* 27 April 1963.

50. Text of the Communique issued to that effect, *National News Agency,* 15 March 1963; for more details see, *Naya Sandesh,* 15 March 1963; also *The Hindustan Times,* 15 march 1963; *The Statesman,* 27 march 1963.

51. *The Commoner,* 17 October 1963; *Gorkhapatra,* 18 October 1963.

52. Britain, *Parliamentary Debates* (Hansard) (House of Commons), Series V, Vol. 684, 20 November 1963, Col. 98, and Vol. 686, 8 December 1963, Cols. 97-99, 115, 11 December 1963, Cols. 368-70. Also see *Gorkhapatra,* J 7 April 1964.

53. *The Times* (London), 7 December 1966; *Gorkhapatra,* 4, 6 and 8 December 1966.

54. *Gorkhapatra,* 6 and 7 June 1958.

55. *Speeches,* n. 9, Vol. I, Part Two, 113-125. Also *Naya Samaj,* 22 June 1958; *Halkhabar,* 23 June 1958.

56. Text of the Joint Communique in original made available by the Ministry of Foreign Affairs, HMG, Nepal, Kathmandu. Also see, *Samaj.* 24 and 25 June 1958; *The Commoner,* 25 June 1958;

Kalpana 25 June 1958.

57. Joint Communique, *ibid.;* also *Gorkhapatra,* 13 June 1958.
58. *The Commoner,* 4 February 1960.
59. *Speeches,* n. 9, Vol. I, Part Two, 164-66.
60. Joint Communique issued at the end of the visit, *The Hindustan Times* 7 February 1960. Also *Kalpana,* 11 February 1960.
61. Soviet Vice-Premier Kozlov accompanying President Voroshilov refused to express any opinion on this question in a press conference in Kathmanau, *The Commoner,* 5 February 1960; *The Hindustan Times,* 5 February 1960.
62. *The Statesman,* 8 October 1960.
63. *Nepal Samachar,* 21 October 1959; also of 29 February 1960; *Halkhabar,* 21 October 1959; *Kalpana,* 22 October 1959.
64. *The Commoner,* 6 and 7 June I960. Home Minister S. P. Upadhyaya's statement in the *Pratinidhi Sabha* in this context, *The Commoner,* 9 June 1960; *Kalpana,* 2 and 4 June 1960.
65. *The Times of India,* 15 July 1960; *Nepal Samachar,* 9 July 1960; *Halkhabar,* 12 July I960.
66. *Kalpana,* 24 October 1960; *The Times of India,* 26 October 1960.
67. *The Times of India,* 27 September 1961; *The Statesman,* 29 September 1961.
68. Survey of East-West Highway may be mentioned here, *The Sunday Standard,* 12 November 1961. Also *Asian Recorder,* February 26-March 4, 1962, 4447.
69. Text of the Joint Communique made available by the Ministry of Foreign Affairs, HMG, Nepal, Kathmandu (Document No. 87). Also *Gorkhapatra,* 29 and 31 October 1963; *Motherland,* 31 October 1963.
70. *Naya Sandesh,* 18 January 1964; *Gorkhapatra,* 29 February and 25 September 1964.
71. A copy of 10-point Soviet note sent in reply to the West German proposal regarding disarmament and European Security was forwarded to Nepal, *Gorkhapatra,* 27 May 1966.
72. *Gorkhapatra,* 1, 3 and 4 June 1965; *Matribhumi,* 3 June 1965.
73. *Gorkhapatra, 9* April 1966.
74. Joint Communique issued at the end of Dr. Giri's visit. Text made available by the Nepalese Ministry of Foreign Affairs (Document No. 99), HMG, Kathmandu.
75. Ibid., Nepal Samachar, *3 November 1964.*
76. Joint Communique, *Gorkhapatra,* 19 November 1964.
77. Cyclostyled text of the Trade Agreement supplied by the Commerce and Foreign Trade Ministry, HMG, Nepal, Kathmandu

78. *Gorkhapatra*, 8 and 9 March 196.
79. Joint Communique, *Gorkhapatra,* 11 March 1966.
80. R. K. Shah, *Foreign Policy of Nepal* (typed manuscript), 13. The UN Committee on admission had raised queries about Nepal's past Treaties and Agreements with India, China, Britain, etc. and its status as an independent sovereign nation therein. For Nepal's response to such queries, see, Reply to *Enquiry of United Nations Committee on the Admission of New Members,* typed text supplied by a former Nepali Foreign Minister. Also see, A. S. Bhasin (ed.), *Documents on Nepal's Relations with India and China,* New Delhi, 1970, 1-22.
81. *UN* General Assembly, Official Records (GAOR*), 1955, 8 and 14 December 1955.*
82. It was repeated almost every year in the Nepali delegation's speech in the UN General Assembly. For example see, *GAOR* (1961), para 102; (1963), para 118; (1966), para 102; and Prime Minister B. P. Koirala's speech at the UN General Assembly in 1960, Text, *Policy Speech,* Department of Publicity and Broadcasting, HMG, Nepal, n. d., 4.
83. *GAOR* (1956), paras 3 and 4; (1958), para 3, and *Policy Speech* (1960), 4.
84. *GAOR* (1966), Cyclostyled Text of Nepali Foreign Minister's speech in the UN General Assembly supplied to the author by the Ministry of Foreign Affairs, Archives, HMG, Kathmandu 5 (Here-after referred as *Text).*
85. *GAOR* (1963), para 108; (1965), paras 142 and 143; (1966), Text para 1. Also see *Speeches,* n. 9, Vol. II, 199-200 and 355.
86. *GAOR* (1956), para 16; (1958), para 13; (1959), para 17; (1961), paras 99 and 100.
87. *GAOR* (1958), para 6; (1959), para 19; (1961), para 126; and (1966), Text, 8.
88. *GAOR* (1963), para 117; (1964), paras 125 to 127; (1965), para 106.
89. *GAOR* (1956), paras 7 and 8; (1957), paras 68 and 69.
90. *GAOR* (1963), para 116; (1964), paras 120 to 124.
91. *GAOR* (1963), para 107; (1964), para 116.
92. *GAOR* (1963), para 110; (1964), para 115; (1965), paras 163 to 165; (1966), Text, 5.
93. *GAOR* (1963), para 110; (1964), para 117; (1965), paras 160-62.
94. *GAOR* (1958), paras 10, 11-19; (1963), paras 98, 99 and 102; (1964), paras 97 and 98; (1965), paras 115 to 159; (1966), Text,

3-4.

95. *GAOR* (1963), para 101; (1966), Text, 4.

96. *GAOR* (1961), paras 102-23; (1963), para 103; *Policy Speech* (1960), 3.

97. *GAOR* (1962), para 60.

98. *GAOR* (1963), para 101; (1964), para 96.

99. *GAOR* (1958), para 61; (1961), para 92.

100. *GAOR* (1957), paras 41, 44 and 55-58; (1961), paras 93-97.

101. *GAOR* (1957), paras 53, 54; (1961), paras 82, 88, 89 and 98; (1965), paras 142 and 143. This office had been drawn into a controversy since 1960 with the then Secretary General Dag Hammarskjold's role in the Congo crisis. Nepal sided with Hammarskjold and paid glowing tributes to the statesmanship after his death during the crisis.

102. *Policy Speech* (1960), 4; *GAOR* (1961), paras 81 and 84-87.

103. *GAOR* (1956), para 19; (1957), paras 110 to 112; (1962), paras 62 and 63; (1964), para 99; (1965), para 157; *Policy Speech* (1960k, 2; and Text (1966), 3

104. *GAOR* (1958), para 9.

105. *GAOR* (1957), paras 39 and 45; (1965), para 152.

106. *GAOR* (1957), paras 46, 47 and 59; [(1961), paras 103-105; *Policy Speech* (1960), 6-7.

107. *GAOR* (1961), paras 103-105; (1964), paras 10C-103.

108. Nepal sponsored moves on the questions related to the West Asian problem in 1956; Algeria in 1958, 1959, 1960 and 1961;. Congo in 1960 and Cyprus in 1965.

109. Text of the statement by Head of the Nepali delegation, *Asian-African Conference,* Information Service, Indonesia, Embassy of the Republic of Indonesia, New Delhi, n. d., 110-13. It may be borne in mind that Nepal had not succeeded in securing UN membership by April 1955.

110. *Gorkhapatra,* 1 November 1965. Earlier, Foreign Minister K. N. Bista said that Nepal would follow the consensus developed among the Afro-Asian Foreign Ministers on the question, *Gorkhapatra,* 24 June 1965.

111. *Motherland,* 8 November 1965.

112. Text of the Head of Nepal's delegation, King Mahendra's speeches at the Conferences, *Speeches,* n. 9, Vol. II, 35-42 and 270-77. These texts have been followed in the analysis here.

113. *Gorkhapatra,* 29 September 1964; *The Commoner,* 29 September 1964.

114. *Samaya,* 2 November 1964; *Gorkhapatra,* 2 November 1964;

Motherland, 24 December 1964.

115. Other countries including India, the UAR and Ghana expressed regrets and shock on this point. Nepal expressed its disapproval in this matter in the UN General Assembly, GAOR (1961), para 22.

116. *GAOR* (1956), paras 11 and 13; (I Emergency Special Session), paras 373-77; (1958), para 8.

117. *GAOR* (1958) (II Emergency Special Session), paras 91-97; (II Session), paras 11, 15; (1957). Nepal's former permenent re-presentative at the UN, told the author that on the Hungarian question, Indian leaders—V. K. Krishna Menon, Jaiprakash Narayan, etc. tried their best to influence him to the effect that Nepal should follow India at the UN. But he had strict instructions from Kathmandu to the contrary. (Kathmandu, April 1968).

118. *The Times of India*, 30 December 1964.

119. Foreign Minister K.N. Bista's statement, *Gorkhapatra*, 31 December 1964

120. *Policy Speech* (1960), 2-3.

121. *GAOR* (1959), paras 13, 51-62; (1960), paras 132-33. Also see Appendix III.

6

FOREIGN ECONOMIC POLICY

"The foreign policy of Nepal was characterised by a strong economic bias. Its objective, of domestic economic development through foreign policy, while keeping in view the *Stability* (E) motive, has been outlined in the Second Chapter. The significance of the objective is borne out by subsequent references to economic matters in Nepal's relations with various countries. Highlighting the economic content of Nepal's foreign policy, the Chairman of the Council of Ministers Dr. Tulsi Giri stated in the UN General Assembly in September 1963 :

> We do not say that other values do not matter, but for us, ecomomic development is a challenge which we can only ignore at our own peril.
>
> Our foreign policy, therefore, is directed towards highlighting not the ideological differences, however important they may be, but the economic differences which unless minimized are bound to become a threat to the world peace.

The foreign economic policy of Nepal had two major dimensions. These relate to foreign aid and foreign trade.

FOREIGN AID

The economic development of Nepal remained neglected under the Rana rulers. Their fall and consequent opening up of the country to the outside world, led to a growing awareness towards this neglected aspect. Internal resources being non-existent, Nepal had to look for external assistance to give the initial push to its stagnant economy.[1] Till 1961-62 the developmental expenditure of the Kingdom was almost wholly met by external assistance. Afterwards also, the domestic contributions remained modest and till 1966-67 it was less than 50%. The *allocations* of domestic contributions for the developmental expenditure during this period had been impressive. From 4.48% (or Rs. 5.3 million Nepali) in 1962-63, it rose to 46.98% (or Rs. 126.00 million Nepali) in 1966-67, more than 40% increase in four years. In actual expenditure, however, the amount had been much less than these figures. Serious thought had been given to mobilise internal resources in order to reduce dependence on foreign aid, with the ultimate goal of doing away with it.[2] This is further borne out by Nepal's willingness to invite foreign loans besides aid, significant changes in its fiscal and monetary policies and financial administration[3], and increasing emphasis on the growth and expansion of foreign trade as against aid.[4]

Nepal mobilised assistance from almost every one of its "friendly countries". There was, however, one self-imposed condition for Nepal to accept aid. That the aid given should be without any condition attached. As a protection against pressures from the donor, Nepal diversified the sources of aid and preferred it to be routed through the UN and other international organisations like The Colombo Plan, Asian Development Bank etc. The Nepali delegation in the UN in 1956 strongly supported the move for the establishment of the Special United Nations Fund for Economic Development (SUNFED).[5] Later Prime Minister B.P. Koirala said : "I feel that all foreign aid to underdeveloped countries should be directed to the receiving countries through the UN."[6]

India and the United States were the first counties to make their mark as aid donors to Nepal in 1951. China and the USSR came to the scene in 1956 and 1958 respectively, but became effective only after 1959. The United Kingdom, New Zealand, Australia, Canada, Japan and Pakistan provided aid under the Colombo Plan schemes. Others included Switzerland, West Germany, Isreal, etc. Besides, the UN— through its specialised Agencies like WHO and ILO—the Ford Foundation had also been assisting Nepal regularly.

By 1966-67, Nepal received a total of Rs. 1,255.611 million (Nepali) as foreign aid, of which the highest contribution, approximately 44%, was made by the USA. The next was India with 37% (app.) share. In 1970-71, however, this position stood reversed. India headed the list of aid donors to Nepal with about 50% share of the total foreign aid. The US accounted for only 20% (approximately) (Table I). Initially, foreign aid intake of Nepal was very low. It was only Rs. 27.323 million (Nepali) in 1958-59, as compared to Rs. 175.300 million (Nepali) in 1965-66 and Rs. 142.236 million (Nepali) in 1966-77. Nepal did not show enough capacity even to absorb the estimated aid out of the total, that was made available. The situation was described as "aid indigestion" in economic terms. This was due to various factors like the lack of proper economic environment, the inadequate administrative and financial institutions, the imperfect monetary and fiscal policies and the absence of well thought out priorities in development projects.[7] Confusion in the political situation created by frequent changes of governments proved an additional hurdle In this context, King Mahendra in his call to the nation in 1958, remarked :

> On account of the political instability in our country, what should have been achieved was not achieved. For that very reason, the aid received from friendly countries could not be used to the maximum advantage.[8]

Gradually with the improvement in these aspects, the aid absorption increased.

Foreign assistance came to Nepal generally in four forms : cash, capital and consumer goods, technical assistance, and training facilities. China was the first and the only country to have given cash grant in 1956 amounting to Rs. 20 million in Indian currency. China was also the first country, followed by the USSR, to give aid in consumer goods. The sale proceeds of these goods were used to meet the local cost of the projects undertaken by them. The rest of the modes were used by every donor. Now we shall discuss the main developmental work undertaken in Nepal with the aid from four major donors: the USA, India, China and the USSR.

The US Aid

Expressedly, US aims in Nepal were "bolstering democracy and preventing aggression" as also preserving political independence.[9] The implied source of threat was from communism and communist countries.[10] Economic development was considered an essential and vital aspect of the defence against this threat. Elaborating upon the point, the US Ambassador to Nepal commented in December 1958:

> ...the revolution of rising expectations begins concurrently with the achievement of independence....Unless these expectations can be met, political independence cannot be secured.
>
> Since my country is firmly convinced that this is so it follows that it believes it to be in its own self-interest to assist the newly independent and less developed countries to raise their living standards to develop sound social institutions and to achieve a degree of well being which will make it possible to strengthen and maintain their political independence.[11]

Within this broad objective, the United States placed emphasis on building up democratic institutions and training people in Nepal through aid.

US economic assistance to Nepal commenced with the signing of the Point Four Agreement between the two countries on 23 January 1951. In the context of the US political and strategic objectives, it may be recalled that the signing of this Agreement was preceded by the establishment of Communist China's authority in Tibet. This Agreement was of a general nature which provided for the exchange of "technical knowledge and skill" for economic development of Nepal and the relevant information related to that.[12] Agreements for specific programmes and projects were to be concluded separately between the two sides within the framework of this Agreement.

Exploratory surveys were conducted by the US experts in Nepal in the fields of agriculture, health and mineral resources following the signing of the Agreement. Specific programmes and projects which were undertaken by the US aid after these surveys during the period under study, covered the fields of agriculture, education, health, water supply, transport and communication, administration, industry and power, forest resources and village and panchayat development.

There was a strong bias in the US aid programme in favour of such projects which had political value. It is evident from Table II which shows the major fields of the US aid activity. The bulk of the aid was spent on projects like agricultural development, education, malaria eradication, panchayat development, etc. The economic value of all these projects, except the agricultural development, was debatable. The agricultural development project was also not devoid of political potential. On being badly executed, the size of the project was considerably reduced after 1962.[13] All these projects enabled the Americans to establish direct contact with the land and people in the Kingdom and facilitate the desired values and influence.

An important feature of the US aid programme was its collaboration with India, particularly in road building activity. It started in January 1958 when the US, India and Nepal agreed to establish a Regional Transportation Organisation (RTO). It was proposed to construct 900 miles of roads in Nepal through this organisation within a period of five years, with an estimated cost of $10.7 million.[14] The financial obligations of the parties individually were : the US=$7.5 million; India=Rs.12.5 million, and Nepal=equivalent in kind of $0.7 million. However, the RTO could not function smoothly. It became virtually defunct by June 1962 and was formally dis-solved on 10 January 1963. The causes of its failure listed in the final RTO report were lack of cooperation between its major partners, the US and India, particularly at the technical and the administrative levels; initial underestimation of the nature and the cost of the project; lack of proper communication facilities between the headquarters and construction sites and the inadequate supply of skilled workers. Naturally, the achievements of the RTO fell far short of the goals originally set.[15]

Three years after the dissolution of the RTO, the United States decided to provide certain equipments to the Government of India for use in the construction of the East-West Highway in Nepal.[16] The US/AID Director in Nepal, Joseph S. Toner, stated in June 1964 that this was a better arrangement to expedite the construction of the road. The arrangement also reflected the US reluctance towards road building projects after their experience in the RTO.

The US collaboration with India underlined the similarity in the approaches of the two countries towards Nepal. This similarity had been indicated earlier by the US Ambassador to India and Nepal, Chester Bowles. It was reiterated in the preamble of the RTO agreement which stated that the contracting parties' objectives were "to safeguard basic rights and liberties and to protect the security and independence of free and independent people ....." It may be recalled here that the idea of the RTO was conceived at a time when Nepal had started cultivating relations with China and the USSR much to the displeasure of both India and the US. Similarly, both India and the US joined the East-West Highway project, only after China had been dislodged from it (details later).

The US aid programmes largely failed to achieve their targets. Fate of the agricultural development and road building (RTO) has been mentioned. The expansion of Nepal's administrative machinery brought about by US aid and advice, in the ultimate analysis perpetrated the HMG's heavy dependence upon US aid.[17] The educational development programme was fairly successful but not without much wastage and delay. The Ropeway and the Malaria Eradication programmes were by and large successful ventures. The failure of the programmes was attributed to faulty planning, lack of understanding about the social conditions and economic environment in the Kingdom and the technical and administrative difficulties.[18] Besides, a substantial proportion of the aid allotments was spent on the technicians alone, most of which, in a way went back to the United States.[19]

How far the US aid programme in Nepal served the objectives of the donor, is difficult to say. But one thing became very clear by the end of 1966. The US gained immense influence in Nepal. It was evident from the free access of US diplomats in Nepal to almost every quarter, the confidence reposed in them by the King, and the activities of the Peace Corps Volunteers. During 1958-59 King Mahendra consulted the US Ambassador regarding the fields to be allotted for Soviet aid, and on his advice did not permit Soviet aid to involve itself in fields like education and aviation which were kept apart for US aid.[20] In 1962-63, the US was reported to have asked the Nepalese Government to discourage Chinese and the Soviet aid and to disclose budgetary estimates as conditions for the signing of new US aid Agreements.[21] The fact that these Agreements were signed after a considerable delay and controversy and following the release of the revised budget estimates lends support to the view that the US had put pressure on the Nepalese Government.[22] The US Ambassador and the US/AID Director also reacted very strongly to the officially sponsored paper *The Rising Nepal's* adverse comments on US aid, and that too in the presence of H.M. Queen Ratna. As a result, the paper had to render apologies.[23]

There was considerable resentment in the Nepalese press regarding the working of the US aid. Ulterior motives were suspected behind the aid and it was accused of misplaced priorities and improper execution.[24] Even the officially sponsored paper, *The Rising Nepal* (20 January 1966) demanded a "radical change of attitude" in the US aid programme and asked the US to give up its bias against the capital projects which could help stimulate economic activities in the Kingdom. However, the US aid enjoyed official patronage and appreciation. In the midst of public controversy around US aid in May 1963 King Mahendra stated :

> My Government is very much obliged to our friendly country, the United States of America for their pure-hearted help and cooperation in development projects to be undertaken by the Panchayats.[25]

Evidently, it was King Mahendra's acknowledgement of the contribution of US aid in maintaining and stabilising his regime.

The Indian Aid

India's concern and interest in Nepal were immediate and extensive owing to the Kingdom's vital strategic position. India wanted to keep communist influence out of the Kingdom, preserve its political stability and encourage democratic progress. India's objectives in Nepal have been discussed in the earlier chapters. It was in the background of these objectives and interests that India's "cooperation and assistance" to Nepal was bracketed with its "special friendship" for the latter.[26]

The germs of economic aid to Nepal were present in Indian thinking as early as 1950. It was implied in the letter exchanged along with the Treaty of Peace and Friendship signed in July 1950. Para (4) of the letter read :

> If the Government of Nepal should decide to seek foreign assistance in regard to the development of natural resources, or of any industrial project in Nepal, the Government of Nepal shall give first preference to the Government or the nationals of India, as the case may be, provided that the terms offered by the Government of India or Indian nationals, as the case may be, are not less favourable to Nepal than the terms offered by any other Foreign Government or by other foreign nationals.

The beginning of a more serious thinking in this context was marked by Prime Minister Nehru's comments in Kathmandu during his state visit in June 1951 in which he told his Nepali audience : "If you seek our help, say in technical or other spheres, we will do our utmost to be useful to you."

In response to Nehru's call, Nepal's Prime Minister M.P. Koirala visited India in January 1952 followed by another Ministerial delegation in April, the same year. It was decided during these visits that India should help Nepal draw a long-term plan for economic development, fix priorities for that and build up a sound administrative and financial system to under-take the task of development. The Indian experts visited Nepal in this context.[27] Meanwhile, India had, since 1950, undertaken two major construction projects in Nepal : the Tribhuwan Rajpath—a Highway joining Kathmandu with an Indian border village Raxaul—and the Gauchar airport in Kathmandu. Initially, the expenditure on these projects was covered under a loan but later, it was turned into an Indian grant. Gradually the field of Indian aid expanded with increased number of projects and the amount of expenditure on them. It was also directed to diverse fields. Details of the fields and aid allotments are listed in Table III.

The bulk of the Indian aid was spent on transport, communications, power and irrigation. These projects were to lay down a sound infrastructure for the economic development of the Kingdom. The roads and airports consumed 32.8% and 2.8% respectively, whereas the development of power resources accounted for 25.2% and the irrigation facilities for 15.7% of the total aid expenditures up to 1966-67. Allotment towards the industrial development was comparatively small, only 0.5%. Similarly education, health, forestry, etc. which acquired high priorities in the US aid programme accounted for less than 1% of the total each.

Among the high priority projects in the Indian programme, community development and water supply schemes had no direct economic output, but they were significant from the point of their political and goodwill values. Regarding the roads, airfields and surveys, much was talked about the strategic considerations behind them, but nobody could dispute their immense economic value.[28] The economic potential of power development and irrigation projects was unquestionable. Thus, though not free from strategic and political considerations, the Indian aid programme in Nepal had a strong bias in favour of the projects having direct and immense economic value. This was in significant contrast with the US aid programme.

There was another category of the Indian aid projects called "mutual benefit projects". They included projects undertaken to harness the Koshi and Gandak rivers which had been causing flood havoc both in India and Nepal every year. The Koshi Project Agreement was signed by the two Governments on 25 April 1954 and the Gandak Project Agreement on 4 December

1959. These projects' Agreements were revised on 19 December 1966 and 30 April 1964 respectively, in order to secure more benefits for Nepal. Both the projects, to be constructed in Nepali territory, were to be financed by India and executed by it with the help of Joint Co-ordinating Committee of the two Governments. Nepal's benefits from the Koshi project were to be : flood protection for 1.27 lakh acres, irrigation for 77,000 acres and 9,000 KW of power at a cost of Rs. 50 million (Nepali) to be borne by India, to secure these benefits alone. From the Gandak project, Nepal was to get flood protection for 20 sq. miles, irrigation for 143,000 acres and 15,000 KW of power at the cost of Rs. 80 million (Nepali) to be borne by India.[29]

India's emphasis on its "special position" in Nepal was evident in the context of aid as well. As noted above, under the Treaty of Peace and Friendship India did not want any other country to aid Nepal without its knowledge and approval. This applied more to the Western Powers, the USA and the UK, since only they had relations with Nepal in the early fifties and were willing to assist economically. Nehru's offer of "technical and other help" followed the conclusion of the Point Four Technical Assistance Programme Agreement between the USA and Nepal. India objected to the visits of the US experts to Nepal in connection with survey and explorations during 1951-52.[30] This conflict between the Indian and the US aid programmes perhaps resulted from India's desire not to be surpassed by any other foreign power in Nepal. This tendency was witnessed only during 1951-54 and afterwards, the Indian and the US aid programmes cooperated to compete with the aid to Nepal from communist countries, particularly China, as will be seen below.

The Indian aided projects were frequently criticised by the press and public in Nepal. The Indian advisors and engineers working on the projects were charged with behaving with an "air of superiority", with their Nepali colleagues and sub-ordinates.[31] The mutual benefit projects of Koshi and Gandak were looked upon as examples of encroachment on Nepal's sovereignty and independence, as also of exploitation of its water and power potential by India.[32] Opposition to these two projects in particular, was witnessed ever since 1954.[33] It was responsible for the delay in the signing of the Gandak Agreement, and in the beginning of their execution and ultimately, for their revision. The Indian Aid Mission was also charged for the delay in the execution of some other projects.[34]

It is clear from the nature of these charges that they related to the execution and progress and not to the content, of the projects or to the programme as a whole. Most of the criticism emanated from psychological and domestic factors of Nepal which in a way, had affected the entire gamut of India-Nepal relations. A better appreciation of Nepali sentiments, both at the official and personal levels by the Indian side could remove a great deal of this criticism.

The slow progress of some of the projects was due to various factors. The foremost was the administrative and other difficulties faced by the project authorities, while dealing with the Nepalese Government. Nepal's Foreign Minister Dr. Tulsi Giri's comments made in a press conference in Kathmandu on 20 February 1961 are worth noting in this context. He said :

> There has been a feeling that some of the programmes undertaken were not carried out as expeditiously as was desirable. This might have been due to defects on our side and the Government of India alone is not to be blamed for it. Now we think that if we, on our side, correct ourselves and gear our machinery, the Government of India will also be more active. Besides, all the projects charged of slow progress, suffered from inadequate supply of labour in the Kingdom.[35] The Indian side was slow in settling the claims of compensation for the land acquired from the Nepalis for the projects.[36] Above all, natural calamities like floods, damaged the construction work and hampered its further progress.[37]

A very important factor that affected the smooth working of the. Indian aid programme was the political climate in the Kingdom and overall relations between the two countries. It was evident during the years following King Mahendra's "takeover" from the Nepali Congress government and the consequent developments.[38] Growing criticism of the Indian aided projects during these years led to the transfer of control over their execution from the Indian Aid Mission to His Majesty's Government of Nepal. The minor projects were transferred in November 1964 and the major projects in May 1966. The transfer also helped a great deal, in taking the wind away from the sails of the critics of the projects. Besides, with the gradual improvement in relations between the two countries at the official level, a better appreciation of the Indian aid programme was forthcoming in Nepal.[39]

The Chinese Aid

China's principal objectives in Nepal were to turn the Kingdom into a useful buffer-zone from the area of Indian influence that it was and to counteract the US and Soviet presence there. Economic aid was resorted to, to serve these objectives. China's opposition to US policies was too pronounced to need any detailed discussion. Its objective to neutralize Indian influence in the Kingdom was expressed indirectly. It was also evident in the manner China utilized its aid in Nepal.

More expressedly, the objective of the Chinese aid in Nepal was to help the latter start production and increase its national income.[40] The aid was considered a reciprocal gesture to, and an acknowledgement of, the support given by Nepal to China on the Tibetan question, on the "Two China" theory and regarding China's admission to the UN. During his state visit to Nepal in April 1965, the Chinese Vice-Premier Chen Yi commented :

> ...aid is always mutual. China helps Nepal and Nepal in turns helps China....She informs the world of the truth about China and opposes distortions and slanders against China. This constitutes a great help.

This principle of mutuality of help was endorsed by the Nepalese side as well.

Chinese aid was first promised under an Agreement signed on 7 October 1956 during Nepali Prime Minister Tanka Prasad Acharya's state visit to China. The amount of Rs. 60 million (Indian), one-third of which was a cash grant, promised under the Agreement was not allotted for any specific project and the Nepalese Government was free to spend it. The result was that after four years, the aid, except its cash-grant part, remained unspent. China recommitted this left over amount of Rs. 40 million (Indian) along with an additional grant of Rs. 100 million (Indian) in March 1960 under a new Agreement. This was the real beginning of Chinese active interest in Nepal's developmental activity. Since then, the emphasis in the Chinese aid programme had been on the construction of roads, establishment of industries and development of power resources. Major projects undertaken by China are listed in Table IV.

The figures in Table IV are estimates. Actual expenditures of Chinese aid by 1966-67 were Rs. 109.75 million (Nepali) in the fields of Transport Communication and Power and Rs. 69.55

million (Nepali) in Industrial Development.[41] The emphasis was obviously on capital projects. The industries undertaken to be established were based on the raw material available easily and in abundance in Nepal. Thus, their economic value was unquestionable. So also was that of the roads and the power plant. Besides. China also made goodwill gestures by occasionally presenting gifts. By the end of 1966, most of the Chinese projects, except the Kathmandu-Kodari road, leather and shoe factory and warehouses, were at the preliminary stage of construction.

Political considerations in Chinese aid were implied in what may be called its demonstrative aspects. China made a pronounced emphasis that its aid to Nepal was free from "whatever conditions attached". Cost of the technicians, except their maintenance expenses, was not included in the aid amount and the living standard of these technicians was not to be higher than that of "the personnel of the same level in the Kingdom of Nepal".[42] Apart from their living conditions, the Chinese technicians displayed a remarkable sense of 'comradeship' through work and behaviour, with their Nepali colleagues which added to their popularity.[43] This contrast between Chinese aid and Indian and US aid resulted in a warmer reception of Chinese aid in Kathmandu.[44]

China's keenness to select the sites for their projects near the Indian border or the Indian aided projects also does not seem to have been free from political and strategical considerations.[45] The same was true with China's interests in the field of aviation where it offered in 1963 to construct a number of airports in Nepal. This led India to agree quickly to undertake the same project and persuade the Nepalese Government to reject the Chinese offer in this field of obvious strategic significance.[46] India also secured assurances from the Nepali Government that it would not overlook the former's interests and anxieties while accepting Chinese aid proposals.[47] At times, China blamed India for the delay in Chinese projects since the machinery for construction, etc. had to pass through the Indian territory in transit.[48] China's political and strategic considerations behind the offer of Kathmandu-Kodari Highway have been noted earlier. The speed and interest with which the construction of the highway was undertaken, further underlined these considerations.

Another noteworthy feature of the Chinese aid was the supply of consumer goods as a part of the aid. The local cost of the projects was to be met from the sale proceeds of these goods.

The goods sent mostly included luxury articles, transistors, fountain pens and textiles. These goods had attractive designs and finish, and were sold at comparatively low prices. Thus they favourably competed with the similar Indian goods in the Nepali markets.[49] The goods were also smuggled into India through Nepal. Serious thinking people expressed displeasure on the inflow of such goods but without much avails.[50]

The goodwill earned by Chinese aid in Nepal was marred by two factors. First, the amount of aid was very small as compared to that of India and the United States. China seemed to be conscious of this factor. Vice-Premier Chen Yi regretted in Kathmandu during his visit in April 1965, that "we have not assisted Nepal in the economic development to the extent we should have." He promised more assistance after the economic conditions in China had improved further.

The second factor was China's frequent shifts from one project to the other. In September 1961, China had decided to undertake the establishment of a cement factory, a pulp and paper plant and a leather and shoe factory. After more than two years of survey and exploration, the first two projects were abandoned. No specific reasons were given officially for the change.[51] The funds earmarked for these projects were re-allocated for the construction of a 170 km. of Janakpur-Biratnagar section of the East-West Highway, a bricks and tiles factory, warehouses in Kathmandu and Biratnagar, and irrigation work.[52] Again, after a year of surveys, China with-drew from the East-West Highway project and the irrigation scheme at the request of the Nepalese Government.[53] The financial commitments of these projects were diverted to the construction of a hydro-electric project at Sunkoshi, a road between Kathmandu and Pokhra and a ring road around Kathmandu.[54] These changes formed one of the main targets for the criticism of Chinese aid.[55]

The Soviet Aid

The Kingdom, which was situated on the fringe of China as well as of Central Asia, though not of vital strategic importance to the Soviet Union, was not too remote either, to be overlooked. The Soviet objective in Nepal was simple and limited: to counteract the US and later the Chinese influences. Accordingly, the Soviet Union pleaded its support for the political independence and non-aligned foreign policy of the Kingdom. Economic aid was used as an instrument to further the Soviet objective.

The Soviet Union's offer of economic assistance to Nepal followed soon after the establishment of diplomatic relations between the two countries. However, the finalisation of details took more than two years and an Agreement to that effect was signed in April 1959. Free technical and financial assistance to the extent of 30 million roubles was provided under this Agreement. Major projects for which this and the subsequent grants were allocated are listed in Table V.

Of the total costs given in Table V, the contributions of the Nepalese Government were nominal in the sugar mill and the cigarette factory projects. In the case of Panauti Hydro-Electric Plant, it was Rs. 10 million (Nepali), *i.e.* 40% of the total cost and in the case of Kanti Hospital, it was Rs. 0.15 million (Nepali), i.e. about 15% of the total cost. The rest was borne by the Soviet Union. Nepal's contributions included the amount of loan allotted for these projects out of the total USSR loans of 2.5 million roubles. The East-West Highway section and the agricultural tools factory were to be constructed completely by the Soviet aid.[56] Like China, the USSR also sent consumer goods to Nepal, to meet the local costs of the projects.

Except for Kanti Hospital, the economic value of the projects undertaken by the Soviet Union was indisputable. The quick completion of the projects was stressed in the Soviet aid programme. This approach was disclosed by the Soviet Vice-Premier Kozlov in Kathmandu during President Voroshi-lov's state visit to Nepal in February 1960. In practice, this approach was evident from the fact that the USSR started actual construction work on the sugar mill, the cigarette factory and the hydro-electric plant in 1962 and all the three projects were inaugurated in 1965, in January, February and October, respectively. The new projects, the East-West Highway section and the Agricultural Tools Factory were formally committed to, only when either these projects were very near completion or had been completed.

The fast progress of the Soviet aided projects was in spite of the occasional complaints regarding lack of proper official response and difficulties in the movement of construction materials and machineries within Nepal, as also in-transit through the Indian territory. What proved more disappointing for the Soviet experts and officials in Nepal was the mismanagement of projects, particularly the sugar mill and the cigarette factory, after they were completed and handed over by them to His Majesty's Government.[57]

The Soviet aid programme was found to be in conflict with the Chinese aid programme. There were press reports which remained undenied, saying that the Soviet Premier N. Khrushchev drew Nepali Vice-Chairman Dr. Tulsi Giri's attentiont during his state visit to the USSR in 1963, towards the "increasing anti-Soviet propaganda" of the Chinese in Nepal. He was also believed to have offered a large volume of economic assistance for industrial development of the Kingdom in order to counteract the Chinese influence.[58] It may be underlined here that the fields chosen by the Soviet Union for economic aid in Nepal were the same as that of China, namely : power development, road construction and industrialization. The Soviet Union evinced great interest in the cement factory project immediately after China withdrew from it.[59] There were other evidences also. The Soviet experts working on Panauti hydro-electric project complained that the Chinese were damaging Panauti road in order to delay the completion of the project.[60] It took two months for the Chinese Embassy in Kathmandu to refute the charge which was described as an "attempt to disrupt Nepal-China friendship".[61] The Soviet Union was also willing to work out some sort of co-ordination between similar projects aided by itself and India.[62]

The Soviet Union had limited objectives in Nepal and, therefore, its aid programme was small. But it was planned and executed very successfully, without much complications. As a result, it won appreciation from a wider circle of the press and public opinion. In fact, there was hardly any criticism of the Soviet aid in Nepal.

Competition among the Donors and Nepal

Political objectives of the aid giving countries being in conflict with each other in Nepal, there was a mutual competition among them. Nepal, on its part, encouraged this competition in order to neutralize unwanted political pressures and influences coming through the aid. Various evidences have been pointed out above while dealing with the aid programmes separately. The point can be clearly demonstrated by taking the case of one giant project : the construction of the East- West Highway.

Nepal requested India and the United States to construct the highway under the RTO programme, but the request was not accepted. Then it approached the Soviet Union, which after conducting a preliminary survey during 1959-60 declined to take up the project. Perhaps Nepal's acceptance in 1961 of China's offer to construct the Kathmandu-Kodari road displeased the Soviets.[63]

Disappointed from all sides, Nepal decided to take up the project without aid. King Mahendra, invoking nationalistic and patriotic sentiments of the Nepalis, gave a call to mobilise internal resources for construction of the highway.[64] In reality, however, the call proved futile, largely, because of the big size of the project in terms of both expenditure and skill. External assistance was, therefore, indispensable.

To help Nepal come out of the dilemma, China offered to undertake the construction of a section of the highway (Janakpur-Biratnagar, 170 kilometres).[65] This led the USSR to re-enter the project with a commitment for 120 kilometres, the Simra-Janakpur section of the highway, which was signed on 8 April 1964. China signed its part of the commitment on 27 April 1964.

China's entry into a project, situated in densely populated Nepali Terai, which was also in close geographical proximity with the Indian plains, was of both political and strategic gains to China. This disturbed India, as also the USA who then made attempts to keep China out of the project. They succeeded in it, but only after committing themselves to the construction of a major portion—430 miles out of a total of 640 miles—of the highway. Commenting on China's withdrawal from the East-West Highway project, the official communique and the Chairman of Nepal's Council of Ministers, disclosed that it was because India and the USA had "promised to construct other sections of the highway" in addition to the one agreed upon by China earlier.[66] The bargain struck by the Nepalese side and accepted by India and the USA was clearly evident. It was further emphasired in this context that Nepal "did not make any agreements or commitments with one friendly nation in a manner prejudicial to the other friendly nation's territorial integrity and sovereignty."[67] The UK also joined the highway project.

Thus the project, which had been refused by every one of the donors at one time, was now supported by almost every one. This shows that Nepal, by exploiting competition among its donors through shrewd diplomacy, not only neutralised their respective influences and exercised independence and discretion in decisions, but also mobilised increased external assistance.

FOREIGN TRADE

Foreign trade constituted another important dimension of Nepal's foreign economic relations. Historically, Nepal played the role of a trade *entrepot* between India and Tibet. This position was jeopardised with the consolidation of British power in India and the extension of its influence over Tibet. Particularly, the conclusion of a trade Treaty between British India and Tibet, as a result of Col. Younghusband's mission to Tibet in 1904, gave a serious blow to Nepal's trade with Tibet and its position as trade *entrepot,* in the following years, British India gained a dominant position in Nepal *vis-a-vis* Tibet in trade matters.

Since 1951, Nepal's foreign trade has marked a steady rise. This trend is evident from Table VI. Between 1956-57 to 1964-65, the total trade recorded a three to four times increase. It was more pronounced and steady in imports. The exports, on the other hand, marked only a marginal increase and if the year 1964-65 is not taken into consideration, it remained largely constant between 1960-61 to 1963-64. An obvious implication of this phenomenon was the increasing unfavourable balance of trade for Nepal.

In direction, *i.e,* countrywise, Nepal's trade was dominated by India as shown in Table VII. More than 90% of Nepal's exports to and imports from, were with India. Balance of trade with India from available figures was unfavourable to Nepal. But it was held officially that taking into account the factors of poor and deficient recording and visible trade, the balance was not unfavourable. These factors, besides off-setting the unfavourable balance with India, also narrowed down, to a great extent the unfavourable balance in Nepal's foreign trade as a whole.[68]

Nepal's trade with Tibet accounted for only about 1% of the total. There had been significant fluctuations in Nepal's trade with Tibet. The exports to Tibet touched the lowest mark during 1959-60 and 1960-61. The imports reached a similar point during 1957-58. It could have been due to the disturbances in Tibet and its effect on the Nepali traders there during 1959-61. Considerable rise in the imports from Tibet after 1957-58 was accounted for by this factor alone because the repatriating Nepali traders brought their assets back.[69] Later it was due to the inflow of machinery, consumer goods, and other articles that came from China under the aid programme.

Regarding the overseas trade, no separate account was available till 1961-62 because the goods were first exported to India and then re-exported to the overseas countries. The value and volume of such trade was calculated in trade with India. Separate account for trade with the overseas countries was maintained after the conclusion of a new Trade Treaty with India in 1960 which will be discussed below. Imports from the overseas countries marked a steady rise.

The lopsidedness in Nepal's foreign trade was not confined to the direction alone. It was equally evident in the content of trade. Foodgrains and food products alone accounted for more than 50% of the total trade. The percentage of this commodity was all the more higher regarding the exports. The imports were largely constituted of manufactured products like machinery, consumer goods and chemicals. Comparative figures for commodity trade between 1960-61 to 1963-64 are given in Table VIII.

The commodity trade in terms of direction was largely in conformity with its general pattern. Nepal exported rice, ghee, jute and oilcakes to India and, in turn, imported wheat and wheat flour, sugar and sugar products, beverages and tobacco, petroleum and petroleum products, textiles, machinery chemicals and salt. With Tibet (China), the imports consisted mainly of food and live animals, unedible crude materials except fuels, consumer goods and machinery and the exports were food and live animals, beverages and tobacco, chemicals, machinery and consumer goods, including petroleum and petroleum products. This underlines the *entrepot* characteristics, since Nepal exported many items to Tibet after importing them from India. From the overseas countries, Nepal imported luxury goods and other finished products including synthetic fibre and stainless steel. In return it exported jute and indigenous herbs.

The pattern of foreign trade made Nepal heavily dependent upon India on the one hand and upon the production of foodgrains and other primary goods on the other. The crux of the policy for foreign trade had, therefore, been its diversification both in content and direction. Whereas the diversification in content related more to the pattern of the domestic economy—agricultural products and industrialisation—the diversification in direction was a matter of tact and diplomacy in the field of foreign policy. Before the problems and prospects of trade diversification are taken up, it is necessary to discuss Nepal's trade relations with India, Tibet (China) and the overseas countries.

Trade with India

After the withdrawal of the British from the Indian sub-continent, Nepal and India entered into a new Trade Treaty on 31 July 1950. The pattern of trade between the two countries, as stipulated under this Treaty, was largely the same as during the British period. The Treaty provided for transit facilities on reciprocal basis and re-export of the goods to, and from, Nepal through the Indian territory. (Aits 2, 3 and 4). The foreign exchange account of Nepal was to be maintained by India. Besides, Nepal's tariff policy was also to be in conformity with that of India. In this context, Article 5 of the Treaty stated:

> The Government of Nepal agree to levy, at rates not lower than those leviable for the time being in India, customs duties on imports from and exports to countries outside India. The Government of Nepal also agree to levy on goods produced or manufactured in Nepal which are exported to India, export duty at rates sufficient to prevent their sale in India at prices more favourable than those of goods produced or manufactured in India which are subject to central excise duty.

The Treaty's unfavourable and unequal provisions to Nepal were viewed as symbols of India's economic domination and as such were continuously criticised in the Kingdom.[70] Tanka Prasad Acharya was the first Prime Minister who openly described these provisions as not only economically disadvantageous to Nepal, but also contrary to its independence and sovereignty.[71] In order to change them, to suit Nepal's aspirations and interests, he raised the matter during his state visit to India in December 1956, with the Indian Prime Minister.[72] This was done informally and no concrete outcome was evident. The issue was reopended with greater seriousness during 1959-60, particularly, because the Treaty was due to expire in August 1960. Prime Minister Nehru and the Nepali Prime Minister B. P. Koirala, mutually discussed various aspects concerning the revision of the Trade Treaty -during their respective state visits to Nepal and India in June 1959 and January 1960.

The new Treaty was signed on 11 September 1960. It removed the unequal and disadvantageous position of Nepal *vis-a-vis* India in their mutual trade matters. The foreign exchange reserves of Nepal were transferred to its direct control and it also secured its right and freedom to frame tariff policies. The Treaty had separate sections on Trade and Transit and under the provisions of the later, the Nepalese goods were allowed the freedom of transit through Indian territory. Though these provisions were applicable reciprocally in practice, only Nepal was to use transit facilities. The procedure for the trade "traffic in transit" was separately laid down in detail in the Protocol of the Treaty. Nepal, on its part, agreed to ensure through mutual consultations, that there would be no flow of goods imported from the third countries into India, in case it pursued a different tariff policy from that of the latter. India, on its part, allowed the imposition of "duties" and "quantitative restrictions" on the Indian goods by Nepal towards the protection of the latter's newly established industries.

Transit Facilities through Indian Territory for Nepal's Trade with Pakistan

The implementation of the new Treaty with India led to a number of difficulties. One of the important matters in this context was Nepal's demand for transit facilities for trade with Pakistan which arose after the signing of a Trade Agreement between Nepal and Pakistan on 19 October 1962 in which, the latter had assured the former about the port and transit facilities for its trade with the overseas countries through Pakistani territory.[73] The demand was officially made in July 1963 when, at a periodical trade talk, the Nepali delegation asked for transit facilities at Radhikapur and Wagha on India's borders with the East and West wings of Pakistan respectively.[74] India agreed to this demand, provided Nepal was ready to bear the cost of such facilities.[75] However, cost of the facilities estimated by India for transit through Radhikapur was described by Nepal as exhorbitant, in view of the small volume of its trade with Pakistan.[76] This resulted into a deadlock between the two sides and Nepal criticised India's stand in the matter as 'unfriendly' and 'un-cooperative'.[77] Nepal's Chairman of the Council of Ministers Dr. Tulsi Giri stated in this context :

> Though an independent nation, we are being pressurised from outside. We want to exercise the freedom of trade with other countries but obstacles are put in our way. We are not being allowed to trade freely with Pakistan.[71]

Ultimately India gave into such criticism and, during Commerce Minister Manubhai Shah's visit to Nepal in January

1965 in connection with trade talks, agreed to provide the desired facilities to Nepal at Radhikapur for nominal rail service charges.[79] But before any trade could take place through Radhikapur, the railway traffic at the transit point was disrupted during the Indo-Pak war of September 1965. Later, Nepal was asked to avail of the transit facilities at Radhikapur after the repair of the railway track, or even earlier, provided the Nepali traders could make their own arrangements for the movement of goods from Radhikapur towards the Pakistani side.[80]

Minor Difficulties

Besides the question of transit facilities for trade with Pakistan, Nepal had other complaints against India. Mainly they related to the cumbersome procedural formalities and 'uncooperative' attitude of the Indian customs authorities at Calcutta port and on the Indo-Nepalese border which often resulted in delay in movement of the Nepali goods through the Indian territory as well as harrassment to the Nepali traders. Nepal also complained about discriminatory excise on the Nepali products in India, inadequate number of railway wagons made available to the Nepali traders, difficulties in road transport and finally, irregular and inadequate supplies of important goods like iron and steel.

India on its part was not happy with the leakage and smuggling of goods in transit or otherwise. In view of the differences in excise on, and restrictions on the imports of synthetic fabrics and yarn, stainless steel and other luxury goods in India ; the Nepali traders engaged themselves in smuggling these items. India was also sore about the diversion and deflection of trade, the re-export of petroleum and petroleum products, salt, mica and jute to Tibet as well as Nepal's discriminatory tariff policy towards some of the Indian goods as against those of the third countries. India often justified the detailed procedural formalities and customs security regarding the Nepali goods in transit through India, as protective measures against smuggling, leakage and deflection of goods.

The difficulties and complaints described above were sorted out, discussed and settled through mutual negotiations between the two countries. Such negotiations took place periodically—usually quarterly—under the provisions of the Trade and Transit Treaty of 1960 (Art. XIII), as well as during the exchange of visits at the highest and the ministerial levels. The understandings arrived at, and measures evolved accordingly, were incorporated into formal documents and treated as the part of the Treaty.[81]

A Memorandum of Understanding on Matters arising out of the Treaty of Trade and Transit (1960), was signed on 27 December 1966 (n. 80). It provided for institutional arrangement in the form of a Border Trade Committee and an Inter-Governmental Joint Committee to resolve difficulties concerning the border trade and the mutual trade expansion, respectively (paras 2 and 3). The procedure for transit traffic of the Nepali goods through the Indian territory was revised to meet Nepal's objections and demands (paras 22 to 24). Nepal, on its part, undertook to prohibit the movement of *ganja* (Hashis) towards India and agreed to regulate the traffic of other "sensitive items" so as to prevent their leakage and smuggling into India (paras 23 and 26).[82] Thus, the Memorandum removed many of the irritants in Indo-Nepalese trade relations and those left, were also decided to be removed similarly through mutual friendly consultations.

Trade with Tibet (China)

Nepal had traditional trade relations with Tibet. Though the volume of trade between the two countries dwindled during the British rule in the Indian sub-continent, its basic pattern continued to be operative. It had two major dimensions : the border trade which was largely barter, and the trade conducted by the Nepalis, who were stationed in Lhasa and other trade centres in Tibet. Since 1950, the trade between Nepal and Tibet had undergone significant changes.

The establishment of China's authority and influence in Tibet in 1950 had an adverse effect on Nepal-Tibet trade in spite of the fact, that no restrictions were announced formally on the Nepali traders stationed in Tibet and moving across the border. Later, the Agreement on Friendship, Trade and Intercourse between China and Nepal signed on 20 September 1956 and the Notes exchanged between the two countries along with this Agreement, substituted China for Tibet as the trading partner for Nepal.

Under the Agreement and the Notes of 1956, China and Nepal agreed to "promote and expand" mutual trade relations and give favourable treatment in the matters of excise and customs duty to each other's goods on a reciprocal basis. (Note, Para 6). The establishment of trade agencies and Consulates General of one country in the other on reciprocal basis was also provided for in the Agreement. (Article IV, Paras I and II). Though the traders of the two countries were granted the facilities of movement and residence in each other's territory, (Art. IV, Note, Paras 3 and 7), the Nepali traders living in Tibet were, for the first time, subjected to the passport and visa regulations in their movement across the border. [Art. IV, Para V (2)]. The customary border trade was allowed to continue as such. [Art. IV, Para V (3)]. The Nepali side took 15 months to ratify this Agreement. Accordingly, the Agreement became effective on 17 January 1958 and was to last for eight years.

The Agreement had hardly regulated trade for a year when fresh disturbances recurred in Tibet during 1959-60. The effect of these disturbances was felt all the more by the Nepali traders in Tibet, and thus its impact was greater on the general trade between Nepal and Tibet. The traders had to face difficulties in living, movement and in carrying on their profession. Besides, China's restrictions on the entry of Indian goods in the following years rendered them idle.[83] As a result, they returned to Nepal after winding up their business.[84] China, however, agreed in January 1964, to repatriate their earnings. By this time the trade between Nepal and Tibet was reduced to insignificant proportions.

Further, changes in Nepal's trade with Tibet on the one hand and with Mainland China on the other, were brought about through a new trade Agreement signed in May 1964 by the two countries. The main purpose behind this new Agreement was to cover the sea trade between them. Favoured terms in excise and customs duties were offered by one country to the other on reciprocal basis under the Agreement. The trade on the Chinese side was to be conducted largely through the state agencies and payments for that were to be made in mutually acceptable currencies. Though the barter-border trade was allowed to continue within 30 km. area from the boundary line, in the case of currency-trade along the border, local authorities on each side were to determine prices on the basis of costs and transport charges.[85] This Agreement was valid for two years.

The response of the traders to this Agreement was very disappointing.[86] The Nepali trade agencies in Kutti, Kerung and Rigarcha had to be closed down in late 1965 due to the negligible volume of trade. The Nepali traders, who remained at these centres were issued identity cards. Simultaneously both China and Nepal agreed to conduct trade exclusively through state agencies, except for the border trade.[87]

In 1966, the terms of both the Agreements, of 1956 and 1964, were to expire. In view of it, a new Agreement on Trade and Intercourse was signed between Nepal and China on 2 May 1966.[888] The pattern of trade stipulated under this Agreement was in conformity with that of the existing one. The two parties agreed to make full use of the Kathmandu- Kodari and the Kodari-Lhasa Highways on a reciprocal basis. (Art. III). The Agreement was valid for 10 years. There were, however, no specific provisions in the Agreement to rescue the dying trade between Nepal and Tibet, by improving the conditions of living and work of the Nepali traders in Tibet.

Thus, through a policy of gradual restrictions and insistence on trading through state agencies, China succeeded in changing the traditional pattern of trade between Nepal and Tibet. It was also in conformity with China's desire to close Tibet to the outside world. Nepal reconciled to this changing pattern partly due to helplessness and partly because its trade with Tibet was not substantial and vital from the point of view of its total foreign trade. The construction of Kathmandu-Kodari road was undertaken with the expressed objectives of facilitating and increasing trade which, strictly in economic terms, was not possible.[89] Neither Tibet nor Nepal had adequate surpluses to trade with each other.

Trade with the Overseas Countries

Nepal had long standing trade relations with the United Kingdom and the United States. The trade was regulated under the provisions of Nepal's Agreement on Friendship and Commerce with the USA and the Treaty of Peace and Friend-ship with the UK, signed on 25 April 1947 and 30 October 1950, respectively. Nepal imported luxury goods from these countries for the consumption of a few wealthy families. Its exports to them were negligible. Whatever the amount, the exports mainly comprised primary goods—industrial raw material—and went as re-exports from India till 1960-61.

A breakthrough in Nepal's trade relations with the overseas countries was marked by the conclusion of a Trade Agreement with Pakistan on 19 October 1962. Under this Agreement, the two sides agreed to give "most favoured nation's treatment" to each other in trade matters. (Art. II). The total value of trade envisaged on each side was to be "around One Hundred Lakhs of Pakistani Rupees" (Protocol of the Treaty, Para 2). However, the Agreement could not be fully implemented till the end of 1966 owing to the difficulties in securing facilities for transit across the Indian territory as discussed earlier. In the absence of a land route, the trade was conducted through air and its volume was negligible.

Nepal's next step towards the expansion of overseas trade relations was the conclusion of Trade Agreements with the USSR and Yugoslavia respectively on 13 August and 5 September 1965, and with Poland on 10 August 1966. The patterns of these Agreements were largely similar. All the three Agreements provided for :

1. Most favoured terms in the matters of excise and customs duties and also regarding the conditions of living, movement and work for the traders on reciprocal basis.
2. Trade to be based on the principle of equality. The payments of the balance, if any, were to be made in hard currency, mostly in Pound Sterling, except in the case of the USSR, where the Nepali Rupee was accepted.
3. Mutual consultations in order to facilitate the implementation of the respective Agreements.
4. All the Agreements were initially valid for a period of two years.
5. The goods exported to, and imported from, these countries by Nepal were also listed in the Agreements. Whereas the exports were composed of foodstuffs like oils and industrial raw materials like jute, the imports mainly included machinery, equipments and finished industrial products.

Besides these countries which had formal trade agreements with Nepal, the latter also traded with a number of other countries. They included Germany, Hongkong, Japan, Singapore, etc.[90]

The Question of Diversification

Diversification was the only way to remove the imbalances in Nepal's foreign trade, both countrywise and commodity wise. Awareness in this direction was evident even during the early fifties.[91] The importance of diversification of foreign trade was stressed in the subsequent years and by the successive governments. However, the first concrete step in this direction was taken as late as October 1962 when trade relations were opened with Pakistan. In the following years, Nepal established trade relations with various other countries both formally and informally as noted above. Nevertheless, in terms of the volume of trade with these countries and from the point of view of the overall trade pattern, the objective of diversification was far from achieved.

There were numerous and varied difficulties in the way. Nepal did not have an efficient system of internal transportation to facilitate quick and better movements of goods. More important than that was its being a land-locked state, which made it dependent upon India for the facilities of port and transit regarding trade with the third countries. The agricultural basis of Nepal's economy restricted export items to primary goods. The "export surpluses" were also not adequate to capture different markets and stabilise them. The agency engaged in foreign trade were weak in terms of financial position and experience. Auxiliary services like banking, insurance and availability of market information, research facilities and reliable statistics, were poor.[92]

The question of transit facilities was mainly related to bilateral trade relations between India and Nepal. Though India had granted transit facilities to Nepal, the procedural matters involving delay and damage, as well as the demands of the movement facilities continued to be discussed between the two countries. At times, Nepal, in vain, referred to the pattern of its trade relations with other countries in order to get the procedural matters settled favourably.[93]

Apart from the bilateral exercise, Nepal pleaded for the cause of landlocked countries' right to have transit facilities through the territories of their respective coastal neighbours. It was evident in its interest in and support for the UN convention on the transit rights of the landlocked countries signed in 1965 as also from its stand on related issues in the UN General Assembly from time to time.[94] Nepal's stand was not confined only to secure better transit facilities. At the United Nations Conference on Trade and Development (UNCTAD), the Nepali representative asked for "preferential tariffs, preferential imports and abolition of quota restrictions" on trade from the developed countries.[95] King Mahendra underlined Nepal's concern about the task of trade diversification at the Non-aligned Summit Conference at Cairo in 1964.

On the domestic front, the importance of industrialisation was stressed in the Kingdom in order to introduce diversification in the exports and to reduce imports of consumer and finished goods. The Nepalese Government's efforts to mobilise and use foreign aid for establishing industries as well as laying a sound infrastructure for the same, have been noted earlier. Besides, private foreign capital was invited by Nepal. The policy of incentives like a 10 year tax holiday, re-patriation of profits, etc. in this context, was clearly spelt out first time by the Nepali Congress Government.[96] This policy of incentives towards the foreign investors was followed subsequently.[97]

Incentives were also provided to the local exporters for trading with the overseas countries. The most important of such incentives was the scheme of 'Bonus Vouchers', introduced in 1962-63. Under this scheme, the Nepali exporters were allowed to import the goods they liked, of the value equivalent to a part of their respective foreign exchange earnings through exports. This scheme contributed a great deal to the expansion of Nepal's trade with the overseas countries which in 1966-67 rose to seven times what it was in 1962-63. The scheme had an indirect adverse effect on Nepal-India trade relations since the Nepali traders imported "sensitive items" under the scheme and re-exported them to India though their entry in India was banned or restricted.[98] These in-centives and the diversification thus brought about, did not in any way reduce Nepal's dependence on India in trade matters.[99]

Very little was evidently done regarding the remaining difficulties in diversification such as the production of "export surpluses", securing stable markets and improving auxiliary services. Thus only a beginning had been made towards the goal of diversification. The constraints inherent in the economy were too heavy to be overcome so easily.

Table I

Foreign Aid to Nepal: Major Donors (Actuals)

(Nepali Rupees, Millions)

S. No.	Countries	Years												Total	Remarks
	56	1955-57	1956-58	1957-59	1958-60	1959-61	1960-62	1961-63	1962-64	1963-65	1964-66	1965-67	1966-		
														Approx.	
1.	The USA	24.951	12.753	48.473	17.951	56.225	86.997	n.a.	46.800	74.400	65.530	57.900	34.926	526.906	44.0%
2.	India*	70.018	14.570	9.605	17.102	18.450	22.353	n.a.	13.600	34.000	62.736	93.000	77.633	433.067	37.0%
3.	China	—	—	—	—	32.135	—	n.a.	3.200	14.700	12.144	16.200	24.583	102.962	8.5%
4.	The USSR	—	—	—	—	—	8.456	n.a.	15.000	33.400	0.463	5.000	4.875	67.194	5.5%
5.	Others	—	—	—	—	−18.530	19.291	n.a.	5.100	9.400	0.174	3.200	0.219	55.914	5.0%
	plus 69.568														
	TOTAL	94.969	27.323	58.078	35.053	125.340	137.097	69.568	83.700	165.900	141.047	175.300	142.236	1255.611	100.0%

* The cost of independently managed projcits by India were not included in the figures of total Indian aid expenditures till 1964-65.

n.a. Not Available

Sources : (a) *Nepal Rastra Bank,*

(b) Budget Speeches,

(c) Foreign Aid Division, Ministry of Economic Planning, HMG, Nepal, Kathmandu.

Table II
US Aid : Major Fields of Activity

S. No.	*Fields of Activity*	*Duration*	*Total Estimated Expenditure of US Aid* — *In Dollars (Millions)*	*Equivalent to Nepali Rupees (Millions)*
1.	AGRICULTURE: General Agriculture and Agricultural Credits and Co-operatives	1957—(Current)	17.78°	134.68[a]
2.	Malaria Eradication	1954—(Current)	16.90	128.02
3.	Nepal Industrial Development Corporation	1956—(Current)	13.78	104.38
4.	Education (Primary and Secondary) and Teachers Training	1954—(Current)	12.08	91.51[b]
5.	Panchayat Development	1963—(Current)	6.54	49.54
6.	Power Development	1960—(Current)	5.92	44.84
7.	Regional Transportation	1958—1962	5.40	40.91
8.	Ropeway	1957—1966	5.02	38.03

(a) General Agriculture = $12.42 or Rs. 94.08 and Agricultural Credit and Co-operatives = $5.36 or Rs. 40.60.

(b) Primary Education and Teachers Training = $6.76 or Rs. 51.21 and Secondary Education = $5.32 or Rs. 40.30.

Source: Facts about American Aid to Nepal, US/AID Nepal, Kathmandu, 1967, 5 (upto July 1967).

Table III
The Indian Aid : Major Fields of Activity

(In Nepali Rupees, Millions)

S.No.	Activity 1965-66	Aid upto 1966-67	Aid in Remarks	Total
1.	Roads and Bridges	140.835	38.094	178.929
2.	Power Development	120.870	20.096	140.966
3.	Irrigation	74.024	13.692	87.716
4.	Community Development	48.320	—	48.320
5.	Surveys	35.056	0.823	35.879
6.	Water Supply	24.308	2.211	26.519
7.	Airports: Construction and Improvement	13.929	1.576	15.505
8.	Education and Allied Schemes	5.856	0.640	6.496
9.	Forestry	3.546	0.318	3.864
10.	Horticulture	3.370	0.484	3.854
11.	Veterinary	2.816	0.339	3.155
12.	Industrial Development	2.685	0.417	3.102
13.	Health	1.552	0.068	1.620
14.	Post and Tele-communication	0.811	0.715	1.526
15.	Metereology	0.275	0.036	0.311
	TOTAL	478.253	79.509	557.762

(a) The programme was withdrawn in March 1961 in response to a request to that effect from the HMG, Nepal.

Source: Facts about Technical and Economic Assistance to Nepal from Colombo Plan Countries, 1952-66, Ministry of Economic Planning (Resources Division), HMG, Nepal, Kathmandu, 1967 (Mimeographed), Appendix A. (The table has been rearranged in the descending order of aid-amount).

Table IV
The Chinese Aid : Major Projects in Nepal

S.No.	Major Projects Nepal Rupees[b]	Estimated Cost[a] In millions of Dollars	Equivalent to millions of
1.	Kathmandu-Pokhra Road	17.11	130.03
2.	Kathmandu-Kodari Highway	9.07	73.72
3.	Sunkoshi Hydro-Electric Plant	9.21	69.99
4.	Leather and Shoe Factory	1.32	10.03
5.	Warehouse Construction	1.32	10.03
6.	Brick and Tile Factory	0.66	5.01

(a) All costs borne by China, except the purchase of land.

(b) Converted at the rate of 1 US Dollar=7.6 Nepal Rupees.

Source: Facts on Foreign Aid to Nepal, 1952-68 (Mimeographed) Programme Office, US/AID, Nepal, Kathmandu, February 1968, 8.

Table V
Soviet Aid : Major Projects in Nepal

S.No.	*Major Projects* (*Millions*)	*Duration* *Nepali Rupees*	*Total Cost in*
1.	Birganj Sugar Mill	1959-1965	65.00
2.	Janakpur Cigarette Factory	1959-1965	41.7
3.	Panauti Hydro-Electric Plant	1959-1965	25.00
4.	Kanti Hospital	1959-1963	0.95
5.	Janakpur-Simra East-West Highway Section	1964—	120.00[a]
6.	Agricultural Tools Factory	1964—	10.00[a]

(a) Estimated cost.

Source: Figures computed from Gorkhapatra.

Table VI
Nepal's Foreign Trade : Total Exports and Imports

(Value in Nepali Rupees, Thousands)

	Years								
Items	*1956-57*	*1957-58*	*1958-59*	*1959-60*	*1960-61*	*1961-62*	*1962-63*	*1963-64*	*1964-65*
Total Trade	265,363	231,663	341,327	419,567	607,719	709,6351	891,678	895,600	259,100
Exports	95,472	73,307	117,934	131,740	209,737	265,221	287,653	291,100	440,300
Imports	169,891	158,356	223,393	287,527	397,982	444,414	604,025	604,500	818,800
Balance	−74,419	−85,049	−105,459	−155,787	−188,245	−179,193	−336,372	−313,400	−378,500

Sources: (a) Statistical Abstracts, Investment Promotion and Publicity Division, Nepal Industrial Development Corporation, Kathmandu, Nepal, Vol. 2, No. 3, October-November 1967, 7.

(b) Arthik Survekshan, 2024-25 (Economic Survey, 1968-69), Ministry of Finance, His Majesty's Govern-ment of Nepal. Kathmandu, Table XVIII.

Table VII: Direction of Nepal's Foreign Trade

(Value in Nepali Rupees, Thousands)

S.No.	Countries	1956-57	1957-58	1958-59	Years 1959-60	1960-61	1961-62	1962-63
1	INDIA							
	Exports	93,436	70,489	116,692	131,296	209,172	263,893	283,630
		(97.86)	(96.16)	(98.96)	(99.97)	(99.73)	(99.49)	(98.60)
	Imports	165,832	150,341	218,217	269,926	375,091	439,661	588,053
		((97.61)	94.93)	(97.69)	(93.88)	(94.26)	(98.93)	(95.69)
	Balance of trade	−71,396	−79,852	−91,525	−138,630	−165,419	−175,768	−294,423
2.	CHINA (or Tibet Region of China)							
	Exports	2,036	2,818	1,242	444	565	1,328	1,643
		(2.14)	(3.84)	(1.05)	(0.33)	(0.27)	(0.51)	(0.56)
	Imports	1.967	301	1.349	2,829	2,760	4.753	5,075
		(1.15)	(0.19)	(0.60)	(0.98)	(0.94)	(1.07)	(0.84)
	Balance of trade	+69	+2,517	−107	−2,385	−2,195	−3,424	−3,432
3	OVERSEAS							
	Exports	—	—	—	—	—	n.a.	2,380
								(0.84)
	Imports	2,092	7,714	3,827	14,772	19,131	n.a.	10.987
		(1.24)	(4.80)	(1.71)	(5.14)	(4.80)		(3.47)
	Balance of trade	−2,092	−7,714	−3,827	−14,772	−19,131	—	−8,517

Source: *Statistical Abstracts* (Table VI).

Note: (1) Figures in brackets show the percentage of the total.
(2) (−) shows the unfavourable, and (+) shows the favourable trends to Nepal in the Balance of Trade.
(3) n.a.—not available.

Table VIII
Recorded Foreign Trade : 1960-61—1963-64

(Value in Nepali Rupees, Millions)

	Exports				*Imports*			
	1960-61	*1961-62*	*1962-63*	*1963-64*	*1960-61*	*1961-62*	*1962-63*	*1963-64*
Foodstuffs and raw materials								
Foodgrains and other food products	158.6	174.1	166.8	196.4	55.2	63.8	92.7	97.4
Beverages and tobacco	2.5	2.1	1.9	3.3	21.8	39.3	40.1	35.2
Animal and vegetable oils and fats	0.7	1.7	3.2	3.1	10.3	11.1	12.0	14.9
Inedible crude materials (excluding fuel)	43.5	50.6	67.3	59.2	20.3	25.9	32.8	30.9
Petroleum, kerosene and related mineral oil products	0.1	—	—	0.1	28.3	36.6	46.2	71.5
TOTAL	205.4	228.5	239.1	262.1	135.9	176.7	223.7	249.9
Manufactured products								
Chemicals	0.1	0.1	0.5	1.3	22.5	23.7	23.6	35.3
Consumer goods	3.3	35.9	47.7	27.0	202.3	215.9	323.3	287.6
Machinery and transport equipment	0.1	0.1	0.1	0.5	25.8	24.8	24.8	31.0
TOTAL	3.5	36.1	48.4	28.8	250.6	264.4	379.7	353.9
Miscellaneous	0.9	0.5	0.2	0.2	11.4	3.4	0.6	0.7
GRAND TOTAL	209.8	265.1	287.7	291.1	397.9	444.5	604.0	604.5

Source: Central Bureau of Statistics, Ministry of Economic Planning, HMG, Nepal, Kathmandu.

Notes

1. Y. P. Pant, *Nepal's Economic Development on International Basis,* Nepal Council of Asian Relations and World Affairs, Kathmandu, 1956,4-6.
2. H.M. King Mahendra, *Proclamations, Speeches and Messages,* Department of Publicity, Ministry of Information and Broadcasting, HMG, Nepal, 1967 (Hereafter, *Speeches),* Vol. II, 254-5, 341- 2. Also *Budget Speeches)* (for the Fiscal Years 1964-65 to 1967- 68), His Majesty's Government, Ministry of Finance, Nepal, Kathmandu.
3. *For details see, Y. P. Pant,* Problems in Fiscal and Monetary Policy: A Case Study of Nepal, *Kathmandu, 1970; B. P. Shreshtha,* An Introduction to Nepalese Economy, *Kathmandu,* 1962.
4. For instance see, Statement of Vedanand Jha, Head of Nepali delegation, *Trade and Development Proceedings of the United Nations Conference on Trade and Development,* Geneva, 23 March-16 June 1964, United Nations, New York, 1964, Vol. II, Policy Statements, 285-89.
5. *General Assembly Official Records, (GAOR*), Second Committee 434th Meeting, 245.
6. *The Commoner,* 7 October 1960.
7. Bhekh Bahadur Thapa, "Foreign Aid and Economic Development in Nepal", *Souvenir Issue,* The Nepal Council of World Affairs, Kathmandu, June 1967, 86-93.
8. *Speeches,* n. 2, Vol. I, 105.
9. Ambassador Chester Bowles's statement in Kathmandu, *The New York Times,* 19 February 1953; *The Times of India, 20* February 1953.
10. E. B. Mihaly, *Foreign Aid and Politics in Nepal,* Royal Institute of International Affairs, London, 1965, 28-30.
11. Text of the speech, *Nepal Economist,* 26 December 1958, No. 1, 16-17; also *The National Herald,* 9 July 1958.
12. *Text of the Agreement,* Ministry of Foreign Affairs, Archives, HMG of Nepal, Kathmandu (Document No. 23).
13. Mihaly, n. 10, 125, 133.
14. Text of the primary Agreement and Agreement No. 1 concerning RTO (Texts supplied by the Indian Cooperation Mission in Nepal, Kathmandu).
15. The RTO till June 1962, had paved 380 miles of 2 'track and 134 miles of 10' track, constructed 152 miles of full width roads and 43 miles of truckable roads, laid gravelling on 60 miles, metalled and surfaced 28 miles completed survey and alignments of 361 miles and constructed culverts and small

bridges totalling 296.

16. Facts About, *American Aid to Nepal,* Programme Office, Economic Planning Section, US/AID, Nepal, Kathmandu, 1967, 1.
17. *Samiksha,* 21 February 1964, 25 July 1965; *Samaj,* 29 March 1965; *Nay a Samaj,* 28 July 1965.
18. For details, see Mihaly, n. 10.
19. This accounted for 50.3% of the total dollar aid expenditure in 1964, 56.3% in 1965, 58% in 1966 and 45.1% in 1967. (*Source :* US/AID, Nepal and Research Section of the Economic Planning Ministry, HMG, Nepal, Kathmandu).
20. Mihaly, n. 10, 81.
21. *Motherland,* 28 December 1962, 3 January 1963; *Samaj,* 1 January 1963; *Samiksha,* 3 January 1963.
22. *Motherland,* 8 January 1963; *Gorkhapatra,* 18 January 1963, 8 and 18 February 1963.
23. *Nepal Press Digest,* Vol. X, No. 5, 29 January-4 February 1965, 35-36.
24. *Nepal Press Digest,* No. 1, 12-17 May 1957, 17; *Naya Samaj,* 25 and 26 February 1958; *Kalpana,* 2 June 1958; *Naya Sandesh,* 28 August 1964; *Naya Samaj,* 5 September 1965; *Dainik Nepal,* 18 September 1966.
25. *Speeches,* n. 2, Vol. II, 187. For appreciation of the US aid also see, *The Rising Nepal,* 18 September 1966.
26. Ambassador Bhagwan Sahai at the inauguration of Airfields by King Mahendra on 13 June 1955, *Asian Recorder,* 18-24 June 1955. Also see *Address by D. R. Kohli to The Rotary Club of Kathmandu,* 26 April 1961, Indian Aid Mission, Kathmandu. (Mimeographed)
27. *The Statesman,* 17 January 1952 ; India, *Parliamentary Debates* (House of the People, 16th-26th May 1952). Statement laid on the Table of the House, Appendix I, Annexure No. 27, 58 ; also *ibid.,* Part I, Vol. II, No. 31, 13 May 1953, Q. No. 1640-D, Cols. 3095-96; *Hamro Par Rastra Sampark* (Our Foreign Relations), Publicity Department, Government of Nepal, Kathmandu, n.d., 43.
28. Mihaly, n. 10, 90,147-50.
29. *Co-operation for Progress in Nepal,* Ministry of External Affairs, Government of India, 1966; *Indo-Nepal Economic Co-operation, 1951-1956,* Indian Aid Mission, Kathmandu.

    For more details about these projects, see, *Koshi Yojana* (Koshi Project), Public Relations Office, River Valley Project, Bihar Government, 1965; *Gandak Yojana Aur Nepal* (Gandak Project and Nepal), Public Relations Office, River Valley Project Office, Bihar, 1961; M.P. Sinha (Minister of Irrigation, Power and River Valley Projects, Government of Bihar, India), "Koshi and Gandak Projects : Monuments of Indo-Nepal Friendship" in *The Commoner,*

18 February 1966; also see *The Commoner,* 24 March 1966.

30. Interview with M. P. Koirala in Biratnagar (July 1960). Shri Koirala told the author that the Government of India's objection was raised under that provision of the Peace and Friendship Treaty of 1950 which obliged each government not to employ any foreigner whose activities may be prejudicial to the security of the other. (Para 5, letter). This means that India apprehended strategic motives behind the exploratory visits of these US experts.
31. *Swatantra Samachar,* 19 January 1964; *Gorkhapatra,* 24 July 1964; *Samiksha,* 3 August 1965.
32. This was the contention of almost every political party and paper which disapproved of these projects. For example, see *Mahasabha : Kariyavahi Ko Sankshipt Viveran* (Senate : Brief Proceedings), 21, 22 and 24 *Vaishakh* 2017 (April 1960).
33. There were demonstrations and agitations against these projects. See *Nepal Press Digest,* 8-14 June 1960, 20 May 1963, 102; *Samaj,* 17 January 1964; *Samiksha,* 5 February 1964.
34. *Gorkhapatra,* 1 May and 21 July 1964; *Matribhumi* (Daily), 22 July 1964.
35. *Gorkhapatra,* 15 November 1963; *Samaj,* 31 January 1965; *Nepali,* 19 April 1965. The labour shortage was admitted by the Nepalese side, *Gorkhapatra,* 2 November 1964, 13 May 1965; *Matribhumi* (Daily), 20 May 1965.
36. *Samiksha,* 14 January and 5 February 1964; *Matribhumi* (Daily), 25 June 1965; *Janmabhumi,* 12 December 1965.
37. Floods occurred almost every year. For the example of the damage caused by it to the Indian aided projects, see, *Nepal Samachar,* 15 July 1965; *Gorkhapatra,* 30 July and 22 September 1966.
38. Mihaly, n. 10, 144-45; also, *Naya SJtnaJ,* 28 June 1964.
39. *Nepalese Press on Indo-Nepal Economic Co-operation 1965-67,* (Supplied by The Indian Co-operation Mission, Kathmandu, cyclostyled). Also *Gorkhapatra,* 27 December 1966.
40. Statement of the Chinese Counsellor in Nepal, *Gorkhapatra,* 12 May 1964.
41. *Statistical Abstracts* (Investment Promotion and Publicity Division, Nepal Industrial Corporation, Kathmandu), Vol. II, No. 3, October-November 1967, 12.
42. Text of March 1960 aid Agreement (Art. IV). *New Developments in Friendly Relations Between China and Nepal,* (Ed.), Chinese People's Institute of Foreign Affairs, Foreign Languages Press, Peking, 1960, 26. Also see *Gorkhapatra,* 12 May 1964.
43. Dev. R. Kumar, "Kathmandu-Kodari Road : Utility, Speed and the Behaviour of Chinese Technicians", *Far Eastern Economic Review,*

Vol. XLIII, No. 8, 20 February 1964, 419-21.

44. Prime Minister Acharya while lauding the Chinese aid, stated that it was in contrast to the United States. Mention of India's name in this context must have been avoided for tactical reasons, *The Hindu*, 22 October 1956. For the praise of the Chinese aid, also see, *Naya Samaj*, 30 April 1964, 7 September 1965; *Gorkhapatra*, 10 July 1965; *Samaj*, 13 July 1965; *Matribhumi* (Daily), 10 September 1965; *Samiksha*, 18 February 1964.
45. G. K. Parsai, "Indian Aid and Changing Pattern of the Economy", *Nepal Today*, Vol. V, Nos. 23 and 24/15 November 1966.
46. Mrs. Laxmi Menon, India's Minister of State for External Affairs, disclosing it assured the Lok Sabha that Nepal did not enter into similar agreements with any other country. India, *Parliamentary Debates* (Lok Sabha), Series III, Vol. XXVIII, No. 32, 23 March 1964, Starred Q. No. 693, Cols. 6827-29.
47. The Sunday Standard, *11 April 1965.*
48. Chinese Ambassador's statement on the eve of inauguration of a bridge on K-K Highway, *Gorkhapatra*, 8 June 1966.
49. For the concern expressed in the Indian Parliament about the entry of the Chinese goods into the Nepalese market, see, India, *Parliamentary Debates* (Lok Sabha), Series II, Vol. LIX, No. 1, 20 November 1961, Cols, 5-7; *The Statesman*, 21 December 1963.
50. Some National Panchayat members in the course of a budget debate held the view that these goods would spoil the consumption habits of the people. It was, therefore, suggested that instead, the capital equipments should be imported, *Gorkhapatra*, 10 July 1963.
51. Informally, however, the difficulties in acquiring necessary machineries, the high cost of projects and the inadequate raw material sources were mentioned as some of the factors. *Naya Sandesh*, 8 March 1963; *Samiksha*, 20 October 1963; *Naya Samaj*, 20 October 1963.
52. *Gorkhapatra*, 28 April 1964; *The Commoner*, 28 April 1964.
53. *Nepal Samachar*, 29 March 1965; *Gorkhapatra*, 31 March and 15 April 1965.
54. *The Commoner*, 8 September, 15 November and 7 December 1965, and 21 December 1966.
55. *Dainik Nepal*, 21 April 1964, 8 September 1965; *Swatantra Samachar*, 24 April 1964; *Nepali*, 5 April 1965.
56. *Facts on Foreign Aid to Nepal, 1952-1968*, Programme Office, US/AID Nepal, 1968, 10-12; also *Gorkhcwtra*, 23 October 1965.
57. *Motherland*, 17 March 1965; *Samiksha*, 20 July 1965.
58. *Nepal Samachar*, 22 November 1963.
59. The cement experts were in a majority in the Soviet economic

delegation visiting Nepal in March 1964. These experts conducted surveys for the cement factory project. *Gorkhapatra,* 13 March and 6 May 1964; *Swatantra Samachar,* 26 May 1964.

After surveys, however, the USSR was reported to have turned cold towards the project. *Matribhumi* (Daily), 14 December 1964.

60. *Naya Sandesh,* 10 May 1964.
61. *Naya Samaj,* 7 July 1964.
62. The Soviet Minister of Electricity disclosed in Kathmandu that he would have talks with the Indian Minister for Power, Dr. K. L. Rao in New Delhi, on the question of unifying the power distribution system of Nepal and India, *Nepali,* 28 October 1966. It may be recalled that both India and the USSR had constructed Hydro-Electric Plants in Nepal and any unification, suggested by the Soviet Minister, would have necessarily resulted in the unification of the Soviet and the Indian aided Power Plants.
63. *The Sunday Standard,* 12 November 1961. Soviet sources were reported to have stated in Kathmandu on 1 February 1962 that their experts would not resume survey of the Highway. *Asian Recorder,* 26 February-4 March 1962, 4447.
64. *Speeches,* n. 2, Vol. II, 60-61, 108-110.
65. *Samaya,* 18 January and 22 April 1964.
66. *Nepal Samachar,* 29 March 1965; *Gorkhapatra,* 31 March 1965.
67. Foreign Ministry's Communique, *Gorkhapatra,* 15 April 1965.
68. S. B. Srivastava, *An Appraisal of Foreign Trade Statistics, 1962-63,* Central Bureau of Statistics, Ministry of Economic Planning, HMG, Nepal, Kathmandu, n.d., 9; *Foreign Trade : Fiscal Years 1962-63,* Ministry of Economic Planning, HMG, Nepal, Kathmandu, September 1966, 93.
69. Y. P. Pant, "Nepal-China Trade Relations", *The Economic Weekly,.* Vol. XIV, No. 15, 14 April 1962, 621-24.
70. For example, see, *Rastravani,* Yr. 2, No. 12, 19 July 1953; *Nepal Pukar,* Yr. 6, No. 8, *Jaistha* 2011 (June 1954); *Swatantra Samachar,* 5 September 1960; *Naya Samaj,* 8 September 1960.
71. *Asian Recorder,* 21-27 January 1956, 64; 2-8 June 1956, 873.
72. *The Times of India,* 6 December 1956
73. *Original Text* of the Nepal-Pakistan Trade Agreement and its Protocol, Ministry of External Affairs, Archives, HMG, Nepal, Kathmandu, (Document No. 42).
74. Minutes of the Meeting between the Indian and the Nepalese Delegations to discuss Trade Matters : 27 to 31 July 1963, *Ministry of External Affairs, Archives, HMG, Nepal Kathmandu, (Document No. 5), para 10.*
75. *Ibid.,* para 11; *Gorkhapatra,* 24 October 1963; *The Statesman,* 24 . October 1963.

76. *Motherland,* 6 January 1964.
77. *Gorkhapatra,* 7 February, 5 August, 28 November and 4 December 1964; *The Hindustan Times,* 28 and 30 November 1964.
78. *Naya Samaj,* 4 December 1964.
79. *Gorkhapatra,* 8 January 1965; *The Hindustan Times,* 8 January 1965. The Indian Ambassador Sriman Narayan claimed that the Indian side agreed to provide such facilities as a result of his intervention. Sriman Narayan, *India and Nepal: An Exercise in Open Diplomacy,* Bombay, 1970.
80. "Memorandum of Understanding on Matters arising out of the Treaty of Trade and Transit (1960)", signed on 27 December 1966, para 25. Text in *Nepal-India Talks,* National Trading Limited, Kathmandu, Nepal, n.d., 21.
81. *For example,* Understandings on the Nepalese Transit Traffic Through Indian Territories in Continuation of the Memorandum of the Treaty of Trade and Transit of September 11,1960, Between Nepal and India, *Department of Publicity and Broadcasting, Ministry of National Guidance, HMG. Nepal, Kathmandu, n.d. (signed on 19 May 1961 in New Delhi).*

    Joint Communique, *Gorkhapatra,* 24 October 1963, 8 May 1964, 15 and 16 March 1965, 9 August 1966, *Memorandum of Understandings,* n. 80.
82. The "sensitive items" were listed in Annexure III of the Memorandum (n. 80). They were : cigarette lighters, flints for cigarette lighters, transistor radios, textiles (fine, superfine and synthetic fabrics), fountain pens, watches, cameras, tape-recorders, radios, auto parts, playing-cards, clocks, sewing machines and any other non-industrial goods, the import of which into India was banned or heavily restricted.
83. China imposed customs duties ranging from 20% on stationery goods to 100% on wine and cosmetics. Imports into Tibet of gold, silver, radio sets, books and films from Nepal were strictly banned, *Gorkhapatra,* 26 June 1962.
84. According to a press report, the number of the Nepal Traders in Tibet went down from 25,000 in 1959 to a bare 22 in' June 1963, *Naya Samaj,* 5 December 1963.
85. *Nepali,* 20 May 1964; *Gorkhapatra,* 29 July 1964.
86. Nepal's Industry and Commerce Minister disclosed that by July 1964, no licences had been granted for trade between Nepal and China under this Agreement, *Gorkhapatra,* 13 July 1964.
87. *Gorkhapatra,* 2 March 1966.
88. Text of the Agreement, Ministry of External Affairs, Archives, His. Majesty's Government of Nepal, Kathmandu, (Document No. 111).
89. Y. P. Pant, "Nepal-China Trade Relations", n. 69; also by the

same author, "Nepal's Recent Trade Policy", *Asian Survey,* Vol. IV, No. 7, July 1964, 947-57.

90. K. M. A. Dixit, "Diversification of Trade : An Urgent Need for Nepal", *Nepal Industrial Digest,* Vol. 11, No. 1, September 1967, Table I (B), 104.
91. *Nepal Marching towards Progress,* Department of Publicity, Government of Nepal, Kathmandu, July 1954, 6.
92. For a systematic and detailed discussion of these difficulties see, Y. P. Pant, "Nepal's Recent Trade Policy," n. 89; Ram Prasad Rajbahak, "Foreign Trade of Nepal", *The Economic Affairs Report,* Ministry of Planning, HMG, Nepal, Kathmandu, Vol. IV, No. 4, November 1956, 20-30; K. M. A. Dixit, "Diversification of Trade : An Urgent Need for Nepal", n. 90.
93. For example, the Nepali delegation at trade talks in July 1963 with the Indian side referred to a particular clause of a recently signed Trade Agreement between Nepal and Pakistan in support of its demand for the abolition of the Bond system, *Minutes of the Meeting,* n. 74.
94. Nepali Representative's speech in the UN General Assembly, *GAOR,* (1962), para 75; (1964), paras 125 to 128; (1965), paras 167 to 169; (1966), Text, 8. Also see, The statement of Nepali Minister Vedanand Jha at the UN Conference on Transit Trade of Land-locked States, on 29 June 1965, *Transit Rights,* Department of Publicity, Ministry of Information and Broadcasting, HMG, Nepal, n.d. 4.
95. Speeches of Minister Vedanand Jha, *Nepal Information,* Department of Publicity, Ministry of Panchayat Affairs, HMG, Nepal, Kathmandu, Vol. I, No. 8, May 1964, 5-9; Vol. I, No. 10, July 1964, 6-8; Vol. I, No. 11, August 1964, 5-9. Also n. 4.
96. Dick Wilson's interview with Prime Minister B. P. Koirala reported a *verbatim* in *Far Eastern Economic Review,* Vol. XXVIII, No. 24, 16 June 1960, 1246-48. Also see, *Philingo,* 26 October 1959; *Gorkhapatra,* 3 August 1960.
97. Minister S. B. Thapa in the King's Cabinet in 1961 stated that the new government would by and large retain industrial policy of the ousted Nepali Congress Government, *The Commoner,* 9 March 1961. Also, *Gorkhapatra,* 27 September 1962, 3 January 1963; *Nepal Gazette,* 12 April 1963, *Samaya,* 27 November 1963; and *Investing in Nepal,* Nepal Industrial Development Corporation, Nepal, Kathmandu, 1968.
98. Mohammed Ayoob, "India and Nepal: Politics of Aid and Trade", *The Institute for Defence Studies and Analysis, Journal,* No. 1. III, No. 2, October 1970, 127-156.
99. *Centre for Economic Development and Administration,* Kathmandu, Occasional Paper No. 1: "Trade with the Southern Neighbour".

7

CONCLUSION

The foreign policy of Nepal is not just the sum-total of its external relations and responses. More than that, it has been a well planned strategy for the Kingdom's defence, development and "self-assertion" as an independent sovereign nation in the midst of the international power politics. This was in accordance with the motives of *security, stability* and *status* discussed in Chapter II.

The evolution and pursual of this plan have been dictated largely by Nepal's uncomfortable geographical location between India and the Tibet region of China, its smallness and its highly underdeveloped economic status. The Kingdom's historical background, its cultural and social values and the character of its leaders have also played their due role in the evolution and functioning of foreign policy.

Nepal's limitations arising out of its geographical location, smallness and backwardness constitute its 'vulnerabilities' (*i.e.* weaknesses), as described by David Vital in relation to small powers' international behaviour in general. Owing to such 'vulnerabilities', small powers are often subjected to 'coercion' by the bigger powers, which exploit the 'vulnerabilities' of the former in order to further their own interests.[1] The task of foreign policy of the small powers including Nepal, has been to minimize 'vulnerabilities' and to weaken the sources and channels of 'coercion' in order to further their respective national interest. The ultimate objective in all these cases has remained to be the strengthening of the "safe base" of national power.

Nepal simultaneously worked on the three courses of action in its foreign policy strategy, namely:

(i) The maximization of the scope of manoeuvrability in relation to the sources of 'coercion'. This was done through the exploitation of the differences and clash of interests between the coercive powers.

(ii) The splitting and diffusing of the potentialities of 'coercion' through the diversification and expansion of the sources of dependence.

(iii) The mobilisation of moral and public international pressure on the sources and agents of 'coercion' through participation in the world forums.

The practical application of the first course of action obviously envisages, in the first place, the existence of differences and clash of interests among the sources of 'coercion'. Secondly for exploiting the situation of conflict and competition, it is essential for the 'vulnerable' state to be of some significance in the scheme of things of competing sources of 'coercion'. In that case the 'vulnerable' state has to convincingly impress upon the competitors and "contenders that it holds a strategic position and is open to be cultivated by either of the sides, provided proper incentives are offered. Towards that end, the stand of political neutrality is a must—a stand that is meant to convey that the 'vulnerable' state has no preconceived sympathies or prejudices for either of the sides and is determined, as well as capable, of taking and implementing independent decisions. Lastly, for successful manoeuvring it is also essential for the 'vulnerable' state to have an arrangement of dependable military protection, particularly, in the event of the break-out of military conflict between the contenders, leading to the failure of political neutrality and a threat to the 'vulnerable' state's bare survival.

What facilitates the 'coercion' of the 'vulnerable' state by the bigger powers is the former's dependence in military, political and economic matters, upon the latter. The more the dependence, the greater are the possibilities and probabilities of 'coercion'. Therefore, the diffusion of its dependence through the creation of more and alternate sources in this context by the 'vulnerable' state, is bound to result in more flexibility and discretion for it and thus in the extension of its scope of manoeuvrability *vis-a-vis* the 'coercive' powers.

The mobilisation of international public opinion by the

'vulnerable' state against the acts of 'coercion' by big powers and thus exert moral pressure on the latter, can also be employed to discipline the 'coercive' power. It may prove to be inadequate by itself, but if used along with other factors, this method also works in the desired direction. However, the degree to which method of moral pressure and the diffusion of dependence would yield results, depends upon the 'vulnerable' state's capacity to display sociability and its skill to conduct "public relations" in the international society. Accordingly, it depends upon the number and nature of the state's 'friends' in the community of Nations and its style of participation in the U.N. and other international forums.

The actual working of the above described three courses of action by Nepal should be viewed at two levels corresponding to the possible direction and sources of 'coercion', namely, the immediate neighbours and the super powers.

In relation to the immediate neighbours, Nepal's geographical location between India and China was both, a *liability* and an *asset.* It was a *liability* owing to the vast power differences between Nepal on the one hand and each of its neighbours on the other. This made the Kingdom an easy prey to the pressures from its neighbours, whenever and in whatever form the latter decided to apply them in order to further their respective interests. Nepal's location as its *liability* was all the more pronounced in relation to India owing to its excessive dependence in military, political and economic matters upon India as also owing to very close socio-cultural affinities and easy accessibility between the two countries.

The aspect of *liability vis-a-vis* India dominated Nepal's foreign policy during 1951-54. For this, the historical legacies and the political developments following the fall of the Ranas were largely responsible. The external environment particularly the Chinese attitude towards India-Nepal ties, also made it imperative. Accordingly, Nepal accepted India's dominance and guidance in its conduct of foreign policy and a veiled alliance existed between the two.

Nepal's geographical location between India and China was also an *asset* since it placed the Kingdom in a strategic position and made it an object to be wooed by each of its neighbours against the other. Thus the *asset* aspect underlined the basic prerequisite for Nepal to operationalize the first course of action in its foreign policy. The developments in Nepal's neighbourhood following the *Panchsheel Agreement,* between India and China on the one hand and in the Kingdom's domestic political scene on the other, during 1954-55 opened the prospects of change in Nepal's foreign policy which was hitherto dominated by India. The *asset* aspect of Nepal's geographical location and the corresponding first course of action of foreign policy became gradually active during 1956-59 and thereafter, with the emergence of the clash of interests between India and China.

The sharpening of differences between its two giant neighbours led Nepal to employ one of them to ward off the pressures exerted on it by the other. By way of doing this, the Kingdom subtly encouraged the competition between them *vis-a-vis* itself and thus extracted political concessions and economic benefits from both. During 1959-60, Nepal ensured India's readiness to act as a counter-balance to the actual and probable Chinese pressures pertaining to the boundary dispute between Nepal and China. Similarly during 1961-62, Nepal successfully mobilised its friendly ties with China and Pakistan to counteract India's 'coercion' in the field of domestic politics. We have described such exercises as Nepal's balance of power in the South Asian region.

In conformity with the functional pre-requisites for the application of the first coure of action—the exploitation of the differences and clash of interests between the 'coercive' powers—Nepal underlined its strategic significance in the region and asserted its capacity to take independent decisions. It pro-claimed a neutral stand on the disputes between India and China as well as between India and Pakistan. To a certain extent, the tension situation in the region emanating out of the disputes between the neighbours suited Nepal's interests best and therefore the continuation of this situation was welcomed. Guided perhaps by this consideration, Nepal was not found to be keen to participate in any serious attempt towards the restoration of understanding and the bringing about of a settlement between its neighbours. Nepal's absence in the "Colombo Powers" efforts during 1962-63 to help resolve the Sino-Indian dispute, may be recalled as an evidence. This is not to say that Nepal's participation in such efforts would have made any difference in their outcome. The Kingdom was, in fact, too small and too precariously placed to be effective, but then its foreign policy conduct was not always guided by this consideration.

Nepal's proclaimed neutrality was subtly, but definitely compromised, once the disputes between its neighbours turned into armed conflicts. During the Sino-Indian conflict of 1962 and the Indo-Pak conflicts of 1965 and 1971, Nepal under-played its neutrality in favour of India. This was primarily in response to the mutual understanding in defence matters between India and Nepal under the Peace and Friendship Treaty of 1950 and other arrangements evolved following this Treaty. It was also due to the socio-cultural affinities, and economic intercourse which Nepal had with India along with the Kingdom's stakes in the maintenance of a balance in the region.

These seemingly contradictory postures of political neutrality and defence commitments adopted by Nepal in the regional context, however, did not prove functionally incompatible. In fact, India's military protection assured under the arrangements constituting the mutual understanding in defence matters between the two countries was one of the pre-requisites for Nepal to take a stand of political neutrality in the region. Nepal took every care in demonstrating that while being politically neutral in the disputes between its neighbours, it did not violate its defence commitments with India and also that while honouring defence commitments at a point of time, it did not take sides on the political question nor did it abandon its right to remain politically neutral, once the conflict situation that activized the defence commitments was over. The Kingdom's neighbours also helped it in the successful implementation of these two contradictory postures. China understood the logic and compulsions behind Nepal's defence commitments with India, and notwithstanding numerous protests in this context, Chinese leaders have shown acquiescence towards this relationship. India, on its part, never disputed the fact that Nepal should have friendly and peaceful relations with China. Even in the midst of Sino-Indian border dispute, the Indian leadership encouraged the Nepali leadership in 1960 to settle their country's boundary problem with China, and were not unusually perturbed when the Nepalese Prime Minister B.P. Koirala declared to be neutral on the question of McMahon line.

Intense differences and clash of interests in the neighbouring region coupled with greater potentialities of 'coercion' from the neighbours made Nepal's policy in the region dominated by the first course of action. The second course of action—of diversification and expansion of the sources of dependence—was also pursued vigorously, though, with a comparatively less success. Nepal secured economic assistance from varied and diverse sources but the assistance from neighbours, particularly India, always remained substantial and was found more effective and convenient in technical terms. Nepal made serious attempts to expand its trade contacts and therefore sought additional port and transit facilities through India and also concluded trade agreements with Pakistan, China, Socialist countries, U.S., U.K. and others. However, the economic and geographical limitations inherent in this policy proved formidable. Nepal's bulk of trade (about 90%) was still with India. The Kingdom also received some military assistance from the U.S., the U.K., and lately from the U.S.S.R., but it was largely with the concurrence of India.

The application of the third course of action—of mobilising international pressures against the sources of 'coercion' in the regional context—was relatively mild. Nepal kept the U.N. and the Non-aligned Nations Summit Conferences informed about its concern with the situations created by the regional conflicts. It also used these forums to ask for peace and mutual settlement between its neighbours.

What was true regarding Nepal's policy towards the neighbouring sources of 'coercion' was basically also true in relation to the global sources of 'coercion'. However, the intensity of 'coercion' from the global sources, the super powers, was comparatively far less. More important than this, Nepal's strategic significance in relation to the differences and clash of interests between the super powers was almost insignificant as against what it was between India and China. Hence the application of the first course of action was much less vigorous and pronounced. It maintained friendly relations with both the U.S. and the U.S.S.R. and their respective allies, received aid and assistance from them and remained non-aligned.

The field being much wider and the prospects being encouraging, the operationalization of the second and the third courses of action was more extensive and spirited. Accordingly, Nepal identified itself with the small uncommitted and newly emerging nations. It expanded mutually beneficial political and economic relations with them, and joined them in raising its voice against the undesirable acts and postures of the big powers. Its participation in the U.N. and the Non-aligned Nations Conferences made this further evident. An integrated view of the simultaneous operationalization of three policy options in the global context by Nepal leads to the assumption that it had identified itself with the emerging world order, realizing full well that it should not be alienated from the existing one. In an international system dominated by bipolarity, Nepal opted for the emerging alternative of non-alignment and peaceful co-existence. In fact, it started practising this alternative at the time when the politics of cold war and bloc formation was particularly brisk in this part of the world. Against the long-standing traditions of colonial and imperial regimes, Nepal sided with the forces of freedom and equality. While doing all this, however, Nepal maintained and expanded its friendly bilateral relations with the protagonists of the cold war and former colonial and imperial powers. This kept the Kingdom abreast with the existing reality and helped in pursuing its economic and political objectives. Thus, whereas it criticised the super powers for their "arrogance of power" it sought and secured moral support and material benefits from them.

A very significant recent development in the international system has been the transformation in the bipolar situation. There has been a drop in the cold war tension, a loosening of the military pacts and alliances and clear signs of the emergence of more centres of power. Nepal kept pace with these developments and made suitable adjustments in its policy. It welcomed the trend towards the emergence of more centres of power in the world, since such a development would enhance the prospects for manoeuvrability for small powers among the conflicting and competing sources of 'coercion'.[2] King Mahendra's visit to France after it had taken an assertive posture *vis-a-vis* the United States and his appreciation of the new French creed of 'Gaullism' in foreign policy matters may be recalled as evidences.

With the same logic, the emergence of China should have been welcomed by Nepal.[3] The probability of increase in China's 'coercive' potential resulted in the coming together of the U.S. and the U.S.S.R. to join India in offering a powerful counter-balance to Nepal against China. This naturally led to the availability of more economic and other benefits to the Kingdom. Nevertheless, China is too close to Nepal and its emergence, apart from its other consequences on the inter-national system, tends to upset the regional balance and damage the *asset* aspect of the Kingdom's geographical location. It has created a scare in Nepal's international behaviour.

This takes us to the correlation between the regional and

the global aspects of Nepal's foreign policy, *i.e.*, between its regional balance of power and the global non-alignment. Obviously, the regional sources of 'coercion' have been more powerful and decisive in Nepal's thinking as compared to the global sources. As a result, its policy towards the latter has been supplementary and subservient to the policy towards the former. It is evident in Nepal's mobilisation of its relations with the super powers to meet the pressures from the neighbours. Three instances may be recalled in support of the contention:

1. King Mahendra's visit to the U.S. and the U.K., and Prime Minister B.P. Koirala's meetings with President Eisenhower of the U.S. and Soviet Premier N. S. Khrushev during 1959-60 when the pressures were felt from the Chinese side.
2. King Mahendra's quick efforts to secure recognition from the U.S. and the U.S.S.R., the U.K., etc., for his domestic action of dismissing the Nepali Congress Government and the abrogation of parliamentary system which brought in pressures from the Indian side. Nepal had also utilized the U.N. and the Non-aligned Nations Conference at Belgrade, mostly informally, for the same purpose.
3. After the Sino-Indian conflict, which made Nepal's position all the more precarious, Chairman Dr. Tulsi Giri made a series of visits to the U.S. the U.S.S.R. the U.K. and France and had important discussions with the respective leaders about the regional developments. One significant outcome of these visits was Western arms aid to Nepal.

Thus Nepal's global non-alignment functioned as an essential component of its regional balance of power.

In this context, Cambodia's foreign policy presented a very near approximation to the Nepalese model. Cambodia's policy also operated at two levels : at the regional and at the global. Cambodia while trying to balance the pressures from Thailand and S. Vietnam by mobilising its relations with China, also depended upon the U.S. to counteract the thrust from China.[4] Afghanistan also acted on the same line but less vigorously and with a qualitative difference that one of its neighbours, the U.S.S.R., was a global power and not a regional one.

In the evolution and operationalisation of the courses of action of Nepal's foreign policy, the contributions of King Mahendra and Prime Minister B.P. Koirala (1959-60) had been significant. King Mahendra, being in control of the Executive, for a long time had been responsible for the skilful operationalisation of the options. His contribution had been all the more important with respect to the 'linkage' between foreign policy and domestic politics. 1960 onwards, he successfully employed foreign policy to stabilise his regime and strengthen the political system of 'Panchayat Democracy' established by him. He worked up foreign policy to resolve the crises of legitimacy, identification and stability of his Government, with considerable success, at least during the years immediately following the establishment of Panchayat Democracy. B.P. Koirala's contribution was more at the level of evolving the courses of action and laying down their theoretical bases. His efforts to implement them were cut short by his short-lived Prime Ministership.

Howsoever significant the contribution of personalities and institutions, it was not decisive and complete. In fundamentals the model of Nepal's foreign policy would have evolved even without them. There are enough evidences in history to suggest that it would have been so, essentially because the germs of it were there in the geo-politics of the region and the position Nepal occupied in it.

Endnotes

1. For a detailed discussion of the small powers 'vulnerabilities' and their 'coercion' by the bigger powers see, David Vital, *The Inequality of States* (A study of the Small Powers in International Relations), Oxford 1967. Also see his, *The Survival of Small States*, Oxford, 1971.
2. Vital n. 1. 151.
3. For the consequences of China's emergence on the small powers and the policy of non-alignment, see Robert L. Rothstein, *Alliances and Small Powers*, Columbia University, New York and London, 1968, 255-58.
4. Bernard K. Gord, "Cambodia : Where Foreign Policy Counts", *Asian Survey*, Vol. V, No. 9, September 1965, 433-448.

POST-SCRIPT—I

FOREIGN POLICY DEVELOPMENTS: 1966-70

RECENT DEVELOPMENTS

The end of 1971 marked a watershed in the political scene in Nepal's neighbouring region, which had witnessed a period of turbulence since 1967. China passed through its major internal shake-up under the Cultural Revolution and the 'second' struggle for power, emerging stronger and more stable in the end. In India, the erosion of Congress party's strength was followed by its rejuvenation which resulted from the organisational split in 1969 and the emergence of Mrs. Gandhi as an undisputed leader in 1970-71. Pakistan broke up, giving birth to a new, sovereign nation, Bangladesh, after suffering a humiliating military defeat at the hands of India in December 1971. Consequently, India's status and position in the sub-continent received an additional boost.

The internal transformations in China, India and Pakistan were also matched by radical changes in their respective external postures. China moved towards a *detente* with the United States and was admitted to the U.N. This led to the display of an unexpected flexibility and dynamism in its foreign policy. India moved closer to the Soviet Union and regained confidence in its international behaviour. It also started throwing definite feelers to China for normalisation of bilateral relations.

Nepal being situated in the midst of these significant developments, could not remain unaffected. It had to respond and adjust both internally and externally, with the emerging realities of the regional and global politics. Below we shall deal with Nepal's external responses mainly *vis-a-vis* its neighbours, India and China, since they constitute a vital and decisive dimension of the Kingdom's foreign policy.

Implications of China's Cultural Revolution

The Chinese propaganda in Nepal had increased towards the fall of 1966, with the extension of the Cultural Revolution at home. The notable features of this propaganda were: the distribution of Mao-lockets, Chinese literature and the red flag among the Nepalis, the publication of a photograph and a poem in the official weekly, *Peking Review* (24 February, 10 March and 2 June 1967), depicting the Nepalis as acclaiming Mao's "great leadership" and the criticism of Nepal's friendly countries, in particular, the Soviet Union, the United States and India, by the Chinese diplomats even in Kathmandu. The Nepalese Government expressed its disapproval for such propaganda which the Chinese ignored by and large. It was evident in big anti-Indian demonstrations organised by the Chinese embassy at Kathmandu airport on 17 and 24 June 1967, while receiving the Chinese diplomats who were on their way back to Peking after being expelled from New Delhi.[1]

The restraint observed by the Nepalese Government did not allow the Chinese "misbehaviour" to affect the Sino-Nepalese relations adversely for quite some time. However, the growing Chinese disregard for the Kingdom's sensitivities ultimately gave rise to some strain between the two countries. On 1 July 1967, a group of students and youth disturbed the Chinese stall set up at the *Ramailo mela* (fun fair), organised under the King's birthday celebrations, in protest against the disrespect shown to Nepal's national flag and King Mahendra's portrait at the stall. The same group then led a pro-King and anti-China procession in Kathmandu, burnt a Chinese jeep and ransacked a Chinese literature shop.

This incident led to the exchange of protest notes between China and Nepal. The Chinese side alleged that the Nepalese Government "connived" at the anti-China "outburst" at the *Ramailo mela*.[2] This was refuted by the latter, Nepal's Dy. Prime Minister K.N. Bista regretting the Chinese propaganda on the incident through *Radio Peking* and *Hsinhua News Agency* in Rastriya Panchayat on 13 July 1967, declared:

> No Nepali has ever lagged behind to shed his blood for his independence when the occasion arose, nor will he do so in future. The entire Nepali race is ready to stake their lives for their King, their system and their dignity.

By the end of July, the Chinese Ambassador left Kathmandu

for Peking and nothing was heard thereafter from either side about the incident. It appears that both the governments, having reiterated their respective positions on the issue, were content to leave it at that.

The *Ramailo mela* incident was an isolated one and soon forgotten when normal friendly relations were restored between the two countries. Work on China-aided Kathmandu-Pokhra road in Nepal continued as usual.[3] King Mahendra inaugurated a Chinese built warehouse complex on 27 September 1967. Reports of damage to the Nepalis and Nepal's Consulate General's office at Lhasa by the Red Guards were promptly denied in Kathmandu.[4] On 1 December 1967, letters were exchanged between the two countries under which the Chinese aid was assured for the maintenance of Kathmandu-Kodari highway till 1979. China also extended on 21 March 1968 the period of aid Agreement of 1960 by seven years to enable Nepal to utilise the unspent amount of about Rs. 3 crores.

The complete restoration of normalcy in the Sino-Nepalese official relations was marked by Foreign Minister K.N. Bista's state visit to China from 22-31 May 1968. On 28 May he signed a Trade Agreement between Nepal and China. The Agreement provided for the trade to be conducted through Nepal's State Trading Organisation and by other traders. The trade was to be based on "the principles of equilibrium between the total values of imports and exports" as far as possible. The value of exchange currency—Pound Sterling—was fixed in terms of gold and the methods of payment were provided for in the Protocol of the Agreement.

Bista discussed bilateral economic and political matters and international issues of mutual interest with the Chinese leaders, including Chen-Yi, Chou En-lai, Lin Pio and Mao Tse-tung. The Chinese leaders favourably responded to Bista's request for more assistance, but no concrete commitments were made.[5] The Chinese and the Nepali leaders pleaded to each other for the restoration and consolidation of "mutual understanding and trust" that had partly been shaken during the Cultural Revolution. They also appreciated each other's political system and institutions. Bista utilised this occasion to renew "personal contacts" with the Chinese leaders and to "have a better understanding of the situation prevailing in China".[6]

Viewed in retrospect, therefore, the Chinese Cultural' Revolution caused only a minor distortion in the normal course of Sino-Nepalese relations. The distortion resulted mainly from the uncontrolled excitement of the Chinese to demonstrate their allegiance to the Maoist forces in view of the internal power struggle going on in China under the Cultural Revolution. It appears unlikely that the distortion was an outcome of any conscious and deliberate policy decision in Peking, as might have been the case with China's relations with Burma, Cambodia and Indonesia during that period.

However, the Chinese behaviour and the developments during these two years (1967-68) had a deep psychological impact on Nepal's perception of China. The incidents of the Chinese 'misbehaviour' coincided on the one hand with the increase in China's nuclear capabilities and its consequent leap towards the status of a super power and on the other, with the completion of Kathmandu-Kodari highway. Whereas the first development established China's supremacy in the region, particularly in view of confused political and economic scene in India, prevailing at that time, the second brought China too close to Nepal and thereby exposed the latter to any possible or probable Chinese threat; the strategic significance and economic irrelevance of the highway had been underlined in several quarters. The methods and intensity of the Chinese propaganda also raised doubts in Nepal about China's repeated assurances to observe non-interference in the internal affairs of other countries. All this combined, introduced an element of scare in Nepal's dealings with China during and after the Cultural Revolution.

Nepal's unexpressed scare from China had other implications also. In the domestic context, the Nepalese government launched counter-propaganda in the form of Mahendra-lockets, badges and Panchayat slogans. A new *Gaon Farka* (Back to Village) national campaign was launched on 29 September 1967. Under this campaign the government proposed to establish closer and wider contacts with the villagers; propagate *Panchayat Philosophy* among them and accelerate their economic progress in order to make them immune to "undesirable influences". Indirectly, the fear of communism also facilitated the rapprochment between King Mahendra and the democratic forces.[7] This ultimately led to the release of B.P. Koirala and his colleagues and general amnesty to other Nepali Congress leaders living in exile in India on 30 October 1968. As expected, this development activised the democratic forces in the Kingdom and acted as a counter-weight to the Communist propaganda.[8]

With India, the process of restoration and consolidation of mutual understanding initiated in 1963 (see Chapter IV) received further impetus during 1967-68. A number of Indian aided projects were completed and inaugurated in Nepal during this period.[9] Matters related to the refund of the "excise amount" by India to Nepal and the stabilization of exchange rates between currencies of the two countries were amicably settled.[10] Two joint committees to deal with the difficulties separately, in border trade and the overall trade and transit were constituted by the two governments in early 1967. Provision for such committees had been made in the Memorandum of Understandings signed by the two sides in December 1966 (Chapter VI). The deliberations of these committees led to the conclusion of another Memorandum on the subject on 19 November 1968. Earlier in October 1968, India and Nepal, agreed to have additional consulates in each other's territory. To keep the activities of Indian and Nepali Communists under control along the Indo-Nepalese border, the police officers of the two countries met at Birganj (Nepal) in April 1967. The Indian Government took steps to curb the activities of the Communists and other outlawed Nepalis living on the Indian side of the border.[11]

The leaders of India and Nepal continued to maintain close contacts between them. King Mahendra, on his way back from Europe, had a stopover in New Delhi on 14 May 1967 and had informal talks with Prime Minister Indira Gandhi and President Zakir Husain. India's Dy. Prime Minister and Finance Minister Morarji Desai paid a 3 day goodwill visit to Nepal starting from 22 October 1967. He had a closed door meeting with King Mahendra during this visit. Dr. Karan Singh, India's Minister for Tourism and Civil Aviation, was in Kathmandu on 25 February 1968 on a 3-day official visits And finally Indian President Dr. Zakir Husain undertook a state visit to Nepal from 12 to 16 October 1968.

The Indian and Nepali leaders discussed economic and other matters of their mutual interest during these contacts. China and its emerging postures figured prominently in the discussion and both sides appeared to have a close understanding in this context. In reference to the *Ramailo Mela* and other anti-Nepal incidents by the Chinese in the Kingdom, India's External Minister M.C. Chagla disclosed in Lok Sabha that the Government of India was in touch with their Nepalese counterpart on matters of mutual security and "drew their attention to the danger, the threat and the menace that China poses not only to India but to other countries as well."[12]

In bilateral discussions, however, any direct reference to China was avoided both by India and Nepal. This was perhaps in deference to Nepal's wishes which reflected its low key posture, and thus the element of scare towards China. Any overt reference to the existing Treaty and Agreements related to the mutual security matters between India and Nepal was similarly avoided. This was to respect Nepal's sensitiveness which was offended in 1959 by Nehru's reference to these matters and to spare the Kingdom from any possible embarrassment that such reference could cause in its delicate relations with China. The caution observed in this respect by the Indian leaders was underlined by Prime Minister Mrs. Gandhi in Lok Sabha on 3 July 1967.[13] Morarji Desai during his visit to Nepal, while categorically stating that neither India nor Nepal believed in defence pacts, referred to certain "connections" between the two countries related to mutual defence. He, however, refused to define or explain them.[14] The Indian leaders and diplomats reiterated their respect for Nepal's sovereignty, independence, territorial integrity and Panchayat system on all available occasions. They also tried to alleviate the then growing doubts in Nepal about the vitality and viability of India's economy and political system.[15]

Disturbed Relations with India

The smooth pace of Indo-Nepalese relations took an unpleasant turn almost suddenly by the end of the year 1968. Minor and otherwise manageable issues were allowed to acquire grotesque proportions and fresh controversies surfaced during the following period. Before these issues and controversies are taken up, the factors that dominated the official thinking in the two countries towards each other deserve attention.

India appeared to be gradually giving up its "lying low" profile towards Nepal, pursued since 1963, for a balanced and firm policy. This new posture was symbolised by India's Ambassador Raj Bahadur who arrived in Kathmandu in January 1968. He and the Indian leaders like President Dr. Zakir Husain during his visit to Nepal in October 1968, made it clear that while being ready to extend economic co-operation to Nepal and display unreserved respect for its political, emotional and other sensitivities India expected complete reciprocity from the Kingdom in matters of mutual interest. Raj Bahadur's speeches on various occasions indicated that India was inclined to revive the theme of "special relations" in its dealings with Nepal. The fact that it was so, was made clear by Indian Foreign Minister Dinesh Singh during his visit to Nepal in June 1969. We have seen that Nepal's aversion for the phrase "special relations" was deep and very strong. Nor could Nepal easily reconcile with an assertive Indian posture which reminded the Kingdom of the pattern of relations that obtained during the fifties. Particularly so, because this new posture appeared to be incredible in view of India's internal political and economic difficulties.

Another factor that loomed large on Nepal-India relation was the failure of October 1968 rapprochement between B. P. Koirala and King Mahendra. B. P. Koirala and his senior colleagues, contrary to King Mahendra's hopes, did not subject themselves to the Panchayat system, and after settling in India gradually moved to revive their "struggle" for "complete democracy" in Nepal. This led to an undeclared confrontation between the two.

The Indian Government had officially welcomed October 1968 rapprochement between the King and the Nepali Congress leaders. It was even alleged that Raj Bahadur played a mediatory role in bringing about the rapproachement.[16] For these and other historical reasons, King Mahendra suspected that India's sympathy lay with B.P. Koirala and his supporters, notwithstanding the Indian Government's repeated assurances that no "anti-Nepal activities" would be allowed from its soil. King Mahendra's suspicion became tenable and strong with the Government of India's decision in September 1970 to issue an identity certificate to B.P. Koirala to enable him to visit London and elsewhere in Europe for "medical treatment". This was against the Nepalese Government's expressed displeasure with India on the subject.

Thus India's new posture of firmness and assertion in bilateral dealings with Nepal and its suspected sympathy for King Mahendra's political adversaries, combined together to create tensions in the relations between the two countries during 1969-71. The Chinese and the Pakistani propaganda helped these tensions to grow for well-known reasons. With all these factors in the background, the issues that had arisen between India and Nepal, became complicated, making solutions difficult and delayed.

Susta Border Dispute

There was some dispute regarding the boundary line between

India and Nepal in the Susta region. A fresh controversy sparked off following publication of the reports in *The Rising Nepal* (23 and 25 November 1968) about the arrest of four Nepalis by Indian officials in the area. According to the Indian version, the arrest that had taken place against "trespassing" on 26 October in Rampur village on the Indian side, was in accordance with law and also included three Indians besides the Nepalis.[17] The Nepalese side termed the arrest as "kidnapping". The positions taken by the two sides focussed attention on two aspects of the controversy:

(i) The Nepalese Government considered the arrest of the Nepalis as "illegal" and thus demanded their release immediately. The Indian Government expressed reluctance to intervene and secure the Nepalis' release because the matter was *sub-judice.*

(ii) The ownership of small patch of land in the Susta region was claimed by both the sides.

The first aspect of the dispute was settled when the Government of India, after initial hesitation, released four Nepalis in question on 18 December 1968. Towards the resolution of second aspect of the controversy, India's foreign secretary visited Kathmandu on 27 December 1968 and had talks with the Nepali officials and leaders. Discussions on the subject were carried on between officials of the two sides in January, March April and May 1969, but without any result. Every round of discussions was preceded and followed by anti-India demonstrations, processions and press comments in Nepal. India was accused of harbouring imperialistic and expansionistic designs towards the Kingdom.

The dispute over the ownership of the territory in question resulted from the fact that the boundary markers in the area had been washed out. Nepal wanted to follow the maps of 1817 for re-demarcation of boundary in the region. India held that the Agreement and maps concluded in 1930 on the subject should be followed. To this the Nepalese objection was that they had not been "formally ratified" by the Nepalese Government at that time.

The officials having failed to arrive at a settlement, the matter was taken up at the higher levels. It was discussed by Nepal's foreign minister G. B. Rajbhandari and Prime Minister K.N. Bista with Indian leaders in New Delhi in May and by India's foreign minister Dinesh Singh with Nepali leaders in Kathmandu in June (5 to 9) 1969. As a result of these discussions, a "joint official group" was constituted to go into the 'depth' of the dispute and evolve "recommendations for specific solutions."[18] Thus, the political content of the controversy was taken off and it was reduced to technical proportions. Since then, some steps, reported to have been taken by the Indian side to extend its administrative control in the area, led a small section in Nepal apprehend that the *status quo* was being disturbed there.[19] However, the *status quo* has continued in the region and the process of detailed survey and re-demarcation by the "joint official group" appears to be in progress.[20]

Mutual Security Arrangements Shaken

The Government of independent India inherited certain mutual security arrangements with Nepal from their British predecessors. These arrangements having been extended and strengthened since 1947 were comprised of Gurkha recruits for Indian army, the Treaty of Peace and Friendship concluded between the two countries in 1950, Indian technicians posted on Nepal's northern border checkposts, Indian Military Liaison Group (IMLG) in Nepal and supply of arms and ammunition to Nepal by India.[21]

The future of these arrangements was put into jeopardy by especially arranged interview of Prime Minister K. N. Bista to an officially sponsored English daily, *The Rising Nepal* (25 June 1969). Bista stated in the interview that,

(i) Indian technicians posted along Nepal's northern border and the IMLG be withdrawn since they were no longer needed in Nepal.

(ii) Nepal was no longer obliged to have multual consultations and exchange of information with India pertaining to security matters in accordance with the Treaty of Peace and Friendship (1950) because India had not observed similar obligations *vis-a-vis* Nepal.

(iii) Nepal's purchase of arms and ammunition was not to be guided by the Agreement signed with India on the subject in 1965 because India had refused to incorporate certain amendments suggested lately by Nepal.

The first impression created by Bista's statement was that Nepal was all set to undo its mutual security arrangements with India. But a close reading of the statement, in the light of Bista's subsequent remarks and Foreign Secretary Y.N. Khanal's explanation in New Delhi in early July 1969, suggested that

Nepal was prepared to have some kind of a readjustment in the structure of these arrangements. In fact, the Nepalese side had been asking for quite some time past to make readjustments in the status of Indian technicians and the IMLG posted in Nepal.[22]

India had taken a firm and consistent stand that the mutual security arrangements were an integral part of the overall relationship and open border between the two countries. Therefore, any change in them would mean a change in the total pattern of relations. India's implied threat was that if Nepal insisted on bringing about any "substantial" change in these arrangements, it would seal the border and thus deny trade, economic and other benefits to Nepal resulting from the "open border" between the two countries.[23] India's firmness on this stand was also one of the key factors that led Nepal to scale down its demands underlined in Bista's statements, since the Kingdom could not sustain economic implications of a sealed border with India.

The question of structural readjustments in the mutual security arrangements was discussed by the Indian and Nepali delegations in New Delhi from 28 August to 4 September 1969. As a result of these talks India agreed to withdraw its technicians and the IMLG from Nepal.[24] The withdrawal was completed by August 1970. Nothing was mentioned about the 1950 Treaty and the 1965 Agreement in the joint statement issued at the end of Delhi talks in September 1969 and it can be inferred that Nepal's complaints regarding these provisions were dropped. This was confirmed by Prime Minister Bista on 16 April 1972 when he stated in Kathmandu on the eve of his official visit to India that 1950 Treaty between India and Nepal was working well and there was no need to modify it.

The nature and shape of alternative arrangements in place of the Indian technicians and the IMLG to be withdrawn from Nepal were further discussed through the usual diplomatic channel and also during Nepal's C-in-C, General Surendra Bahadur Shah's visit to India in December 1969, India's Foreign Minister Dinesh Singh and President V.V. Giri's visits to Kathmandu in February and March 1970, and at the meeting between King Mahendra and Prime Minister Indira Gandhi in September 1970 at Lusaka where the two leaders were attending the Non-aligned Summit Conference. As a result, Nepal agreed to:

(i) exchange "military information" with India on

developments harmful to each other; and

(ii) permit India to post a Senior Military personnel at its Embassy in Kathmandu for an "agreed period and job".[25]

Later some Nepalese press reports held that Indian technicians withdrawn from Nepal's northern checkposts were absorbed in the newly set up cultural centres and libraries in Nepal by the Indian Embassy.[26] These reports were not challenged. Thus, whatever be the exact nature or shape of the alternative arrangements, the substance of the mutual security arrangements between India and Nepal appears to be intact.

Difficulties in Trade Matters

The "Memorandum of Understanding" in trade matters concluded in November 1968 could not be implemented properly by the Nepalese Government owing to the pressures of Nepal's synthetic textiles and stainless steel producers.[27] The Indian Government, however, continued on its own to take steps to discourage deflection and smuggling of goods between India and Nepal. A series of talks in January, June, July and August 1970 took place between the two sides to resolve the difficulties that had arisen in the conduct of their mutual trade, but in vain.

In the meanwhile, the question of revision of the ten-year old Trade Treaty, due in October 1970, had also come up. Nepal based its case for the new Treaty on two formulations. First, it asked for two treaties, each dealing separately with the matters related to trade and transit. This was to avoid difficulties in one resulting from the difficulties in the other. Secondly, Nepal demanded adequate facilities in India (at Radhikapur) for its trade with, and through, Pakistan as a "matter of right".

Both these demands were unacceptable to India which viewed them as "politically motivated". In the first, India saw an attempt on Nepal's part to encourage deflection and smuggling of goods under the pressure of the Kingdom's powerful lobby of synthetic textiles and stainless steel producers. For the second, India held that there was no economic rationale behind Nepal's demand but, the Kingdom was trying to embarrass and pressurize India by exploiting its differences with Pakistan. On its part India was prepared to meet the "legitimate" demands of transit, port and other facilities for Nepal's "expanding" trade. In its turn it was firm on having explicit and effective provisions in the new treaty to counteract undesirable trade practices indulged into by Nepali traders at the cost of Indian interests.

A series of negotiations took place between the two sides for the conclusion of the new Treaty at various levels during 1970. Both the sides held their positions rigidly making these negotiations futile. The Nepalese Government stepped up its propaganda at home and abroad against the Indian stand. It also tried to mobilise international pressure and opinion against India to secure desired concession. Even the presence of Indian President V. V. Giri in Kathmandu in February-March 1970 along with other foreign dignitaries on the occasion of Crown Prince Birendra's marriage was not spared from this kind of propaganda. India, on the other hand, refused in December to repeat the monthly extension of the old Treaty granted since October, and unilaterally decided to continue the flow of certain essential goods to and from Nepal, from 1 January 1971.

This course of diplomatic confrontation continued for about three months. The softening of the attitude appeared to have begun towards the end of March.[28] The real breakthrough, however, came after King Mahendra's talks with Mrs. Gandhi in New Delhi on 10 June 1971. This led to a fresh round of negotiations on the subject in Kathmandu where the new Treaty of Trade and Transit was concluded between India and Nepal on 13 August.

The new Treaty contained provisions on trade as well as transit. The idea of a common market between the two countries, stipulated in the Treaty of 1960, was replaced by the principle of "most favoured nations treatment" on reciprocal basis. India agreed to provide adequate market facilities and preferential tariff to such Nepalese industrial products, that contained not less than 90% of Nepalese or Nepalese and Indian materials (Arts. III, IV, V and Protocol). Detailed procedures were laid down in the Protocol and Memorandum attached to the Treaty, to check deflection and illegal conduct of trade. Provisions for satisfactory port and transit facilities in India for Nepal's overseas trade were also laid down in detail in the Treaty. Nepal gave up its demand for overland route at Radhikapur (near the erstwhile East Pakistan) in view of India's assurances that such "routes will be provided to Nepal through regional or sub-regional co-operation agreements" if and when possible. (Letters exchanged with the Treaty).

It was clear from the provisions of the new Treaty that Nepal had compromised on its initial stand. This was primarily due to India's firmness and Nepal's limitation, geographical, economic and diplomatic. Then, the domestic political situation in the Kingdom —marked by communal riots and the growing unpopularity of Panchayat system—and the fast changing global and regional power equations, warranted Nepal to patch up its differences with India. The emergence of Bangladesh movement which had gained considerable momentum by June-July 1971 was of particular relevance to Nepal's trade relations with India. In view of this development, Nepal found it prudent not to press for its demand for overland routes at Radhikapur.

Thus the issues that had arisen between India and Nepal since the fall of 1968 were settled one by one by the end of 1971. India remained firm regarding the matters vital to its interests. The gradual but definite improvement in domestic and political situation and the consequent restoration of self-confidence in India ultimately led Nepal to readjust its posture with India's realistic firmness. It was evident from the fact that on all the three major issues, the Susta dispute, the mutual security arrangement, and the trade matters—the Nepalese Government softened its initial stands to adjust with the Indian Government's positions. The Government of India's sincere efforts to discourage "anti-Nepal" activities of the Nepalis living in India and show that to the Nepalese Government—excepting in the case of identity certificate to B.P. Koirala—proved further conducive to the change in Nepal's posture. The Nepalese Government also co-operated with the Indian Government in curbing the activities of extremist elements (Naxalites) who were using Nepalese territory in their operations during this period.

Nepal's response to the emergence of Bangladesh provided yet another evidence of the shift in Nepal's policy towards India during this period. Initially, Nepal had termed Bangladesh movement as an "internal affair" of Pakistan. But in September 1971, when Swaran Singh visited Kathmandu to explain India's stand on Bangladesh issue, Nepal expressed "concern" and "distress" for the "events" and asked for a solution "acceptable to all the concerned parties". In the Indo-Pak war of December 1971, Nepal's undeclared sympathies were with India. The Kingdom promptly recognised Bangladesh as an "undeniable political reality" in January 1972. Care was, however, taken by Nepal to avoid any displeasure to Pakistan, to the extent possible.[29]

Nepal continued to maintain and strengthen its friendly and balanced relations with China during the period of its disagreements and misunderstandings with India. Closer contacts between China and Nepal were renewed occasionally at the higher levels. The Nepali Minister, Rudra Prasad Giri visited China in 1969 to participate in the anniversary celebrations of October Revolution. He met Chairman Mao tse-tung and had talks with Premier Chou En-lai there. A Chinese delegation headed by Kuo-Mojo, Vice-Chirman of the Standing Committee of People's Congress, represented its government at Crown Prince Birendra's marriage in Kathmandu in February-March 1970. Kuo-Mojo had talks with King Mahendra, Prime Minister K. N. Bista and other Nepali leaders and officials. He signed an Agreement with his Nepalese counterpart on 6 March, to further strengthen economic co-operation and increase cultural and goodwill exchanges between the two countries.[30] It was under this Agreement that Nepali Princess Sharda Shah led a Sports delegation to China in May 1971 when she met Dy. Premier Ly Hsiennieh and Vice-Chairman Kuo-Mojo.

The disturbed Indo-Nepalese relations eminently suited China's interests. It, therefore, fanned these differences as much as it could. Chinese leaders and diplomats consistently pleaded their usual rhetorical support to the Nepalese Government and people in their "struggle for independence and sovereignty against foreign interference and expansionism".[31] The indication was obviously towards India. Such propaganda was often conducted through Chinese publicity media and was carefully served to aggravate Nepal's displeasure with India. The Chinese propaganda in Nepal was not confined to anti-Indian outbursts. Some encouragement to Indian extremists (Naxalites through Nepali territory and spurt in Maoist activities in the Kingdom) were also reported.[32] Not unconnected with this aspect were the closer contacts established by the Chinese diplomats with Nepal's lower tiers of Panchayat and the Class Organisations.[33]

It is difficult to say whether China played any role in hardening or otherwise influencing Nepal's attitude towards India during this period, but certain facts need mention. The first anti-Indian demonstration of December 1968 in Kathmandu on Susta issue followed the Chinese propaganda through official media on the subject. About the mutual security arrangements, China's interest in jeopardising them was obvious. At the time of the *Ramailo mela* controversy between China and Nepal in 1967, the Chinese Charge d'Affaires in Kathmandu was reported to have presented a note to the Nepalese foreign ministry demanding similar arrangements between China and Nepal.[34] The implication was that Nepal should withdraw from these arrangements with India. The Nepalese Government had rejected the note at that time but it had made them prone to think about the readjustment in the said arrangements. Later, the "unprovoked" expulsion of the Dalai Lama's respresentative in Kathmandu, Sunam Wamgyal Serga, a couple of weeks before Prime Minister Bista's statement of 25 June 1969 on the mutual security arrangements was a strong indication of Chinese pressure on the Nepalese Government.[35]

There was no resentment in the Nepalese official circles against the anti-Indian content of the Chinese propaganda: a contrast with the similar situation in 1967-68. Instead, the Chinese stance was considered a welcome gesture in Nepal's bid to mobilise counter pressure on India. Following the failure of trade talks with India in December 1970, the Nepalese Government approached various countries including China, to help develop the Kingdom's transport facilities and industrial potential. In response, China agreed to establish cotton textiles factory. Agreement for surveys by Chinese experts in Nepal Terai—the region bordering with India—was concluded on 16 July 1971. China also undertook to conduct geological surveys in the Terai, the letters for which were exchanged on 27 October 1971. The Government of Nepal showed deliberate disregard to the Indian interests and sensitivity in this context. India's Foreign Minister Swaran Singh in vain raised this question with Nepali leaders during his visit to Kathmandu in September 1971.

Basic Pattern of Nepal's Policy Sustained

Nepal's external responses to the developments in its neighbouring region since 1967 reinforced the basic pattern of its foreign policy behaviour, which has been defined and enumerated in the foregoing chapters. The motives of *security, stability* and *status* played a dominant role and the Kingdom continued to aim at the minimization of its "vulnerabilities" and the weakening of the sources and channels of its "coercion". Accordingly, Nepal endeavoured, as before, to work out the strategies of political balance and economic aggregation through its participation in international affairs.

The developments in relation to Nepal and its neighbouring region during 1967-68 and 1969-71 had a close similarity respectively with those obtaining during 1959-60 and 1961-62

Nepal experienced pressures from the Chinese side during 1967-68 as was the case during 1959-60, though the pressures and strains were of different nature. Nepal adopted a two- pronged approach to meet those pressures. One, issues involved were localized and bilaterally settled with China. They were not allowed to affect other aspects of the Sino-Nepalese relations. Two., Nepal maintained close contacts and understanding with India and explored the possibilities of meeting the situation if the Chinese pressures were to acquire dangerous proportion.

During 1969-71, the direction of pressures on Nepal was changed from the north to south. India had become assertive, the Nepali Congress leaders living in the self-imposed exile in India, particularly B.P. Koirala, were becoming active against the Panchayat System and a number of economic and political problems had come up between the two countries. To deal with these pressures, Nepal had direct negotiations with India which were marked by ups and downs. When ever Nepal found India unyielding, it resorted to the tactics of creating counter pressures. Within Nepal, the issues involved were inflated and an anti-Indian opinion was subtly allowed to gain strength. Externally Nepal activised its relations with China and Pakistan within the region and at times tried to play one side against the other. When trade talks were facing difficulties between India and Nepal, President Yahya Khan of Pakistan visited Nepal in September 1970. King Mahendra explored the prospects of extending trade with Pakistan during this visit.[36]

Functionally, however, Nepal's exercise in the regional balance of power during the two sets of situations, during 1967-68 and 1969-71, was mild as compared to the one during 1959-60 and 1961-62. This was largely due to the fact that the intensity of pressures was also mild during 1967-68 and 1969-71. The Chinese pressures had no military aspect as was the case with border dispute and the Mustang controversy during 1959-60. During 1969-71, the Nepali Congress in India was active against the Panchayat System but not violently and vigorously as in 1961-62.

Another factor that explains the functional mildness of Nepal's policy towards its neighbours was that both India and China had gained in stature and strength during this period. It, therefore, could neither go too close to the one, particularly China, nor sustain a strong posture against the other, India as in the past. Most important constraint on Nepal in this context was the absence of open and intense hostility between China and India. Instead the two countries had quietly started probing each other for normalisation of their relations. This had considerably reduced Nepal's scope for manoeuvrability in the region. While facing difficulties with the neighbours, Nepal activised the global dimensions of its foreign policy. Contacts with the super powers were maintained at high levels. King Mahendra visited the United States in November 1967 and the Soviet Union in June 1971. Nepal's Foreign Minister, G.B. Rajbhandari was in Moscow in September 1969 and Kathmandu welcomed the US Vice-President, Sprio Agnew in January 1970. Besides other things, Nepali leaders discussed the developments in their neighbouring region with American and Soviet leaders. Soon after King Mahendra's visit to the USA, an American Army General, T. Z. Conway visited Nepal in November 1967 where he inspected Kathmandu-Kodari highway and the Mustang region. This visit was significant in view of the then prevailng apprehensions regarding strategic motives behind the Chinese built highway. The activities of the US Peace Corps in Nepal witnessed further increase during 1967-71. The Soviet diplomats, also undertook frequent visits to the Kingdom's enterior like Dharan, where the Maoists had been reported to be active. The Soviet interest in Nepal's economic development had lately marked a notable increase. All these facts combined, confirm that the close co-ordination between the regional and the global dimensions of Nepal's foreign policy continued to operate as before.

Since the emergence of Bangladesh in South Asia and the radical realignment of global and regional powers that had taken place recently, it appears that Nepal is inclined towards the "Indo-Soviet line up''. This should, however, not lead any one to conclude that the Kingdom would give up, or even weaken, its other policy options. While recognising Bangladesh, Nepal did not write off Pakistan. It approved of both, the Sino-US *detente* and the Indo-USSR Treaty of Peace and Friendship. Thus it is trying to adjust itself with the new trend of "parallelism" in international politics. The new global and regional power alignments would further integrate the regional and global dimensions of Nepal's foreign policy. Nevertheless, the prospects of normalisation of relations between China and India would further restrict Nepal's manoeuvrability in the region but in no case it would force the Kingdom to revert to the position of early fifties.

Notes

1. For details, see *Nepal Press Digest* (Weekly), 18-24 June and 25 June to 1 July 1967.
2. For the text of the Chinese statement, see *Peking Review,* Vol. 10, No. 29, 10 July 1967, p. 39.
3. *Gorkhapatra,* 9, 10 and 12 September 1967.
4. *Gorkhapatra,* 22 and 26 September 1967.
5. Jont communique issued at the end of the visit, *Gorkhapatra,* 1 June 1968.
6. *Gorkhapatra,* 29 May 1968.
7. The softening of King Mahendra's attitude towards his Nepali Congress adversaries was evident in his remark, during a state visit to the U.S. in November 1967, saying that he was inclined to release B. P. Koirala provided Koirala's "colleagues in India" behaved properly. *Gorkhapatra,* 6 November 1967.
8. Some of the Chinese literature bookshops were burnt or forced closed in Biratnagar and Bhaktpur by the student sympathisers of the Nepali Congress. *The Motherland,* 6 December 1968 ; *The Times oj India,* 17 December 1968.
9. The projects and the dates of their inauguration were : General Post Office building (29 January 1967), Trisuli Hydro-Electric Plant (24 February 1967), Lumbini Airport and Bhairawa Water Supply Scheme (March 1967), Janakpurdham Airport and Hardinath irrigation project (24 September 1967), Forest Training Institute at Hitaura (30 September 1967), National Archives building at Kathmandu (3 October 1967), Bagmati River bridge (11 June 1968),, Concrete surfaced Airport at Biratnagar (22 June 1968) and Foreign Post Office building (20 August 1968).
10. For details see *Gorkhapatra,* 20 to 25 March 1967.
11. *Naya Sandesh,* 28 April 1967 and 2 February 1968 ; *Gorkhapatra,* 12 August 1967, 22 and 23 January 1968; *The Hindu,* 22 January 1968.
12. *Lok Sabha Debates,* 4th Series, Vol. V, No. 30, 3 July 1967,. col. 8928.
13. *Ibid.,* col. 8931.
14. *The Times of India,* 25 October 1967.
15. For example, see Morarji Desia's address to Nepal Council) of World Affairs, Kathmandu, on 23 October 1967. *The Hindustan Times,* 24 October 1967.
16. *Samiksha* (Weekly), 27 November 1968.
17. *Lok Sabha Debates,* Vol. XXIII, No. 23, 11 December 1968, cols. 127-30.

18. This was indicated in the Joint Communique issued at the conclusion of Dinesh Singh's visit to Nepal. *The Times of India,* 10 June 1969 ; *Gorkhapatra,* 10 June 1969.
19. See *Njya Samaj,* 21 January 1971 ; *Malribhumi* (Weekly), 6 April, 6 July and 9 November 1971 ; *Naya Pailo,* 24 October 1971.
20. The issue was reported to figure in the talks to be held by Prime Minister K. N. Bista with Indian leaders in Delhi during his official visit in April 1972. *The Statesman,* 17 April 1972.
21. The evolution of these arrangements has been referred to in the foregoing chapters (III and IV, in particular). For further details see author's, "India's Mutual Security Arrangements with Nepal'V *The Institute for Defence Studies and Analysis Journal,* Vol. 4, No. 1,. July 1971, p. 26.
22. The question was discussed between the two countries during Nepal's Foreign Minister G. B. Rajbhandari's and Prime Minister K. N. Bista's visits to New Delhi in May and Indian Foreign. Minister Dinesh Singh's visit to Nepal in June 1969.
23. Dinesh Singh's press conference in Kathmandu. *Gorkhapatra,* 16 June 1969 ; also see *Lok Sabha Debates,* Vol. XXX, No. 1, 21 July 1969, cols. 230-244.
24. Joint statement issued at the end of talks. *The Rising Nepal,* 5 September 1969 ; also see *Lok Sabha Debates,* 4th Series, Vol. XXXVI, No. 4, 25 February 1970, cols. 65-66.
25. This was disclosed by King Mahendra in a specially arranged interview to an Indian press representative. *The Times of India,* 21 October 1970.
26. *Jan Jagriti* (Weekly), 24 January and 6 December 1971.
27. For the reaction of synthetic textiles and stainless steel producers lobby in Nepal, see *Gorkhapatra,* 4 and 6 December 1968, 6 January, 4 February, 13 February and 2 April 1969; *Motherland,* 13 December 1968.
28. This was evident in the relaxation allowed in March by India in the categories and quantitites of the goods to be trade with Nepal. For the changed tone of the Indian and Nepali leaders's statements, see *Gorkhapatra,* 12, 14 and 18 april, 5, 7 and 9 May 1971.
29. For details, see Urmila Phadnis and S. D. Muni, "Emergence of Bangladesh: Responses of Ceylon and Nepal", in S. P. Varma, Virendra Narain, edited, *Pakistan, Political System in Crisis,* South Asia Studies Centre, Jaipur, 1972, 173-92.
30. For details, see *Gorkhapatra,* 2, 6 and 8 March 1970.
31. See, for instance, *Gorkhapatra,* 1 April, 13 June, 28 July and 11 September 1969, 25 January, 8 March and 6 October 1970, 11

January, 1 May and 2 October 1971 ; *Nepalese Perspective,* 13 June 1970.

32. *Samiksha,* 11 September 1970, 19 February and 23 July 1971 ; *Arti* (Weekly), 3 December 1969, 23 May 1970; *Dainik Nepal,* 27 July 1971 ; *Samaj,* 12 April 1970 ; *Pratidwani* (Weekly), 31 May 1970 ; *Nepal Press Digest* (Weekly), 20 April 1970.
33. *Gorkhapatra,* 1 April 1969, 25 January 1970.
34. *The Hindu,* 21 and 29 November 1967.
35. *The Hindustant TImes,* 30 May 1979.
36. *Pakistan Observer,* 29 September, 3 October 1970.

POST-SCRIPT—II

NEPAL AS A ZONE OF PEACE

One of the most important strategic moves made by Nepal in order to project its changing security perception and, in the process, undermine the Treaty of Peace And Friendship of 1950 with India, particularly its mutual security component, was to get itself recognized as a Zone of Peace (ZOP). This proposal had indeed been unique because it seeks to project only one country as a ZOP. Before being a Nepali proposal, it was a proposal, closely identified with the personality of King Birendra and came to assume the emotional significance of being a symbol of the Nepali Monarch's major contribution to his Kingdom's national life. He often mentioned this proposal as "my zone of Peace proposal". Before we take up the substantive issues of this proposal's implications for India-Nepal relations, we must keep in mind the Nepali Kings' tradition of projecting their personal identities through specific policy moves.

Every ruler wants to leave his imprint on his polity so as to strengthen his rule and also to be remembered by his posterity. The Nepali monarchs tried to build up and project their respective national and international images by making some new contribution during their rule in the realm of domestic politics and foreign policy and identifying their own personality with that specific contribution. King Tribhuwan came to be known as the first monarch who ushered in democracy in Nepal by removing the anachronistic rule of the Ranas. King Mahendra's contribution was the establishment of Panchayat system on the demise of Parliamentary Democracy. In the field of foreign policy, he diversified and expanded Nepal's diplomatic relations by pursuing a vigorous participation in world affairs in contrast to his father's policy of relying heavily upon India with which a pattern of "special relationship" was carefully nursed.

King Birendra generally followed his father's framework both in domestic politics and foreign policy and adjusted this framework so as to make it responsive to the emerging challenges and contingencies. This was evident in the significant changes brought about in the form and content of the Panchayat system. He held the national referendum in May 1980 and introduced constitutional provisions (Third Amendment, February 1981) for adult franchise and a representative and responsible (at least in appearance) legislature. Through these acts, he sought to secure popular legitimacy for the Panchayat system, particularly at a time when its credibility and relevance had come under serious clouds. That even after ten years of the new constitutional facade, such clouds hovered again, and in a far more threatening gesture, as subsequent events (1989- 90) showed. It is however in the field of foreign policy that King Birendra claims to have made a novel contribution, in the form of ZOP. This proposal sharply underlined the linkage in King Birendra's perception of his concern for internal instability and international recognition.

The Proposal

The ZOP proposal had been a major pre-occupation of Nepal's foreign policy since mid-1970s. Apparently a foreign policy proposal, it had vital and far-reaching implications for domestic politics, including the sustenance and survival, not only of the Panchayat system but even of Monarchy. Though the proposal was officially announced in February 1975, initial moorings could be discerned as early as in 1973 in the King's speeches and statements. In his address to the Nepal Council of World Affairs on 26 July 1973, he said:

> I would further like to point out that in our scheme of things in Nepal, we neither have enemies to fight against nor battles to win. If fight we must, the battle lies well within the territory; it is a battle against backwardness and destitution, to fight which I have exhorted the need for development... we are therefore, desirous to see to it that our foreign policy has a bearing on our aspirations for peace, for security and for our economic development. It seems to me that it is not enough to harp upon the theme of non-alignment. As we extend our hands of friendship to nations and to our neighbours, we expect co-operation and reciprocity in our development efforts.

He carried forward the germs of this idea in the prepared text of his speech to the Algiers Non-aligned Summit in September 1973 when he stated that "Nepal situated between the two of the most populous countries in the world, wishes within her frontiers to be declared a zone of peace".[1] Owing to unexplainable factors (allegedly Indian pressure), this formulation was however deleted in the actual delivered speech, wherein he confined his remarks to saying that Nepal welcomed "the idea of creation of peace zones and their further extension". He added in that speech after referring to the UN Declaration of Indian Ocean as a Zone of Peace:

> In our view, Mr. President, that the advocacy of zones of peace, being established in one region and extending therefrom to other parts of the world, will represent reinforcement of the principles of non-alignment. In the absence of clearly demarcated peace zones, accepted as such by every country in the world, countries with smaller size and population are bound to feel insecure. In such a world as we live in, which is still dominated by power politics, it is our carefully considered opinion that the non-aligned countries require safeguards against outside interference and aggression.

The formal announcement of the ZOP proposal by King Birendra came on 25 February 1975 in a farewell address to the foreign dignitaries who had assembled in Kathmandu to attend his Coronation. After underlining his major concern for preserving Nepal's sovereign integrity, independent identity and political stability, he declared:

> We adhere to the policy of non-alignment because we believe that it brightens the prospects of peace. We need peace for our security. We need peace for our independence and we need peace for development. . . And if today, peace is an overriding concern with us, it is only because our people genuinely desire peace in our country, in our region and everywhere in the world. It is with this earnest desire to institutionalize peace that I stand to make proposition, a proposition that my country, Nepal, be declared a Zone of Peace.
>
> We believe that only under a condition of peace will we be able to create a politically stable Nepal with a sound economy which will in no way be detrimental to any country. I also wish to declare that in making a proposition for the zone of peace, we are not prompted out of fear or threat from any country or quarter. As heirs to a country that has always lived in independence,

> we wish to see that our freedom and independence shall not be thwarted by the changing flux of time when understanding is replaced by misunderstanding, when conciliation is replaced by belligerency and war. It is with such a perspective view of the future that with the help of our friends, we seek peace.[2]

Then onwards, the King, his ministers and his government continued to emphasise the necessity and importance of the proposal of zone of peace being endorsed by various countries, particularly its neighbours. There was however no precise indication as to what the King meant by this proposal. It took the Nepalese government six long years to give a shape to the King's initial ideas. Some details of the proposal were formulated as late as May 1981 and the formulation was officially made known in February 1982 when the then Prime Minister, Surya Bahadur Thapa, addressing the Nepal Council of World Affairs enumerated seven points defining the ZOP proposal.[3] Before we come to those seven points, the themes that were emphasized with regard to the ZOP proposal between Feb my 1975 and February 1982 may be recalled here.

One theme was Nepal's desire to maintain neutrality in all possible regional conflicts without legally becoming a neutral state like Austria or Switzerland. As an essential corollary of this, emphasis was laid on keeping basically equal relations with the Kingdom's two giant neighbours: India and China. In order to rationalize this stance, the King started projecting a new strategic doctrine for the Kingdom by reinterpreting its geo-strategic location; taking clues from those small parts of Nepal's Western Himalayas in the Mustang region where Nepalese territory stretched to the northern Himalayan plateau in contiguity with the Tibet region of China. Along with the early signs of his ideas on ZOP in September 1973, King Birendra rejected the idea of a "buffer state" as "outmoded" and told an American weekly in an interview that:

> Nepal is not a part of the subcontinent, it is really that part of Asia which touches both China and India. Our historical experience is that we maintain friendly relations with both these countries.[4]

The basic thrust of this contention was subsequently elaborated and reiterated through various official and unofficial statements. Towards building the rationale for equidistance from India and

China in the context of the ZOP proposal, the official daily *Rising Nepal* refuted the contention that Nepal's geopolitical importance was more to India than to China.[5] In 1976, the then Prime Minister Dr. Tulsi Giri made several statements of a similar nature.[6] In the same year, Nepal established direct air link with the Tibet region of China when the King visited the Szechwan region. Since then, such articulation of the ZOP proposal became essential part of any major foreign policy statement or writing in Nepal.[7] In the continuing effort to justify the ZOP in the context of the new strategic doctrine enunciatedby the King, Nepal's Foreign Minister, Randhir Subba, in July 1985 in a hard-hitting interview to an Indian English daily said that Nepal did not perceive any security threat from China and added that Nepal's security interests did not converge with that of India's.[8]

The second theme was that the ZOP proposal aimed at ensuring domestic political stability and economic development. This aspect was clearly mentioned in the King's initial statements announcing the proposal and was reiterated subsequently on many occasions. Both these themes, of equidistance and internal stability, found important place in the seven-point definition of the proposal. These seven points were:

1. "Nepal will adhere to the policy of peace, non-alignment and peaceful coexistence and will constantly endeavour to develop friendly relations with all countries of the world regardless of their social and political system, and particularly, with its neighbours on the basis of equality and respect for each other's independence and sovereignty.
2. Nepal will not resort to the use or threat of force in any way which might endanger the peace and security of other countries
3. Nepal will seek peaceful settlement of all disputes between it and other state or states.
4. Nepal will not interfere in the internal affairs of other states.
5. Nepal will not permit any activities on its soil that are hostile to other states supporting this proposal and in reciprocity, states supporting this proposal will not permit any activities hostile to Nepal.
6. Nepal will continue to honour the obligations of all the existing treaties which it has concluded with other

countries as long as they remain valid.

7. In confomity with its policy of peace and non-alignment, Nepal will not enter into military alliance nor will it allow the establishment of any foreign military base on its soil. In reciprocity, other countries supporting this proposal will not enter into military alliance nor they will allow establishment of military bases in their soil directed against Nepal".

This definition of the proposal is more in the form of a declaration of intent. It ostensibly reiterated broad principles of Nepal's foreign policy. Most of these principles, separately or together, had been stated several times earlier on various occasions. The only notable feature in the ZOP proposal's definition was para fifth which was concerned with the domestic aspect of Nepali politics and was relevant generally in the Kingdom's relations with immediate neighbours. The significance of this provision will be discussed below.

The seven point enumeration of the ZOP proposal as mentioned above also did not clarify as to how the proposal is sought to be pursued. All available indications were that Nepal sought bilateral endorsement of the proposal in a very broad sense through official declaration, in the form of a political statement or incorporation in a joint communique, from a given country. To that extent, it was of very limited and almost token significance which may not even involve any mutual obligations in a bilateral context. This, however, did not rule out Nepal's intentions to eventually get its proposal endorsed, even as a multilateral resolution or convention, by the United Nations. There were strong indications of Nepal thinking along these lines. Suggestions to this effect had been made even before the proposal was defined. The Nepali foreign office also argued in favour of this line of action. King Birendra in a press conference in Paris on 4 September 1981 clearly stated the possibility of Nepal taking the ZOP proposal to the United Nations for endorsement.[9] During his official visit to the United States in the first week of December 1983, he again said:

> Zone of Peace essentially calls for non-alignment, non-aggression, peaceful settlement of disputes and peaceful economic and social development in Nepal. We think that this proposal is distinct from all such precedents in that it implies the creation of peaceful status for an individual state but is given *legal force* by its recognition by other

states (emphasis added).

Besides the King, Nepal's Prime Minister, Foreign Minister and other lesser officials also occasionally underlined this aspect during the Panchayat period.

It is interesting to note in this respect that the Nepali side sought only a token statement of endorsement from India for the moment. A close probing of the Nepali thinking on the question of the ZOP proposal's intended international status suggests that once a token endorsement could be secured from India, Nepal would have then raised it in the United Nations on the lines of the Pakistani proposal for South Asia as a nuclear weapons free zone. Without India's token endorsement, the proposal could face a rough weather at the UN because according to the world body's norms, any proposal to be endorsed by it should have the consent of concerned regional and neighbouring countries. India objected to the Pakistani proposal because it lacked such a regional consensus. Nepal wanted to avoid such controversies in pursuing its proposal. However, the fact that Nepal had all the intentions to seek international endorsement of the proposal could be seen in its attempt to get the proposal introduced in the Asian-African Legal Consultative Committee. (See Doc. No. AALCC/XXIV/9, Text in *Strategic Studies Series,* no. 2, Winter 1984-85, Kathmandu.)

MOTIVATIONS

Nepal's zone of peace proposal in its than defined form appeared to be quite ordinary and insipid on the face of it. It essentially presented the famous five principles of peaceful coexistence (Panchsheel) in a slightly elaborated and redefined form. Since Nepal and its two neighbours, India and China, had already committed themselves to the principles of peaceful coexistence, the proposal even appeared as redundant and superfluous. Particularly so because Nepal since long, concluded treaties of peace and friendship both with India (1950) and China (1960), and enjoyed settled, demarcated, stable and demilitarised borders with them. The kingdom also generally remained unaffected by their mutual conflicts in the region. Yet so much of Nepal's diplomatic effort and emotional involvement was evident regarding the zone of peace proposal that one needs to understand the possible motives behind it.

In a very significant way, the proposal can be seen as the continuation of Nepal's efforts to undo its special relations with

India and redefine them on a balanced and 'equal' footing. Such efforts were initiated during the mid-1950s by the late King Mahendra. Nepal's urge to assert its identity as an independent nation by eroding and undoing its security relations with India has been a long-term policy pre-occupation. Besides this urge there were immediate and pressing factors that prompted the proposal of zone of peace; the most important being the challenge posed by the Nepali Congress armed activities against the King's Panchayat system. Notable among such activities were the attack on Haripur police station in Nepal Terai in August 1972, hijacking of a Royal Nepal Airlines Corporation plane on a domestic flight and looting of Rs 30 lakhs (Indian) by B.P. Koirala's associates in June 1973 and a devastating fire in July 1973 that gutted a large part of the famous *Singha Durbar* building (Central Secretariat) in Kathmandu. Accompanying all these activities was B.P. Koirala's call, from his self-imposed exile in India for armed revolt against the Panchayat system. Reports were rife about Nepali Congress operated camps for armed training of its volunteers in India.[10] In 1974, there were even reports of an armed encounter between the Nepali Congress activists and the Nepalese Army in the Kingdom's Okhaldunga area.[11]

For King Birendra, all this was a matter of deep concern, amounting almost to a scare in view of the related developments in South Asia. The emergence of Bangladesh was one such development in which the mass upsurge against the military regime was actively supported by India in December 1971, only a few weeks before Birendra's coming to power. The emergence of Bangladesh had acted as an impetus for the democratic forces in the subcontinent, particularly the Nepali Congress whose leader B.P. Koirala, while in India, was actively involved in mobilising support in favour of the cause of Bangladesh in association with the Indian leader, Jayaprakash Narayan, throughout the year 1971.[12]

Subsequently, India's blessings to the democratic forces in Sikkim, comprising mostly the Sikkimese of Nepali origin, resulted in the protectorate Kingdom's integration with India in September 1974. The Sikkim issue had been active since early 1973. Nepal's political divide between the King and the Nepali Congress got directly involved in the Sikkim developments with the King extending support to the Chogyal and the Nepali Congress joining hands with the popular forces. The King foresaw a possibility of Indian backing to the Nepali Congress in its revolt against the monarchy, even while the Government of India, in deference to the King's fear, had restricted the movement of the Nepali Congress leaders (to 50 kms) along India's border with Nepal. King Birendra was further assured explicitly, during his visit to India in October 1973, that "no hostile activities" would be allowed against his regime from the Indian soil.[13] These assurances were in response to the King's gesture of accommodating Indian concern on the ZOP announcement at the Algiers Non-aligned Summit as we mentioned earlier. Such assurances also, perhaps, delayed the formal announcement of the proposal to February 1975. But the culmination of Sikkim developments in late 1974 undermined the marginal improvement in the King's sense of fear from the activities of the Nepali Congress based in India and acted as a catalyst. The tensions between the monarchy and the Nepali Congress between 1973 and 1975 were at their worst since 1960-62 and one of the major objectives of the ZOP proposal was to ensure that the King's adversaries did not receive any international, particularly Indian, support. Here, attention may be drawn to King Birendra's speech made on 18 November 1976 in Moscow, wherein explaining the rationale of his ZOP proposal, he said:

> Geographically, we are placed between two of the important emergent forces of Asia . . .In our view, it is for every country to contribute what it can towards the maintenance and consolidation of peace. In ensuring on a reciprocal basis that the territory of one country is not used for conflict against another country, which is why my Zone of Peace proposal aims at for Nepal, we are reducing to a degree, the possible areas of tension. . .[14]

The possibility of interested external powers having exploited the King's apprehensions *vis-a-vis* India and prompted him about the ZOP proposal cannot be ruled out. China, Pakistan and the USA may be mentioned here. China and Pakistan have always encouraged Nepal to weaken its dependence upon, and security relations with India as we have already mentioned in the previous chapters. The ZOP proposal eminently suited their objective in the then prevailing context of regional politics in the sub-continent.

Some reliable observers in Nepal also attributed the idea of ZOP to Kathmandu-based American and Chinese diplomats. While the authenticity of such attribution cannot be conclusively established, this may not be too far-fetched either, because the US was equally interested in "restraining India" particularly, in the subcontinent, in the aftermath of the emergence of Bangladesh. If there was any hesitation in this regard, it was removed following India's peaceful nuclear explosion of May 1974 and, thereafter, the integration of Sikkim with India as an 'associate state'. In the wake of developments in Sikkim, the US connections with the Chogyal through his American wife and the CIA activities in the subcontinent had come under strong criticism in India which continued through the 1975-76 emergency period. It was in the background of these developments that Pakistan was encouraged to initiate and pursue the proposal of South Asia as a nuclear-weapons-free zone. Another zone of peace proposal in the region such as that of Nepal was bound to embarrass India in its pursuit of the proposal of the Indian Ocean as a zone of peace. India's expected reservations on Nepal's proposal could be used to put a blame on India that it was not serious in the pursuit of peace in South Asia. Both the Nepali and the Pakistani proposals succeeded in creating the impressions that there were serious dissensions on strategic issues within South Asia from where the Indian Ocean proposal had emanated. These dissensions which also highlighted smaller neighbours' apprehensions *vis-a-vis* India gave credibility to the western view that India was pursuing Indian Ocean proposal seeking withdrawal of the great powers, to establish its hegemony in the region as India was the most powerful country among the Indian Ocean littorals. The American opposition to the Indian Ocean proposal was well known. King Birendra also frequently referred to the Indian Ocean as a zone of peace proposal while describing the context for his own proposal.

The Nepali proposal was compatible with the implications of Sino-US rapproachement developing since 1972. It was to nurse this new found friendship with China that the US had withdrawn support to the Khampa armed operations against the Tibet region of China. These operations were launched from bases in Nepal's Mustang region with the backing of the United States. As a result of the US disinterest in the Khampa operations, following President Nixon's visit to China and the Shanghai Communique of 1972; Nepal got a green signal to remove this irritation in its relations with China. By 1974, the Khampas were forced to lay down arms and were rehabilitated away from the Tibetan border. Having achieved that, Nepal could have an easy conscience and make bold claims for being declared as a zone of peace because since then Nepal could not be blamed for allowing its territory to be used for hostile activities against one of its neighbours. Earlier, any one could accuse Nepal of allowing Khampa hostile activities against China (Tibet). China's interest in and its prompt support for Nepal's ZOP proposal could also be seen as China's attempt to ensure that Khampa type operations were not encouraged in future from the Nepalese soil.

INTERNATIONAL SUPPORT

King Birendra made vigorous diplomatic efforts to secure international support for his ZOP proposal. During official state visits abroad by himself or his Ministers and other senior officials as also during the visits of foreign dignitaries to Nepal, the Nepali government tried to get endorsement for this proposal. It is claimed that by the end of the 1980s, nearly eighty-five countries had endorsed the proposal. The American support for the proposal during King Birendra's visit to the US in December 1983 was highlighted. The US in fact was mentioned as one of the early supporters of the proposal along with China, the Soviet Union and Pakistan.[15] What added importance to the US endorsement in December 1983 was the statement made to that effect by President Reagan himself as we shall see below.

The most unqualified, enthusiastic and immediate support extended to the proposal came from China and Pakistan—naturally, since the proposal in effect aimed at qualitatively changing the existing nature of Indo-Nepalese relations to India's disadvantage. Chinese support was elaborated in May 1976 when the then Chinese Premier Hua Guofeng said: "We firmly support the just stand taken by His Majesty the King of Nepal, in declaring a zone of peace. We are ready to assume appropriate commitments arising thereform". Interestingly, the occasion for this Chinese assurance was the Pakistan Prime Minister Bhutto's visit to Beijing. This was reiterated in early June, 1976 when King Birendra visited China" The Chinese Premier, Hua Guofeng, said:

> The proposal put forward by His Majesty King Birendra to declare Nepal as a Zone of Peace reflects the strong desire of the people of Nepal to safeguard national independence and state sovereignty. The Chinese government firmly supports this just proposition. The Chinese people will, as always, stand together with you for ever in the struggle against hegemonism and expansionism.[16]

Subsequently, the Chinese tried to interpret it in the context of growing need for cooperation and understanding in South Asia. This perhaps was intended to tone down its anti-Indian facet in view of the growing process of Sino-Indian normalisation. Pakistan considered the proposal as being in consonance with its own move to get South Asia recognised as a nuclear-weapon-free zone.

Support from most other countries had been more of a routine and can be seen as a token gesture. The Soviet Union was the first to support the proposal when the Deputy Chairman of Presidium of the Supreme Soviet, Tura Bai Kulatov, who led the Soviet delegation to the King's coronation, endorsed it in Kathmandu on February 26,1975.[17] This was perhaps done without properly understanding all the implications of the proposal or in the hope that Nepal would reciprocate by endorsing the Soviet proposal for collective security in Asia. But as the anti-Indian implications of the King's proposal became clear to the Soviet Union and as Nepal did not endorse the Soviet collective security scheme, the Soviets almost withdrew their support from the King's proposal. Accordingly, the Soviet Ambassador K.B. Udumyan told a press conference in Kathmandu on March 5,1976 that the Soviet Union's initial gesture in favour of the zone of peace proposal was only a support for Nepal's non-alignment so that it did not become an area of tension and a centre for hostilities against other countries.[18]

Nearly the same thing happened in the case of French support which was extended by President Mitterrand on May 2,1983 during his visit to Nepal. The next day, explaining the French position, the French Ambassador to Nepal clarified that the precise formulation of the French stand was to be declared later, as legal and political advisers were to be consulted. Even the British support was of a token nature because it was clearly impressed upon the Nepalese side that, the only effective support to the proposal could be of Nepal's neighbours, particularly India.

While the US could have been associated with the King's proposal in its initial stages, as has been discussed above, official support to it was extended only through quiet diplomatic channels. US enthusiasm for the proposal declined as Indo-US relations became relaxed as a result of the political change in 1977 in India. Subsequently, though President Reagan, through his personal statement raised the level of support from 'quiet diplomatic' to 'open political', it should not be viewed as all that unqualified, notwithstanding the fanfare attached to this in the officially geared Nepali media.

There were two notable aspects of the US support which were obscured by the euphoria of American endorsement in the Nepali official media. One, President Reagan emphasized that this proposal will help Nepal in avoiding the use of its "scarce resources for military purposes". This is in contrast to the principal objective behind the proposal which had been defined more in terms of internal political stability rather than for conserving economic resources spent on military expenditure. Nepali budgetary expenditure on defence and internal security had in fact been steadily rising over the past few years. This expenditure which was Rs 253.2 mn (Nepali) in 1978-79 increased to Rs 638.2 mn (Nepali) in 1983-84, and nearly Rs 1,000 mn (Nepali) by the end of the 1980s. The expenditure under this head has always been more than the budgetary expenditure on social and economic services put together. Reagan's hopeful statement did not make any change in this situation.

Secondly, Reagan urged upon Nepal to work closely with her neighbours to make the peace zone proposal a reality. This in practical terms, cautioned Nepal that the US had limits in going along with the Kingdom and supporting its apprehensions and idiosyncracies *vis-a-vis* its bigger Asian neighbours, particularly India. The qualification added to the US support was definitely aimed at showing deference to India's reservations on Nepal's ZOP proposal. Accordingly, it dampened the King's enthusiasm and was accordingly taken note of in the Nepali press. Further, while extending even this cautious support to the ZOP proposal, the Americans impressed upon the Nepalese side that it was in return for Nepal's pro-US policy on Afghanistan and Kampuchea. The US also appreciated Nepal's friendly relations with Israel, which, until the opening of the "Israeli interest section" in Colombo in June 1984, was an exception in South Asia. Nepal's readiness to send troops to work as part of the UN peace force earlier and then in 1982 in Lebanon was also viewed by the US leaders as a positive aspect of the Kingdom's foreign policy. Significantly, King Birendra, while in the US in December 1983, told a press conference: "Nepal is willing to participate and can be counted on to contribute troops if such an action would bring about peace in other parts of the world".[19] One wonders if the US had quietly made equiries in this regard. But such gestures from the developing countries suited the US policy.

The King in making this statement had, however, ignored the domestic criticism of this aspect of Nepal's foreign policy, particularly in the context of developments in Lebanon.

While one must understand the US support for ZOP proposal of Nepal in its proper context, it should however, be noted that the US had decided to take an open stand on the issue which involved India's susceptibilities. Viewed in the light of the then prevailing phase of US policy towards the subcontinent, particularly Pakistan, Sri Lanka and Bangladesh, it created the impression that the US was not averse to making a careful use of the small-power psyche of India's neighbours to further its strategic objectives in the Kingdom. Strong sympathetic sentiment that existed in the US Congress and media, as also in some sections of the Bush Administration with regard to Nepal's difficulties with India on matters of trade and 1950 Treaty during 1989-90, may also be seen in this context.

The number of countries endorsing the ZOP proposal steadily increased, particularly so since 1980 when Nepal stepped up its attempts to secure increasing support. The forms in which support to the proposal was extended varies from a political statement to a 'simple note', through diplomatic channel. It was, however, of an insignificant nature and in most of the important cases, polite suggestion had been made to Nepal to get endorsement from its neighbours which was of greater relevance. Accordingly, Nepal cannot be seen as having succeeded in using increasing international support as a pressure-factor in inducing India to endorse the ZOP proposal. Notwithstanding this, Nepal continued to attempt in persuading more and more countries to lend support to its proposal. This was one of the major issue on the agenda any time a Nepali dignitary visited a foreign country or a foreign dignitary paid an official visit to Nepal.

INDIA'S RESERVATIONS

All the countries in South Asia, with the exception of Bhutan and India, had endorsed Nepal's ZOP proposal. Nepal was acutely conscious of the fact that the proposal would not make much sense in effective terms, without India agreeing to it. The question of India not endorsing it was a subject of much internal debate in the Kingdom. While the lack of positive response on the proposal on India's part had been criticised in some sections of the Nepali official circles and public opinion, others blamed His Majesty's government for not being persuasive enough with their Indian counterpart in securing the desired response. One of Nepal's senior and balanced foreign policy maker and analyst Y.N. Khanal's observations in this respect were pertinent. After the announcement of the seven point definition of the ZOP proposal, he said in a Foreign Ministry seminar in 1982:

> Support for Nepal's proposal is growing but is not enough. Is it because the proposal is not specific enough? Is it the indifference or perversity of the international community that is standing in the way? Why is India so reluctant and so suspicious? ... Comments in an important section of the Indian press suggest that the proposal does indeed need an intensive dialogue between Nepal and India on one hand and between Nepal and China on the other, so that the interests, of all the three countries could be balanced to mutual satisfaction and to the satisfaction of the international community... It is expected that the growing concretization of the concept through new definitions, new turns in exposition and successive clarifications is bound to invite progressive acceptance from the international community in general and from India in particular.[20]

India's initial response to the proposal was that of disapproval—as being unnecessary because Nepal has treaties of peace and friendship both with India and China. India also sought clarification from Nepal about what precisely it wanted to achieve through the proposal. Its seven-point definition which was put forward by Nepal after six years of the announcement of the proposal still left things ambiguous as was evident from Y.N. Khanal's statement cited above. After the formulation of this definition India's formal reaction was that the proposal is being studied seriously. This was disclosed by Foreign Minister Narasimha Rao in Parliament on March 11, 1983. Later in November 1983 Mrs. Gandhi again asked Nepal to clarify as to from which source it feared threat to its peace and security. This was an obvious indication of India's displeasure with the proposal and hence its reluctance to endorse it.

India has had reservations about the proposal in terms of its timing and context on the one hand and substance on the other. India did not quite relish the idea of Nepal formally announcing the proposal in the context of the developments in Sikkim as also at a time when reservations on the Indian Ocean peace zone proposal had started being voiced by some neighbours.

King Birendra had invited the Chogyal of Sikkim to participate in his coronation functions where the proposal was announced. The King also had long talks with the Chogyal who was allowed to make anti-India statements in Kathmandu. India's quiet diplomatic persuasion with the Nepalese government to avoid announcing the proposal on the occasion of the coronation, when a large number of foreign representatives were present in Kathmandu, was scornfully ignored.

India's reservation on the substance of the proposal appeared to be on three major counts. One was that India abhors the Nepali stance, originating mainly from the Royal Palace, of equidistance with its neighbours, which is being sought to be pursued through the ZOP proposal. There was considerable understanding and appreciation in India for Nepal's desire not to get involved in regional conflicts. It was being argued that India respects Nepal's this desire and accordingly, never wished Nepal to be directly involved or even affected by India's regional conflicts with China (1962) and Pakistan (1948,1965 and 1971). During 1959-60, with the intensification of tensions with China, India encouraged and helped Nepal, in whatever manner possible to reach a boundary Agreement (March 1960) and the Treaty of Peace and Friendship (April 1960) between India and China. It was due to the deterioration in the Sino-Indian relations and tensions in the Himalayas that India accepted the rationale of Sino-Nepalese Treaty of Peace and Friendship, on which it otherwise had serious reservations from the beginning. However, while respecting Nepal's desire to keep aloof from regional conflicts, India could not endorse Nepal's attempts to ignore the geopolitical reality between the two countries which intertwines them to such an extent that the security of one cannot be separated from the security of the other, whether a particular regime likes it or not. In India's perception, Nepal's ZOP proposal was heavily preoccupied with the concerns of the regime security of the monarchy where it views India as a source of threat. This Nepali preoccupation was stretched so far that it ignored the external dimension of security of the Kingdom which was common with that of India's.

Even King Mahendra who initiated and championed Nepal's assertive stance *vis-a-vis* India had to accept though grudgingly, this geopolitical reality. He had to allow, as was evident in his statement on the subject on December 19, 1970, the basic essential structure of mutual security arrangements between the two countries to exist. In India's perception, Nepal's zone of peace proposal will negate or seriously undermine these vital arrangements. This would be harmful not only to India but to Nepal itself in the long run. It may be recalled that Nepal found these arrangements reassuring when it experienced disturbances along its northern border during 1949-50, 1960, 1966-67 and also 1971 (Bangladesh crisis). With these past experiences in mind, India's Foreign Minister Narasimha Rao cautioned Nepal during his visit to Kathmandu in November 1981 that it was not wise to embarass or weaken India in the region.

In order to meet India's susceptibilities in this regard, Nepal incorporated a provision in the definition of zone of peace (sixth point) reaffirming its "respect for all existing Treaties". But this formulation did not include arrangements other than Treaties. Further, even in relation to the Treaties, the provision in the proposal at the sixth point was in contradiction with its first point regarding "friendly relations... on the basis of equality ..." This is particularly so because Nepal's Peace and Friendship Treaty with India is much more comprehensive and precise than any other comparable Treaty or Agreement it has had with any other country. This Treaty reflected not only the convergence of security interests between the two countries but also the multi-dimensional economic and socio-cultural relations that were rooted in geographical compulsions and historical evolution of Indian and Nepalese societies, since times immemorial. How then will Nepal try to establish relations with neighbours on the "basis of equality" it was asked. Nepal could not provide any satisfactory explanation for this obvious contradiction between the proposal and the then existing reality. The only possible way in which Nepal could do so was to upgrade its strategic ties with other neighbours like Pakistan and China. Nepal's decision in the recent years to send its military officers to Pakistan for training and its import of lethal and non-lethal military equipments from China were pointers in this direction.

In addition to this, the formulation of seventh point of ZOP proposal was disturbing and intriguing for its implications for India's strategic interests in the region. Nepal's refusal to "enter into military alliance" or "allow the establishment of any foreign military base on its soil" had been assured within the framework of its policy of "peace and non-alignment". But then what was the credibility of such unilateral and one sided assurances? In South Asia, the moves of Pakistan and Sri Lanka during the early eighties, to expand and consolidate their strategic ties with the West and China were also been taken while swearing with "peace and non-alignment" at the same time. This became technically possible because "non-alignment" prohibits only those "military alliances" and "foreign military bases" that were conceived in the "context of the great power conflict". Once a country says that it is entering into "alliance" and "allowing bases" outside the "context of the great power conflict" it could do so without violating its non-aligned status. This distorted application of the non-aligned criteria had been resorted to by many a members of the non-aligned movement. Theoretically, at least, the possibility of Nepal following the same model while harping upon its ZOP proposal clearly exist.

The formulation in the seventh point of the definition further said that a country supporting Nepal's proposal "will not enter into military alliance nor will they allow establishment of military base on their soil directed against Nepal". This sounded meaningless because the Third World countries generally do not explicitly declare that their "bases" or "alliances" are directed against a particular country. This formulation also allowed an aligned country with military bases (as they would not be "directed against Nepal") to extend support for Nepal's ZOP proposal and secure reciprocal commitments from the Kingdom.

In the light of all these strategic implications, India's endorsement of the Nepali proposal would have meant India's acceptance of Nepal's separation from India's south of the Himalayas, security parameter and shifting of India's northern security line from Indo-Tibetan to Indo-Nepalese border, in the heart of Indian mainland. The logic of security interests would accordingly demand sealing of the Indo-Nepal border as closely as possible with security posts and regular armed patrol. This would involve enormous expenditure and even after that, would be most ineffective barrier because of the length and openness of the border. Indo-Pakistan border is a case in point, the porousness of which is so clearly evident in the context of internal turmoil in the Punjab and Jammu and Kashmir states. The idea of barbed-wire fencing on Indo-Bangladesh border has also not been very inspiring to be pursued in other sectors of India's boundaries with neighbours.

The second area of India's reservation was concerning the actual and the intended legal status of the ZOP proposal. India was not clear about the oft-repeated reference to take the proposal to the United Nations and "adding legal force" to it. What could be the form of this? The implication as may be generally understood, was obvious that it would inter nationalization of Nepal's bilateral relations with India (as also other countries) since the endorsement of the proposal can not but be at the bilateral level. India wanted to know Nepal's thinking on the role that the UN or any other international agency will play, if and when the obligations arising out of the ZOP status were violated by Nepal or another country which has endorsed the proposal.

India's third and strongest reservation on the ZOP proposal had been with regard to its fifth point of definition concerning "hostile activities". There could be two broad categories of "hostile activities", namely criminal and political. The criminal activities may include offences like dacoity, murder, economic crimes etc. India and Nepal have a Treaty of Extradition signed in 1953 to deal with this category of "hostile activities". The provisions of the Treaty had been invoked and the criminals extradited. However, this treaty could not be applied against political activities. Article 5 of the Treaty says:

> Neither Government shall be bound to surrender any person if the offence in respect of which the surrender is demanded be of a political character, or if he proves that the requisition for his surrender has in fact been made with a view to trying or punishing him for an offence of a political character.

Thus, the reference to "hostile activities" in the ZOP proposal meant hostile political activities. Here again, two types of political activities may be involved i.e. (i) those involving armed attacks and violent assaults, and (ii) those of peaceful protests agitstion and propaganda. It was not clear if Nepal officially extended any clarification about which of these two types (or both) of "hostile activities" it has in mind regarding the ZOP proposal. But some definite clues available from the past thinking[21] and present projections[22] on the subject suggesed that both violent and non-violent activities were meant to be contained through the proposal. The list of "hostile activities" based on these clues was very broad and a long one that included any "unfriendly act which may undermine the security or internal stability or the system of the Government"[23]. This could be 'arms traffic', 'armed expeditions', a political resolution or even a press statement of a political leader in exile. Consequently, the obligations expected of a country supporting the ZOP proposal could also be very heavy. (See Annexure IA and IB of the Chapter.) Particularly so for a Nepal's neighbour like India which had an open border with the Kingdom and a tradition of extensive and intimate people to people contacts in all walks of life including politics.[24]

India, on its part, had repeatedly assured Nepal that armed activities aimed against the King and his Panchayat system were not be permitted from its soil. Those assurances have been executed many times to the satisfaction of the King and his government; whenever the latter so demanded. It may be recalled that the deposed Nepali Congress leader B.P. Koirala after his release in late 1968, came to India for medical treatment and also in self exile. He, owing to his close association with Jaya Prakash Narayan and other socialists, had actively supported the cause of the emergence of Bangladesh in 1971 as well as democratization and integration with India, of Sikkim in 1974-75 as mantioned earlier. These developments activized his Nepali Congress workers in India and Nepal, and had encouraged them to step up their activities against the Panchayat system. This worried King Birendra as noted earlier. In response to the King's anxieties, the government of India restricted the activities of the Nepali Congress leaders to a 50 miles limit within India along the Indo-Nepalese border. Subsequently, following the imposition of internal emergency in India, B.P. Koirala found himself compelled to go to Nepal in December 1976 where he was arrested and put under trial for treason. One is not sure if this was the *quid pro* quo for Nepal to contain the activities of some of the opponents of Mrs Gandhi's emergency regime who sought sanctuaries in Nepal. B.P's trial could have led to the passing of death sentence on him. Some of his associates were in fact shot dead in Nepal after being charged for indulging in anti-national and subversive activities. The King, the His Majesty's Government, and the then Prime Minister Tulsi Giri had expressed satisfaction with India's cooperation in dealing with the activities of the Nepali Congress rebels in this context.[25] Later, on her coming to power again in 1980, Mrs. Gandhi's unexpressed sympathies lay with the King's Panchayat System in the national referendum. Her son Rajiv Gandhi also tried his best to support the Monarchy until the Nepali side irritated his government on Trade and 1950 Treaty issues.

In the larger context however, Nepal' s experience of India's cooperation on the question of anti-regime political activities of the Nepalis from the Indian territory had been a mixed one.

The events of 1960-62, (until the break out of Sino-Indian conflict on 20th October 1962 which changed India's attitude suddenly) may be recalled here. Similarly, during 1969-75; the Nepali Congress enjoyed considerable amount of support and sympathy in India. The problem with Indian policy towards Nepal on this question is that it has traditionally (even during and before the British consolidation in India) been approached by conflicting expectations of political support from Nepal; namely the expectations of the ruling regime as well as the opponents of the regime. In recent times, this was evident during the anti-Rana revolution; during King Mahendra's coup and subsequently since the early seventies. India had responded to these conflicting demands through a mixed degree of accommodation depending upon the assessment of its specific interests at the given point of time. Such a mix had often left one or the other or even both the parties unhappy.

A complete alliance with either side has not been viewed as prudent in India. The acceptance of the ZOP proposal demanded precisely such a total commitment in favour of the royal regime that can be offered at the cost of flexibility and resilience in India's long term policy on the one hand and alienation from Nepal's democratic forces on the other. These democratic forces constituted the natural political constituency of India in terms of the nature of popular interaction and political values. A total commitment to the royal regime expected under the ZOP proposal from India was hard to fulfil for any government in New Delhi, particularly against the forces of democracy and progressive change. This was so because of the nature of people to people contacts between the Nepalese and the Indians as well as due to the long and contiguous border between the two countries. Irrespective of any official sympathy or support from the government of India, opposition groups from Nepal have always found it possible to use Indian territory and political connections to advance their political goals in the kingdom. For instance, presence of Nepali communist extremists in India during the seventies when "Naxalite" movement was stronger in Bihar, U.P. and North Bengal areas, may be recalled here. This was evident to a lesser extent even later, when many active communist and non-communist extremists (such as Ramraja Prasad Singh) frequently crossed the India-Nepal border.

Under the circumstance, it was extremely difficult for the government of India to extend assurances that no political activity will be allowed by Nepalis in India. More so when the possibility always existed that the state governments in India, like that of Bihar and West Bengal, may not accept some of the Central Government's policies in this respect. Therefore, if India endorsed Nepal's ZOP proposal, it could be called upon to undertake police operations against Nepali political activists residing in India. This could bring the Indian government directly in conflict with the Nepali democratic or anti-monarchy forces as well as their Indian sympathisers and supporters. Failing to carry out such police operation at the Royal government's behest would lead to irritations in Indo-Nepal relations. Then, Nepal could also hold India guilty of not fulfilling its international commitments. It could then, even threaten to invite third party intervention such as U.N. observers etc. and create embarassing situation for India. No sensible government in India would have liked to land themselves in such an avoidable mess.

The provision of "hostile activities" was aimed at ensuring political stability in Nepal. In the given context, this meant perpetuation of a reigning monarchy and the Panchayat system. That was why the King got the ZOP proposal incorporated into the Nepali Constitution following the Third Amendment in December 1980. The support for ZOP proposal, thus in a way, implied support for Nepal's then prevailing constitutional system. India's Foreign Minister Narasimha Rao referring to this aspect in 1981 questioned whether it would be proper for other countries to endorse a particular provision of the Constitution of another country. There is nothing to suggest that India had done anything consciously to disturb the present system in Nepal but since the ZOP proposal was so closely identified with specific aspects of internal politics, it was not possible for any country, particularly the one placed in India's position, to extend a categorical support for it without becoming controversial within Nepal.[26]

Particularly so because the Panchayat system could not yet secure a viable popular legitimacy and it was passing through a rather critical phase. None of the major non-Panchayat political groups including B.P. Koirala of Nepali Congress, had given unqualified support to the proposal in 1981 (mainly in the context of his "national reconciliation" policy), but added that the King needed to evolve a firm national political consensus in the Kingdom which by itself would be the best guarantee of political stability and peace. The successors of B.P. Koirala deviated even from this qualified support and their position on ZOP proposal became increasingly unsympathetic to the King. For instance,

Ganesh Man Singh, the Supreme leader of the Nepali Congress said in 1984:

> The objective of the peace zone proposal may be good but the people will think that it will be used only to sustain the undemocratic regime so long as they have to follow the line laid by the rulers. Indeed, people seem to be withholding support for the peace zone proposal because they apprehend that it is being used as means to mobilise external support for suppressing their voice.[27]

The pro-Chinese communist groups had hailed the proposal for its. "anti-India" and "anti-hegemonistic" thrust but even they did not endorse the fifth point on "hostile activities". Subsequently the M.L. (Marxist-Leninist) and the Mashal extremist groups further revised their stand on the proposal and completely rejected it. The pro-Soviet communist groups consistently disapproved of the proposal.

Within the Panchayat system, political support for the proposal had not gone beyond sycophancy and lip service. A number of resolutions and statements supporting the proposals were adopted on various occasions at different levels of Panchayat. However, many of the district and zonal level panches and the members of Rastriya Panchayat revealed in quiet, informal conversations that they sang the song of ZOP mainly because it had been composed by the King and he was emotionally identified with it. Otherwise they did not find anything of special significance that could serve Nepal's enlightened national interests. Therefore, they did not have their heart in it. At the international level, seminars and discussions, sponsored by the foreign ministry and the Tribhuvan University in 1983 and 1984 raised more doubts and questions about the ZOP proposal's relevance, utility and viability. In open debates and discussions, one could hardly find an intellectual speaking in Nepal in favour of the proposal with sound arguments and logical explanations.

Thus India's reluctance to endorse the Nepali proposal and undertake obligations inherent in the proposal arise from all the factors discussed above. It is because of these factors that even most sympathetically oriented Indian Prime Ministers have not been able to please the king on the question of the ZOP proposal. Both Morarji Desai (in 1977) and Rajiv Gandhi (in 1985) initially promised to consider the proposal favourably but once they were acquainted with its various facets affecting immediate and long term Indian interests, they had to back out from such promises. Morarji Desai after raising King Birendra's hopes on India's positive response to the ZOP proposal finally side-stepped its endorsement by India by saying that "It was enough if the *nations of the subcontinent contributed their* mite towards making the region free from tensions and strife".[28] Rajiv Gandhi also raised similar hopes on his first meeting as Prime Minister, with King Birendra in Delhi in early 1985, but his term ended on serious tensions between the two countries on all important issues. The National Front government that came to power in India in 1989 was also not able to change India's known position on the proposal notwithstanding its declared intent of improving relations with all the neighbours.

It is therefore clear that there was no possibility of Nepal's ZOP proposal being accepted by India. The proposal was dectined to die its natural death, and so at did when the panchayati system ended in 1990 and Nepal had a new multi party democatric constitution.

Notes

1. *The Rising Nepal,* 9 September 1973.
2. *The Rising Nepal,* 26 February 1975.
3. For the Text of the Speech, see: Special issue of *The Weekly Mirror* (Kathmandu) on Nepal's Zone of Peace Proposal, Kathmandu, 1982.
4. *Newsweek,* 10 September 1973.
5. *Rising Nepal,* 23 February 1976.
6. Ibid; also *Times of India,* 28 January 1976.
7. See for instance, the Special issue of *The Weekly Mirror,* op. cit. (n.3); also Govind R. Agarwal, Rajeshwar Acharya and Pustun Pradhan (ed.) *Fundamentals of Nepalese Foreign Policy,* CEDA, Kathmandu, 1985.
8. *The Hindustan Times* (New Delhi), 10 July 1985.
9. Text of the King's speeches emphasizing various aspects, particularly that of Nepal keeping out of tensions and conflicts, may be found in Bishwa Pradhan, *Nepal: A Peace Zone,* Kathmandu/ New Delhi, 1982. Also, Review of Developments in Nepal's Foreign Affairs (1973-83); Ministry of Foreign Affairs, HMG of Nepal Kathmandu, n.d.
10. *SeePermanand,* The Nepali Congress Since Its Inception, *Delhi 1982; Lok Raj Baral,* Opposition Politics in Nepal, *New Delhi, 1977.*

11. As mentioned in Sashi P. Misra, *BT. Koirala : A Case Study in Third World Democratic Leadership,* Konark Publisher, Bhubneswar, Varanasi, 1985, p. 92.
12. For instance, see B.P. Koirala's speech at the International Conference on Bangladesh held in New Delhi from 18th to 20th September 1971. He said in that speech: "We in Nepal know that if Bangladesh people win, half of our struggle will have been won already".
13. *Indian Express,* 14 October 1973.
14. Text in Bishwa Pradhan, n. 9.
15. Foreign Minister Krishna Raj Aryal's Statement in Kathmandu on 23 May 1975.
16. Text in, *Foreign Affairs Journal,* May-August 1976, no. 2.
17. *The Rising Nepal,* 27 February 1975.
18. The Rising Nepal, *6 March 1976.*
19. For President Reagan's Statements and King Birendra's speeches during the latter's State visit to the U.S. see, *Department of State Bulletin,* February 1984.
20. Y.N. Khanal, *Essays in Nepal's Foreign Affairs,* Kathmandu, 1988, p. 20.
21. Two official publications of 1962 released by the Department of Publicity and Broadcasting, Ministry of National Guidance, HMG, Nepal may be mentioned here. They are: S.P. Gyawali (the then Attorney General of Nepal), *Friendship on Trial,* Kathmandu, n.d.,p. 25; Prakash Bahadur *K.C. Hostile Expeditions and International Law,* Kathmandu, April 1962, p. 62. These publications were brought out to focus attention on India's alleged connivance with and support for the Nepali Congress activities against King Mahendra's drastic action of 16 December 1960. Nepal's Foreign Minister Khatri referred to the second publication when I was discussing the fifth point of the ZOP proposal with him in Kathmandu in 1982.
22. Bishwa Pradhan, n. 9, p. 173. This is a private publication. Though its author at the time of the publication of this book, was Special Secretary in the Nepalese Ministry of Foreign Affairs. Some friends in the Nepalese Foreign Ministry suggested that this book was printed in India with the help of the Nepalese Embassy in India so as to informally draw the attention of Indian government towards the definition of "hostile activities".
23. Ibid.,p. 29.
24. For some Indian reactions on the ZOP Proposal see: Mavin Kurve "Nepal's Peace Zone Move: Attempt to Change 1950 Treaty", *Times of India,* 14 January 1981; Jampa Sangva "Nepal: Zone of Peace Still A Dream", *Deccan Chronicle* (Hydera-bad) 6

March 1978; S.D. Muni, "Nepal As a Zone of Peace" *Strategic Analysis*, Vol. VIII, January 1984.

25. See the outcome of Dr. Giri's visit to India in April 1976. *Hindustan Times*, 10 April 1976; *Amrita Bazar Patrika*, 12 April 1976.
26. It may be useful to recall the comments of a perceptive Nepali intellectual known for his sympathies for the Nepali Congress regarding the domestic political bias of the ZOP proposal. An eminent lawyer, Ganesh Raj Sharma said: "If there were no national crises and was no need for national unity, there was no rationality of His Majesty's proposition that Nepal be declared a Zone of Peace". As cited in Lok Raj Baral, *Nepal's Politics of Referendum: A Study of Groups, Personalities and Trends*, Vikas, New Delhi, 1983, p. 26.
27. Matribhumi (*Weekly*, Kathmandu), 3 April 1984.
28. *Times of India*, 10, 11 and 12 December 1977.

    The Statesman, 10 December 1977; *The Rising Nepal*, 11 December 1977.

POST-SCRIPT—III

REGIONAL BALANCING FOR REGIME SECURITY

The foregoing pages clearly underline two principal areas of Nepal's foreign policy, namely engaging with the world and reinforcing the regional balance of power. Of these two, the first area has almost been reduced as a routine matter, often influenced by the second, in substantive policy matters. Acknowledging the priority of the regional relations, the Ministry of Foreign Affairs of Nepal states that "Because of its geographical proximity to and historical links with China and India, Nepal's foreign policy was focussed mainly on maintaining close and friendly relations with these two countries and on safeguarding its national security and independence". This priority of regional relations is also clearly reflected in the various writings on Nepal's foreign policy, specially by Nepal's influential policy makers and analysts like Y.N. Khanal, Rishikesh Shah, Bishwa Pradhan, Shailendra Kumar Upadhyaya, Shambu Ram Simkhada, Dr. Prakash Chandra Lohani and Ramesh Nath Pandey.

Global Engagements

For keeping engaged with the world beyond its regional concerns, Nepal continued to swear by the policy of non-alignment, and peace and cooperation with all. Nepal has also continued to expand its diplomatic relations with various countries of the world as also with international organisations to keep diversifying and extending its global reach and protect and promote its interests concerning with economic and other matters related to Nepali diaspora. More and more Nepalese have been seeking jobs and economic opportunities abroad, in far and distant places, owing to lack of development at home. By 2016, Nepal has established diplomatic relations with 142 countries and it maintains 50 diplomatic missions (Embassies, permanent

Missions and Consulates) abroad. The Ministry of Foreign Affairs of Nepal defines its Vision/Mission as to:

> ...project and protect Nepal's independence, sovereignty, territorial integrity, to promote friendly relations with all the countries of the world and particularly with its immediate neighbours, to play an active role in the United Nations and other international organisations in order to promote international peace and security, and development, to play an active role in the promotion of regional cooperation in South Asia, to act as the country's first point of contact for the outside world and also serve as Nepal's window to the world.

Republican Nepal's new constitution of 2015 defines its foreign policy goals in broader terms. Under its Directive principles, it is stated that the objective of foreign policy will be:

> "... enhancing the dignity of the nation in the world community by maintaining international relations on the basis of sovereign equality, while safeguarding the freedom, sovereignty, territorial integrity and independence and national interests of Nepal (Clause 50.4)
>
> ...conduct an independent foreign policy based on the Charter of the United Nations, non-alignment, principle of *Panchsheel,* international law and the norms of world peace, taking into consideration of the overall interest of the nation,...reviews treaties concluded in the past, and make treaties, agreements based on equality and mutual interest... (Clause 51(m1 and 2).

Nepal has maintained amicable relations with global players like the US, Russia, UK, Europe and Japan and has participated in regional organisations including the United Nations and BIMSTEC (Bay of Bengal Initiative for Multi Sectoral Technical and Economic Cooperation). The thrust in approach towards these countries has remained on mobilising developmental support, trade and investments, as also on seeking political and diplomatic support on occasions when neighbourhood relations become difficult and challenging. Nepal has only periodically been stressed on some aspects of its engagements beyond the immediate neighbourhood.

An important aspect of Nepal's engagement with the United Kingdom has been on the issue of Gurkha recruitment for the

British army that represents a 200 year old legacy of the British Empire in India. Issues regarding the equality of pay and compensations to British Gurkha soldiers with the British national soldiers and the right to residence for the former in UK have been raised since the British withdrawal from Hong Kong in 1997. They were finally settled in 2009. The Nepali Maoists raised, during their ten year long insurgency, the question of withdrawing the Gurkha recruitment facility, but quietly dropped the issue when they came to power in 2008 on the consideration of job opportunities and economic benefits. The British Ambassador in Nepal doubted in 2012 if the practice would end during his life time.[1]

Similarly the question of Nepal army's role in UN Peacekeeping operations has also been linked with the vital economic dimension. But in recent years, examples of corruption in recruiting UN Peacekeepers and deploying them, as also violations of human rights by these peace keepers have been contested by Nepal's foreign policy.[2] The question of human rights violations by the Nepal Army during the Maoist insurgency was also raised in the UN Human Rights Council (UNHRC), Geneva.[3] During the King's direct rule in 2005-2006, raising of human rights issues was seen as a conspiracy blamed on the leaders of the peoples' movement (*Jan Andolan-II*)like G.P. Koirala of the Nepali Congress. He was alleged to have been working in coordination with the countries like Britain, Denmark, Norway and Sweden, and supported by India, to put pressure on the King and the Royal Nepal Army (its participation in UN Peacekeeping Operations).[4] The question of human rights violations has been raised in the context of Nepal's new constitution; first with regard to the killing of Madhesi protesters when the UNHR Commissioner ZeidRa'ad Al Hussein included Nepal as one of the violators in his opening address to the 30th session of the UNHRC in 2015. India supported this contention to the much displeasure of Nepal.[5] Subsequently, human rights activists and analysts have also underlined incompatibilities between Nepal's new constitution and the rights for Dalits and criteria for citizenship.[6]Reacting to these charges, Prime Minister K.P. Sharma Oli has strongly defended Nepal's democratic constitution. Referring to international human rights criticism and, while admitting that laps might have been there in Nepal's position, Oli asserted that Nepal's record on rights has been historically better than that of many European countries.[7]

Nepal has maintained amicable relationship with the US. These relations have been invoked for economic and technical support but more to counter uncomfortable regional pressures. Nepal's tacit support for the US backed anti-Chinese (led by Khampa tribal warriors) operations in Tibet from Nepal's Mustang region during the 1960s until early 1970s, and the US support for King Birendra's Zone of Peace proposal, much against India's displeasure during mid-Seventies have been discussed in previous chapters. The US expressed greater sympathy for King Gyanendra's take over and direct rule in February 2005 in the name of fighting the Maoist insurgency and even supplied arms to the royal regime towards that end when India had frozen such supplies. However, the US, in view of growing strategic understanding with India, followed the Indian political line in urging the King to broaden democratic base of the regime by cooperating with the mainstream political parties so that the Maoists could be isolated and strongly dealt with.[8] At a seminar on "Nepal's Foreign Policy: The Way Ahead" in Kathmandu on November 22, 2010, Dr Prakash Chandra Lohani, former Foreign Minister was reported to have said; "...America has consistently supported and remained sensitive to Nepal's political interests of strengthening sovereignty, integrity and independence".

Regional Balance

While global engagements have a significance of their own in Nepal's foreign policy, the thrust of this policy has been on, as already mentioned, keeping a desirable balance between its immediate and principal neighbours, specially between India and China. Developments on two fronts, particularly since the beginning of the 1990s, have shaped and defined Nepal's efforts towards maintaining regional balance. One is regarding Nepal's internal politics and political transformations and another is regarding developments in India and China. On the domestic political front, Nepal has been undergoing significant changes with the Panchayat System under an assertive Monarchy yielding place to multi-party democracy in 1990 and then, the rise of Maoist insurgency after ten years of violence and mayhem (1996-2006)eventually leading to a Republican and Federal Nepal. This transition is still in the process of stabilising and institutionalising itself.

On the neighbourhood front, the post-Mao China under the leadership of Deng Xiaoping undertook extensive economic and political reforms to make China rise phenomenally and emerge as a resurgent player in Asia-Pacific and global affairs. Internally China has also undertaken strong initiatives to integrate its periphery, Yunnan, Xinjiang and Tibet, through infrastructure, economically and politico-administratively. An economically strong China which needs help and support of its neighbours in stabilising and developing its periphery opens up several economic and strategic opportunities for the countries like Nepal to harness. India has also economically grown since 1990 to emerge as the second most successful growth story in Asia and the world after China. India has invited all its neighbours including Nepal to join in its growth and prosperity. India's democratic vibrancy has been radiating influence and support to the rising democratic aspirations of people in its neighbouring countries. Both India and China have increasingly come under pressure from the rising threats of terrorism, internally as well as across the borders and they need and expect their respective neighbouring countries like Nepal to help and cooperate in dealing with their security concerns.

The combined impact of both Nepal's internal transformations and changing dynamics of the growth and strategic concerns in the neighbouring region has precipitated situations where Nepal has felt pressured and interfered by India. The thrust of Nepal's regional balance has accordingly been to mobilise support to balance this pressure from the south which has been felt in almost all areas of national life but mainly in three sectors. In matters of trade and transit, Nepal seeks greater freedom to meet the growing demands of its developing economy. India's restrictive trade regime and constrained transit infrastructure, including poor port, road and rail network, has come in the way of freedom in moving goods, people and services aspired by Nepal. India has periodically responded to Nepal's demands and tried to accommodate its concerns, but not to the complete satisfaction of Nepal.

Then Nepal has felt uncomfortable in responding to India's changing needs in the security sector. India's security concerns in Nepal that were largely confined to border security during 1950s through 1970s have become more complex and diversified. They now include the flow of fake currencies, drugs and other contrabands, and terrorists from third countries (particularly from Pakistan), through Nepal using open border and free movement of people provided under the Treaty of Peace and Friendship concluded in 1950 between the two countries. The hijacking of an Indian Airlines flight (IC814) from Kathmandu by terrorists from Nepal in December 1999 may be recalled in this respect. There is also the problem of controlling the movement of anti-social and criminal groups across the open India-Nepal border. India's demands for regulating the undesirable traffic has been found difficult for Nepal to respond to effectively and satisfactorily. The difficulty arises on two counts; one, due to laxity in and inadequacy of the law and order structure and two, the sense of Nepal's sovereignty which is perceived to be compromised in meeting any given Indian demand.

Nepal's sensitivity on sovereignty has always been a critical factor in Nepal's relations with India in view of the former's geographical, economic and socio-cultural proximity and dependence on the latter. It is widely known and accepted that Nepali nationalism has often been expressed in terms distinct, different and incompatible with India. Nepal's sovereign sensitivity has been reinforced by the Nepali rulers' sense of regime security. Since the emergence of modern Nepal and the rule of King Prithvi Narayan Shah, India has been viewed as a source of threat to regime security. The Rana rulers of Nepal bought their internal political autonomy and regime security from the British Empire in India by accepting to work within the framework of India's regional security and economic interests. The Ranas extended the same arrangements with independent India's leadership in the form of the Treaty of 1950 and were quite upset when they found India becoming a party to the end of the Rana autocratic system in 1951. Thus disturbed politically, Ranas were the first in prompting and encouraging demands for the revision or revocation of this Treaty. This Rana inheritance of approach towards India was passed on to the Nepali Monarchy which became increasingly assertive since the rise of King Mahendra. We have discussed some of these issues in previous Chapters. The point that the Ranas and the post-Rana Kings of Nepal failed to appreciate was that in Indian perspective, the treaty of 1950 represented a sincere balance between India's security concerns in Nepal and Nepal's developmental concerns in India; the latter being enshrined in the provisions of open border, free trade and equal treatment to Nepali national in India. In Indian perception, the thrust of mutual security reference in the Treaty of 1950 was with regard to external threats to the contracting parties. The consequences of Nepal's political turbulence and transformations and Indian response to their spill-over in India did not fall within the framework of the Treaty of 1950. While those in Nepal fighting against the regime excesses and atrocities have sought and secured India's support for their cause, the regimes in distress, for failing to get Indian support have sought to erode the undesirable provisions of the Treaty and invoked the strategy of regional balance to contain Indian pressures and ensure regime security.[9] King Birendra's "Zone of Peace" proposal has already been discussed as an innovative foreign policy move of Nepal in this respect.

Nepal's regional balance strategy to contain pressures from India has been driven by its concerns for greater freedom in the matters of trade and transit, its inability and unwillingness to accommodate India's security demands and ensuring regime security and internal political independence. This can be illustrated by looking somewhat closely at three of the major recent developments that precipitated crises in Nepal-India relations and witnessed the operation of Nepal's regional balance strategy. These developments were Nepal's first *Jan-Andolan* (Peoples' Movement, 1989-90), the second *Jan-Andolan* (Peoples' Movement 2005-2006) and the regional balance strategy of Republican Nepal.

The First *Jan-Andolan (1989-90)*

The first *Jan-Andolan* was formally launched in February 1990 as a Movement for Restoration of Democracy (MRD) with the joint efforts of the Nepali Congress (NC) and a coalition of left forces, the United Left Front, forged under the leadership of Smt. Sahana Pradhan, the wife of the founder of Communist Party of Nepal, late Pushpalal Shreshtha. The objective was to force Nepal's absolute Monarchy to become constitutional Monarchy under a multi-party parliamentary democratic system. The movement attained its objective in April 1990, when 28 years old Partyless Panchayat System was eliminated.

MRD had been launched in the background of strained India Nepal relations. These strains were triggered from the coldness which had been prevailing between the two countries regarding King Birendra's pursuance of the Zone of Peace proposal and attempts to erode the provisions of the Treaty of 1950. In order to show its resentment against India, Nepal had also raised questions against India's intervention in Sri Lanka's ethnic conflict during 1987.[10] On June 05, 1987, Nepal deplored air dropping of supplies by India for the beleaguered Tamil population in Sri Lanka's Jaffna province. Then using this as an excuse, Nepal bought anti-aircraft guns, along with AK-47 and small fire arms from China ostensibly for defending Kathmandu against any similar intrusion by India. This was in violation of the provisions and spirit of 1950 Treaty. India's Minister of State K. Natwar Singh visited Nepal to protest against this move but in vain.[11] With the question of 1950-Treaty, dispute on trade relations also got added. The bilateral Treaty of Trade and Transit was to expire in March 1989. A new "package" for a new Treaty which envisaged a unified trade and transit Treaty was worked out and initialled by both sides in October 1988. Nepal however refused to work according to this understanding and became disinterested in negotiating and signing the new unified Treaty. As a result, India's Rajiv Gandhi government withdrew all the special provisions for the flow of trade between the two countries when the Treaty lapsed, resulting in severe difficulties for common Nepalese.[12]

The Nepalese government called India's action as an "economic blockade" and mobilised international support for putting pressure on India. Nepal also, in April 1989 imposed work permits on Indians working in Nepal as a retaliatory measure which further hardened India's position. It sought to mobilise domestic protests and resistance against the Indian action by raising the question of nationalism, sovereignty and non-interference. The King's objective was also to use this mobilisation to defeat the MRD that was gathering momentum. This proved counterproductive after marginal success. People held the King's regime responsible for the difficulties of common people for its failure in concluding the Trade Treaty in time, and joined the MRD in larger numbers. So far as international support was concerned, China's support did not matter much in Nepal's domestic political developments. International community, particularly the Western nations led by the US had sympathies for the King's regime against India's "economic blockade", but there were no international provisions under GATT or MFN where India had faulted and which could be invoked to put pressure on India. Moreover, the US and its European allies were hesitant in supporting the King's regime as in the internal struggle, as that was for the restoration of democracy dear to all these countries.

Nepal's actions on India's intervention in Sri Lanka, purchase of arms from China, imposition of work permit on foreign/ Indian workers and whipping up of anti-Indian nationalism further displeased India. In spite of its hard posture on trade and transit issue, informal and active support for the MRD came from India. In the international conference called by the

NC in Kathmandu in January 1990 where MRD was formally launched, nine members of Indian Parliament, including a national leader of Chandra Shekhar's stature (who soon became India's next Prime Minister) participated. There were also a number of other foreign representatives to attend this conference. In his address at the NC conference, Chandra Shekhar was reported to have said:

> As a neighbour, we have a vital interest in what happens in Nepal. We cannot forget that B.P. Koirala had fought the British imperialism and suffered imprisonment for our independence. It is natural therefore, that the sympathies of Indian people are with B.P. Koirala and with the people of Nepal now fighting for the restoration of their democratic rights and liberties.[13]

It may be noted here that in Novemebr 1989, Rajiv Gandhi's government, that imposed "economic blockade" on Nepal, had been defeated in India and the new government headed by V.P. Singh had promised not to interfere in Nepal's affairs and normalise trade and other relations soon. But this government could not stop Chandra Shekhar and other political activists and media from supporting the MRD in Nepal. Not only this, when eventually the King was forced to concede the MRD demands and eliminate the Panchayat System in April 1990, New Delhi welcomed the change. Then Foreign Minister of the V.P. Government, Sh I.K. Gujral made a statement in Indian Parliament on April 9, 1990, saying:

> The winds of liberalisation, freedom and democracy have been blowing across our planet. India is a democracy and our people are committed to democratic values. We are full of hope and faith in the aspirations of our Nepalese brethren for a liberal and truly democratic polity. There has been an arduous struggle, under a courageous and united leadership. It has borne fruit. In securing these political changes, the people of Nepal have opened a new chapter in the history of their land. The chapter must be full of promise, the beginning of a new dawn of peace, progress and national reconciliation.

In his application of foreign policy strategy of regional balance for ensuring regime security, King Birendra was inspired by his father King Mahendra who succeeded in containing Indian pressures during the 1960s. However, King Birendra could not achieve what he wanted as the Panchayat System had to be removed and defence ties with China curtailed. There were a number of factors behind King Birendra's failure. The credibility of the royal regime, particularly the façade of Panchayat System had been considerably eroded over the years. The opposition looked far more united, with both the NC and the left forces getting together, and confident, and waged their MRD struggle peacefully from within Nepal, without seeking sanctuaries in India. India-China equation was no longer of active hostility as during the early sixties. Both the countries were moving towards normalising their relations following the return of Indian Ambassador in Beijing since 1978 and Rajiv Gandhi's successful visit to China in December 1988. And above all, India was far from feeling as vulnerable in its security as in the aftermath of military humiliation at China's hands. The emergence of Bangladesh in 1971, integration of Sikkim in 1975, nuclear explosion, nay implosion, in 1974 and a reassuring military skirmish with China in the Sumdorong Chu valley in Arunachal Pradesh region in 1987 had helped India regain some of its regional self-confidence. King Birendra, nevertheless, managed to do some damage control after his unsuccessful regional balance approach. He succeeded in keeping Monarchy's position critically central to Nepal's power structure in the new post-Panchayat constitution. This constitution also denied easy harnessing of Nepal's natural resources like hydro-power by making 2/3 parliamentary approval necessary for any such international agreement or treaty. India was to be affected adversely most by such provision.

The Second *Jan Andolan (2005-2006)*

The next test for Nepal's regional balance came during the second *Jan Andolan* which emerged in the context of Maoist insurgency raging since 1996.[14] There is considerable credible literature available on this development.[15] The conditions for *Jan Andolan-II* started building up soon after one of the most unusual event of Palace Massacre in June 2001, in which King Birendra and his entire family was eliminated. This led to his brother Gyanendra assuming Kingship on the pattern of the Ranas where succession line flowed from one brother to another. The new King dissolved elected parliament on May 22, 2002 and from October 2002, onwards, started ruling through personally chosen Prime Ministers. To protest against the King's arbitrary action, the NC and the mainstream left parties gradually came together under *Jan Andolan*-II. To deal with the uniting opposition, King Gyanendra assumed direct power on February 01, 2005 by imposing emergency and arresting all the mainstream party leaders. The King tried to justify his action for fighting Maoist terrorism. The king's move further reinforced opposition unity and the *Jan Andolan-II,* bringing subsequently the Maoists also in anti-Monarchy united front. Eventually following massive demonstrations of popular unity in Kathmandu and throughout Nepal from April 6-21, 2006, the King had to concede the demands of the *Jan Andolan-II,* paving way for an elected Constituent Assembly, elimination of Monarchy and establishment of a Republican Nepal.

India strongly opposed King Gyanendra's takeover of direct power in February 2005, as it was seen to be in violation of India's clearly stated "two pillar" policy since 1990, of supporting parliamentary democracy under constitutional monarchy. With reference to the dissolution of parliament in 2002 and ruling Nepal through nominated cabinets by King Gyanendra, Foreign Minister of India Natwar Singh voiced strong objections and India's Ambassador Shyam Saran said in Kathmandu on August 13, 2003, "The peace process in Nepal cannot succeed without the involvement of the political parties...Constitutional Monarchy and multi-party democracy are the two pillars for peace and political stability of Nepal".[16] There were strong apprehensions in India that King Gyanendra, since his assumption of power, was moving towards the revival of the discarded Panchayat System as the King, soon after taking over, had appointed diehard Panchayat leaders to assist him and also sounded the Indian leadership for support in letting him have a free hand in dealing with Nepali political parties and the Maoists insurgency.[17] In various interactions, India clearly expressed its apprehensions to the Nepali side. On the lines of its reaction to King Mahedra's take over in December 1960, India's response to King Gyanendra was to revoke emergency, give up direct role, cooperate with mainstream political parties and then deal with the Maoists, preferably peacefully.[18] Indian assessment was that Nepal's security forces would not be able to control the Maoists militarily. In support of its stand, India kept in touch with and allowed its territory to be used by the Nepali opposition, including the Maoists, to coordinate their mutual efforts, restrain (stop-start-stop) supply of its weapons to the royal regime and tried to persuade other nations, including China, US and UK, not to endorse or support the King's autocratic move.

Nepal's strategy of regional balance for regime security was put in operation to counter Indian pressures. There were two broad dimensions of this approach; one was to keep India engaged and the second to mobilise international support from whatever sources available to counter Indian pressures. India was kept engaged through a number of formal and informal emissaries sent from Kathmandu to New Delhi, as also by keeping direct personal contacts with Indian leaders and decision makers at various levels. Some of the most important personal contacts took place between Indian Prime Minister Dr. Man Mohan Singh and King Gyanendra of Nepal. Two of these meetings were important, one in Jakarta on April 23, 2005, on the side lines of Afro-Asia Commemorative Summit and another in Dhaka, on November 14, 2005, on the side lines of SAARC summit.

At both these meetings, the Indian leader insisted on the King to move fast in restoring democratic process in Nepal. In both these meetings, King Gyanendra tried to assure the Indian leader of his commitment to democracy and promised to move in the desired direction. This was however not done. The King kept on fudging the issue of cooperating with the democratic leaders, first by lifting emergency in April without removing restrictions on rights and freedoms. Then he announced elections at municipal levels for 2006 and parliamentary levels in 2007. The King was also willing to accommodate India's economic interests in Nepal such as the case of United Telecommunications Ltd.[19] He, however, made no move towards either leaving his direct control over the state or cooperating with the political leaders. This alienated India and resulted in the *Jan Andolan-II* agitations that forced the king to compromise. India in November, 2005 facilitated a Twelve Point understanding between the mainstream parties and the Maoists to jointly launch the anti-King agitations. Even after signing of the Twelve Point understanding and the decision to launch the agitations, India organised a secret visit by the King's foreign minister Ramesh Nath Pandey in December 2005, to send a stern message to the King for the last time, but in vain.[20]

In mobilising external support, the King directly monitored relations with the US and China. The biggest success was naturally achieved by him in relation to China which was willing not only in supplying arms to the King's regime but also shared Nepal's concerns about pressures from India on its independence and sovereignty. China criticised the Maoists for wrongly using

Chairman Mao's name. During Foreign Minister King Gyanendra's visit to China in August 2005, China offered support for Nepal's candidacy for the non-permanent UNSC membership and offered cash budgetary support as desired by Nepal. Nepal's aspiration to become the transit trade point between India and China was also endorsed by China. In return, the Chinese were keen that Nepal helped them "deter international conspiracies against China" and helped them in stabilising Tibet. From the Chinese side, Foreign Minister Li Zhao Xing visited Nepal in April 2005. Assuring support to the King's moves he said:

We respect and would like to help the Nepalese have their own way in their nation's specific political development... Nepalese people have full authority to take their own decisions regarding their internal politics and development.[21]

In this visit, China also conveyed to Nepal not to allow military presence to the US for arming and training Nepal army in fighting the Maoists, as there were reports to that effect.[22]Another important visit from China to Nepal was of the CPC's State Councillor Tang Jiaxuan in January 2006, who reiterated China's support for Nepal's internal independence while assessing the situation unfolding in the context of *Jan Andolan-II*. Nepal tried to keep Chinese support a low key affair as that was not acceptable to US and European countries along with India.

Nepal's efforts to secure US support were only partially successful. The US endorsed the King's initial 100 day road map for controlling the Maoists insurgency, improving security situation and then reopening democratic process. US supplied about 5000 Belgium guns to Nepal and an Amnesty International report gave details of Nepal securing arms from UK, South Africa and France.[23] Nepal also managed to get arms and political support from Russia and Pakistan.[24] It may be kept in mind that Indo-US relations were getting close by this time and there was a reasonably effective coordination between them on Nepal barring some nuances. The US had also sounded Nepal on supplying troops to support American war in Iraq. Though Nepal responded favourably to such soundings but could not really send troops in view of domestic concerns and resistance from countries like India. UK and the European countries were also strongly committed to the question of democracy and human rights in Nepal and were willing to go along with India that the King must not prolong his autocratic control of the state any longer. All these countries knew that the Royal Nepal Army was not capable of meeting the Maoist challenge, that any military approach would result in greater human rights violations and therefore, political approach was the only desirable course to be pursued. Unfortunately King Gyanendra failed to grasp this message and had to suffer political humiliation.

Regional Balance under Republican Nepal

India's critical role in facilitating the success of *Jan Andolan-II* was widely appreciated by all the major political players; the NC, Other mainstream parties (clubbed in Seven Party Alliance), the Maoists, the Nepali civil society and the people at large. Only King was unhappy with India. In view of the goodwill earned by India and the major political transformation in Nepal, there were hopes that India-Nepal relations would now be cast in an enduring and positively cooperative dynamics. This however did not happen. Both, Nepal's internal developments as well as serious flaws in India's approach were responsible for this failure.

Domestically, the coalition of forces that brought the *Jan Andolan-II* to its successful culmination soon started getting fragmented. The national popular ideological consensus to build a "New Nepal" on the basis of republican and inclusive democratic polity proved to be only rhetorical and fragile. It seems that the Maoists and the mainstream parties had joined hands with different goals in mind, otherwise wrapped up in the agenda of "New Nepal". The Maoists wanted to build their "peoples" new democracy and the traditional mainstream parties were content to tame an "absolutist" monarchy. Both were driven by strong desire to assume power and control the Nepali state. In their struggle for power, the Nepali political parties and leaders replaced the King with India's blessings and support. With tthe breakdow national political consensus became clear as soon as the first Constituent Assembly was elected in 2008; giving the Maoists an impressive victory but clearly short of dominance. Under these competitive drives for power, this Constituent Assembly could neither deliver a constitution, nor provide stable and effective governance. Nepal got its first popular constitution in September 2015, under the second Constituent Assembly elected in November 2013. The electoral verdict still being fragmented and the competitive drives for assuming unchallenged power still shaping Nepal's political agenda, stable and effective governance looks like a distant dream.

India also seemed not seriously committed to the idea of a "New Nepal" and was happy only to get rid of an obstinate and uncooperative Monarchy. The rise of the Maoists in 2008 Constituent Assembly elections came as a shock to India and a large section of international community. While it was not possible to block Maoists from assuming power under democratic norms, India strived to strengthen other constitutional and political institutions in Nepal like the Army and the President to ensure balance in domestic political structure of Nepal. As a consequence of its growing involvement in domestic political equations in Nepal, India also could be blamed for indulging in undue interference, political fragmentation, micromanagement of political developments and delay in drafting of the constitution by the first Constituent Assembly.[25] The result was a great loss in the goodwill earned by India. Lack of high level political visits from India, absence of any major developmental projects and delays in delivering on the promises of economic assistance precipitated considerable alienation between Nepal and India. India's new Prime Minister Narendra Modi who assumed office in May 2014 tried his best to undo this alienation. He visited Nepal twice in August and November 2014, established a personal rapport with the diverse sections of political elite as well as people at large and promised to make India close and dependable partner in Nepal's development. India also came forward with prompt and generous assistance to help Nepal meet the consequences of severe earth quake in May 2015. All these efforts were however washed out by India's strong and negative reaction to Nepal's new Constitution.

India's official policy and its Prime Minister Modi repeatedly urged upon Nepal to take on board all the stakeholders and important social group so as to draft a broad based constitution acceptable to everyone in Nepal. Nepal's constitutional process, however, marginalised Madhes and Janjati groups and produced a Constitution that was rejected by these groups. The Madhesis in particular agitated against Constitution which was found by them to be heavily tilted in favour of the hill upper caste groups. In this anti-Constitution agitation, the Madhes parties blocked the supply of goods being traded between India and Nepal, causing unprecedented hardships to the people of Nepal. India backed the Madhesi agitation and informally restricted the supplies of essential goods like fuel and food for nearly five months to put pressure on Nepali leaders. India also encouraged other countries to urge upon Nepal to ensure a broad-based and widely acceptable constitution. Nepal called India's action as an economic blockade and questioned uncalled for interference in its domestic affairs giving rise to strong anti-Indian feeling in Nepal.[26] Efforts were made to normalise the strained bilateral relations through high level visits of Nepal's Prime Minister in February 2016 and President in May 2016. Nepal was forced to amend its constitution to address Madhes demands. However all Madhes demands were not addressed nor scars in bilateral relations between India and Nepal were fully healed.

The fragmented *Jan Andolan-II* national political consensus drove a wedge between the Maoists and the Nepali Congress and pushed the former closer to the other communist groups, specially the Communist Party of Nepal-United Marxist Leninist (UML). In foreign policy, India's approach towards Nepal alienated the latter and drove it closer to China. As China was already looking opportunities to expand its presence in Nepal in the post-*Jan Andolan-II* period, as a part of its overall economic and strategic push into South Asia, Sino-Nepalese relations started improving fast. China made impressive infrastructure development proposals of constructing airport in Pokhara, linking Nepal with Tibetan rail and road network and helping Nepal harness its hydro-power potential.[27] There was also noticeable increase in important political Chinese visits to Nepal and the visits of the Nepali leaders of different parties to China. Concessions were offered to Nepal in trade, scholarships were increased and large number of China studies Centres were opened in areas of Nepal's borders with India.[28]

Nepal's Republican government, having a new constitution, sought to activate Nepal's regional balance strategy under Prime Minister K.P. Oli's leadership to counter Indian pressures on Madhesi demands and their constitutional accommodation. International support was sought by projecting Nepal's new constitution as the most democratically adopted and having extensive rights for the citizens. The constitution was also projected as the most inclusive of marginalised social groups. India's approach was strongly criticised and questioned even through the United Nations. Nepali diaspora was encouraged to organise protest demonstrations against Prime Minister Modi during his foreign visits. Prime Minister Oli not only threatened to visit China on his first foreign trip, flouting the usual norms of Nepali Prime Ministers first visiting India, but oil and other essential supplies were also arranged from China and through third countries. During his visit to China in March 2016, Prime

Minister Oli also concluded extensive agreements of economic cooperation including transit rights through China. In all ten agreements/understandings were signed between the two countries covering infrastructure projects, trade and financial credits.[29] Though the implementation of these projects will involve huge costs and take considerable time, the agreements were widely hailed in Nepal as a strong cushion against future Indian pressures and as creating an alternative to its heavy dependence upon India.

The enthusiasm aroused by the outcome of Prime Minister Oli's China visit in the context of pressures felt from India have considerably revived the hopes of Nepal to emerge as a link between India and China. The idea of being a link was inherent in Nepal's traditional role as a trade-entrepot between India and Tibet. This role was lost with the military takeover of Tibet by China in 1951, followed by Sino-Indian hostilities and conflict of 1962. Nepali Kings have periodically expressed the sentiment of becoming a link but regional dynamics did not leave much scope. We have noted earlier that in 2005, King Gyanendra's foreign minister Ramesh Nath Pandey conveyed this sentiment to the Chinese when he proposed that Nepal be a transit point between India and China. In the post-Monarchy period, the idea has been more actively articulated by the Maoist Prime Ministers. While the Maoist supremo Prachanda envisaged Nepal's role between India and China in strategic and developmental terms, Baburam Bhattarai articulated it strongly in economic terms. In his very first address to the Constituent Assembly as Prime Minister, Bhattarai said that Nepal was no longer a buffer between India and China but was a "friendship bridge". Acknowledging that it is in Nepal's interest to gain from Asia's two fast growing economies, Nepal would not be a "barricade" but a "bridge" between them.[30] Prime Minister Oli also expressed similar sentiments during his visit to China in March 2016.

In view of its geostrategic and economic initiatives in South Asia, China is both willing and capable of linking Nepal with its "Belt Road Initiative". Nepal's access to Chinese built infrastructure connectivity may then provide Nepal access to Central Asia and even Europe in the long run. If and when India joins this Chinese connectivity network, Nepal's "bridge" role may become a reality. However, India has strong reservations with regard to the Chinese initiative and does not seem to have made up its mind on how to respond to China's "Belt

Road Initiative". Accordingly, Nepal's vision of becoming a link between India and China looks more theoretical in view of the challenges inherent.[31] To begin with, as noted earlier, building of the infrastructure connectivity and linking Nepal with it is still far away in time and expenses. One of the most essential precondition in this regard is political stability in Nepal and a robust national consensus, sans different political parties and possible ruling coalitions, to pursue the "bridge" objective in a determined and sincere manner. Nepal will also have to ensure that its proposed "bridge" role in the developmental context remains cautious and scrupulously avoids offending strategic sensitivities of India and China. This would be a formidable challenge because strategic underpinnings of the Chinese initiative are inevitable and strategic competition in the Asian region, including South Asia is more likely to intensify involving China, India and also the US. It remains to be seen as to how will Nepal cope with such a competition not only in crafting its strategy of regional balance but also in pursuing overall objectives of its foreign policy.

Notes

1. Dhruv Adhikari, "Maoist Nepal to end Gurkha tradition", Asia Times, January 20, 2015
2. See for instance, Maskey, Bishwa Kesher and Dahal Dev Raj (Eds.) "Nepal's Participation in the United Nations Peacekeeping Operations: Report of the Round Table", UN Association of Nepal, Kathmandu 1995. Rajan Bhattarai, "Peace Keeping Contributor Profile: Nepal", Nepal Institute for Policy Studies, Kathmandu, 2013.
3. Ramesh Nath Pandey, Kootniti Ra Rajniti: Atmakatha (Diplomacy and Politics: Autobiography), Sangri-la Books, Kathmandu 2015, pp.612-624.
4. Ibid, p. 698.
5. Himalayan Times, Kathmandu, September 14, 2015; Hindustan Times, New Delhi, November 15, 2015.
6. Mohna Ansari, "Human Wrongs", Kathmandu Post, Kathmandu, April 12, 2016.
7. See Prime Minister Oli's address to the Nation on the Nepali New Year on April 12, 2016. Paras 13 and 14th of the text.
8. Ramesh Nath Pandey, op.cit, pp. 650-670.
9. The erosion of the Treaty of 1950 from India's perspective has been discussed in S.D. Muni, India and Nepal: A Changing Relationship, Konark Publishers, New Delhi 1996, See Chapter 3., pp. 32-62.

10. Avtar Singh Bhasin (Ed), Nepal-India, Nepal-China relations: Documents 1947-June 2005, Published in Cooperation with the XP Division, Ministry of External Affairs, Government of India, New Delhi, 2007, p. 752.
11. Arvind Dev, "Prelude to Nepal's First Jan Andolan", Oral History Section, Indian Foreign Affairs Journal, Vol. 3, No. 4, October-December 2008, pp. 107-119. Also see, Shailendra Kumar Upadhyaya, Tryst With Destiny, New Delhi 1991, p. 76, Sangeeta Thapliyal, Mutual Security: The case of India-Nepal, Lancer Publishers and Distributors, New Delhi 1998, p. 134.
12. India's External Affairs Minister P.V. Narasimha Rao gave a detailed statement on the crisis in India-Nepal trade relations in Indian parliament on April 26, 1989.
13. As quoted in D.P. Kumar, Nepal: Year of Decision, Vikas Publishing House, New Delhi, 1980, p. 26.
14. Mahendra Laowti and Anup K. Pahari (Eds.) The Maoist Insurgency in Nepal: Revolution in the Twenty-first Century, Routledge, New York, 2010. Michael Hutt (Ed.) Himalayan People's War: Nepal's Maoist Rebellion, Indiana University Press, Bloomington, USA, 2004. S.D. Muni, Maoist Insurgency in Nepal: The Challenge and the Response, Rupa & Co., New Delhi, 2003.
15. See for instance studies by Prashant Jha, The Battles of the New Republic: A Contemporary History of Nepal, Aleph Book Company, New Delhi 2014. Sudheer Sharma, Prayogshala: Nepali Sankraman Ma Dilli Durbar Re Maovadi (Laboratory: Role of New Delhi, The Palace and the Maoists), Fineprint Publishers, Kathmandu, 2014. See the author's Chapter (No.12) in Sebastian von Einsiedel, David Malone, Suman Pradhan (Eds.) Nepal in Transition: From People's War to Fragile Peace, Cambridge University Press, 2012.
16. Bhasin, op.cit, p. 1193.
17. Sudheer Sharma, p. 122.
18. The details of India's role in the Nepali crisis have been discussed elsewhere, Sudheer Sharma, op.cit. S.D. Muni, in Nepal in Transition...op.cit. Also see, Sandra Destradi, "A Regional Power Promoting Democracy? India's Involvement in Nepal (2005-2008)", CIGA Research Unit, Working Paper No. 138, June 2010.
19. Ramesh Nath Pandey, op.cit, pp.591-92.
20. Ibid, p.606.
21. As quoted in Dr. Pushpa Adhikari, China: Threat in South Asia, Lancer International, US, Frankfort and New Delhi, 2012, p. 115.
22. Ibid.
23. Amnesty International, Press Release, 15 June 2005.
24. Ramesh Nath Pandey, Op.cit, p. 691-692; 698.
25. Based on author's close and informal interactions with the key players and policy makers both in Kathmandu and New Delhi.

Also see Sudheer Sharma, Reports of the International Crisis Group (ICG) on Nepal, particularly No. 120, 173, 194, 211, 233, 234 and 276. V R Raghavan (Ed.) Internal Conflict in Nepal: Transnational Consequences, Vij Books India Pvt. Ltd., New Delhi, 2011.

26. Issues involved have been widely discussed in Indian and Nepali media. Also see S.D. Muni, "Nepal's New Constitution", Economic and Political Weekly, Vol. 50, No. 40, October 03, 2015. Deepak Thapa, " State of Siege", Kathmandu Post, October 08, 2015. Mani Shankar Aiyer, "A Modi-Made Disaster Hits Nepal", NDTV Blog, December 07, 2015. Rakesh Sood, "Nepal: Finding A Way Forward", Observer Research Foundation, New Delhi, January 2016.
27. Swaran Singh, China-South Asia: Issues, Equations, Policies, Lancer Books, New Delhi, 2003. Ranade Jayadeva, China Unveiled: Insights Into Chinese Strategic Thinking, Knowledge World, New Delhi, 2013. Pushpa Adhikari, Ties That Bind An Account of Nepal-China Relations, Sangam Institute, Kathmandu, 2010. Nihar Nayak, Strategic Himalayas: Republican Nepal and External Powers, IDSA; Pentagon Press, New Delhi 2014, See specially Chapter 4, "China in Nepal: From Political to Strategic Engagement', pp. 75-109.
28. Jigme Yeshe Lama, "China and its Periphery: Securing Nepal in South Asia", IPCS Issue brief No. 232, Institute of Peace and Conflict Studies, New Delhi, August 2013.
29. Himalayan Times, Kathmandu, March 21, 2016; Kathmandu Post, Kathmandu, March 22, 2016; Economic Times, new Delhi, March 21, 2016; The Hindu, New Delhi, March 22, 2016.
30. See the Maoist Chief Prachanda's interview in Kantipur, Kathmandu, November, 11, 2010. For Baburam's statements, see Kathmandu Post, Kathmandu, September 16, 2011, and August 28, 2012.
31. For a discussion on some of the issues involved, see Pramed Jaiswal and Geeta Kochhar (eds.), India-China Nepal: Decoding Trilateralism, GB Books, New Delhi, 2016.

ANNEXURE IA

UNDER customary international law and practice and under the constitution and laws of India His Majesty's Government of Nepal are empowered to ask the Government of India to take the following preventive measures in order to stop and eradicate the armed raids, loot, arson and murder carried out in the southern districts of Nepal by anti-national elements from their base in India;

(i) (a) Promptly liquidate their organization in India;

(b) Confine them to a particular place and carefully watch their movements. Prevent them from indulging in anti-Nepal political activities;

(c) Under the Indian Foreigners' Act to deport those against whom His Majesty's Government of Nepal can furnish prima facie evidences of anti-Nepal activities;

(d) Under the Preventive Detention Act to arrest and detain those against whom the Government of Nepal can supply evidence that they have been aiding and abetting persons to commit acts of sabotage and subversion in Nepal from their haven in India.

(e) Request the Government of India to issue necessary instructions to the State Governments to pass on orders to the district magistrates and border check-posts to co-operate with their Nepalese counterparts to apprehend the hostiles when chased by the Nepalese Army or Police or in the alternative to allow the Nepalese army or police to enter India in the course of hot pursuit of the hostiles.

In India executive branch can fulfil these international obligations without intervention from the judicial organs of the state. Even without requisition made by His Majesty's Government of Nepal to apprehend the fugitives the constitution and municipal laws of India enable the Government of India sui sponte to implement her international obligation,

(ii) If genuine difference of opinion on factual circumstances exist such cases might he submitted to a Mixed Tribunal composed of one *Nepal as a Zone of Peace* representative each from the two countries and the presiding judge from a third country or a nominee of the International Court of Justice or of any recognized international organization.

Source: Hostile Expeditions and International Law, published by the Department of Publicity and Broadcasting, Ministry of National Guidance, HMG, pp. 60-62.

ANNEXURE IB

The term "Hostile Activity" which is considered as an action short of war, generally means any threat or use of force against the territorial integrity or political independence of any state or in any other manner inconsistent with the purposes of the U.N. and this term includes the following actions;

(a) any act of aggression;

(b) any propaganda for aggression;

(c) any violation of existing international boundaries of another state or use of force to solve territorial or other disputes;

(d) acts of reprisals involving the use of force;

(e) acts of organising or encouraging the organisation of irregular forces or armed bands, including mercinaries, for incursion into the territory of another state;

(f) acts of organising, instigating, or participating in acts of civil strife or terrorist acts in another state or acquiescing in organised activities within its territory directed towards the commission of such acts, when the acts referred to in this paragraph involve a threat or use of force;

(g) acts of military occupation or acquisition of any territory from the threat or use of force;

(h) any act of intervention, directly or indirectly, for any reason, whatever, in the internal or external affairs of any other state;

(i) armed intervention and all other forms of interference or attempted threats against the personality of other state or against its political, economic and cultural elements;

(j) any use or encouragement on the use of economic, political or any other type of measures to coerce another state in order to obtain from it the subordination of the exercise of its sovereign rights and to secure from it advantages of any kinds;

(k) any act to organise, assist, foment, finance, incite or tolerate subversive, terrorist, or armed activities directed towards the violent overthrow of the regime of another state or to interfere incivil strife in another state;

(l) any use of force to deprive nationals of another state or aliens of their national identity;

(m) any interference in another state's right to choose its political, economic, social and cultural systems;

(n) any action aimed at the partial or total disruption of the national unity and territorial integrity of any other state.

Source-. Bishwa Pradhan, *Nepal: A Peace Zone* (Kathmandu, 1982), pp. 29-30.

APPENDICES

Appendix I

A Fact Sheet of Nepal's Diplomatic Relations, 1951-71

S.No.	Name of the country Relations	Date of Establishment of Nepal's Diplomatic in Nepal	Important Treaties and Agreements Mission	Important exchange of visits lomatic Mission	Residen-tial Dip-Diplomatic	Nepalese residential	Remarks
1	2	3	4	5	6	7	8
1.	The United Kingdom Renewed in	Since 1816 uitment for the October 1950	(i) Agreement, Gurkha recr- British Army (1885, renewed in November 1947). (ii) Treaty, Friendship Peace Peace (October 1950). (iii) Army aid (1964). (iv) Agreements, Aid.	(i) King Mahendra's visit to Britain (October 1960). (ii) Queen Elizabeth's visit to Nepal (February 1961). (iii) Chairman Dr. Tulsi Giri's visit to Britain (October 1963)	Yes	Yes	
2.	India	August 1947	(i) Agreement, Gurkha recruitment for the Indian army (ii) Treaty, Peace and Friendship (July 1950). (iii) Treaty, Trade and Transit (September 1950 revised in October 1960, renewed in August 1971). (iv) Treaty, Extradition of Criminals Agreement (1953).	See Appendix IA(A).	Yes	Yes	

1	2	3	4	5	6	7	8
			(v) Agreement, Arms purchase (1955). (vi) Agreements, Aid and Cultural Exchanges.				
3.	The United States of America	April 1947	(i) Agreement, Friendship and Commerce (April 1947). (ii) Agreement for American Investment protection (1960).	(i) King Mahendra's visits to the USA (April 1960 and November 1967) (ii) Chairman Dr. Tulsi Giri's visit to the USA (September 1963). (iii) U.S. Vice-President Sprio Agnew's visit to Nepal (January 1970)	Yes	Yes	Nepalese
4.	France	May 1949		(i) Chairman Dr. Tulsi Giri's visit to France (October 1963). (ii) Foreign Minister K.N. Bista's visit to France (October 1964). (iv) Foreign Minister G.B. Rajbhandari's visit to France (September 1963).	—	—	—

1	2	3	4	5	6	7	8
5.	China	July 1955	(i) Agreement, Trade, Intercourse and Friendly Relations (September 1956) (ii) Agreement, The Question of Boundary (March 1960) (iii) Treaty, Peace and Friendship (April 1960). (iv) Treaty, The Question of Boundary (October 1961)	See Appendix IA(B).	Yes	Yes	—
6.	Japan	July 1956	Agreements, Aid (October 1956).	(i) Prime Minister T.P. Acharya's visit to Japan	Yes	— February 1968.	Opened in Katu in
				(ii) King Mahendra's visit to Japan (April 1960). (iii) Japanese Crown Prince and princes' visit to Nepal (December 1960). (iv) King Mahendra's visit to Japan (March-April 1970).	—	Yes	—

1	2	3	4	5	6	7	8
7.	The USSR	July 1956	(i) Trade Agreement (August 1965) (ii) Agreements Aid and Cultural and Scientific exchange.	(i) King Mahendra's visit to the USSR (June 1958) (ii) President Voroshilov's visit to Nepal (February 1960). (iii) Chairman Dr. Tulsi Giri's visit to the USSR (October 1963) (iv) Foreign Minister G.B. Rajbhandari's visit to the USSR (September 1969). (v) King Mahendra's visit to the USSR (June 1971).	Yes	Yes	The Nepalese Prime Minister B.P. Koirala and the Soviet Premier N.S. Khrushchev had talks at the UN Headquarters, New York, (October 1960)
8.	Switzerland	November 1956 Upgraded to Ambassadorial level in 1960	Agreements, Aid Aid	—	Yes	Yes	Switzerland maintained a Swiss Technical Co-operation Mission in Nepal since 1949-50.
9.	Egypt (The UAR)	April 1957	—	—	Yes (headed by Change Affaires)	—	—

1	2	3	4	5	6	7	8
10.	Ceylon	July 1957	—	(i) King Mahendra's visit to Ceylon (March 1957).	—	—	—
11.	The West Germany	June 1957	Agreements, Aid	(i) King Mahendra's visit to West Germany (May 1964). (ii) K.N. Bista's visit to West Germany (November 1966). (iii) President Luebe's visit to Nepal (March 1967). (iv) Foreign Minister G.B. Rajbhandari's visit to West Germany (September 1969).	—	—	—
12.	Austria	August 1959	—	—	—	—	—
13.	Italy	August 1959	—	—	Yes	Yes	Nepalese Embassy in Rome was closed down w.e.f. September 1957 on account of economy measures.

1	2	3	4	5	6	7	8
14.	Yugoslavia	October 1950	(i) Agreement, Trade (September 1965).	(i) Chairman Dr. Tusi Giri's visit to Yugoslavia (October 1964). (ii) Premier Peter Stambolic's visit to Nepal (March 1966).	— —	— —	King Mahendra visited Belgrade in September 1961 to participate in the Non-aligned Summit Conference.
15.	Poland	November 1959	(i) Agreement, Trade and Payment, (August 1966)	—	—	—	—
16.	Thailand	November 1960	—	—	Yes (Headed	—	Diplomatic relation were upgraded from ministerial to ambassadorial level in May 1969.
17.	Czechoslovakia	January 1960	—	(i) Foreign Minister Milostav Huruzo's visit to Nepal (December 1971)	—	—	—
18.	Malayasia	January 1960	—	(i) Prime Minister Tunku Abdul Rehman's visit to Nepal (July 1968).	—	Yes	Nepal had a Consulate in Malayasia since 1947-48.

1	2	3	4	5	6	7	8
19.	Greece	February 1960	–	–	–	–	–
20.	Australia	February	–	(i) King Mahendra's visit to Australia (April 1971).	–	–	Relations were upgraded from Ministerial to Ambassadorial level.
21.	Philippines	February 1960	–	–	–	–	–
22.	Burma	March 1960	–	(i) Prime Minister B.P. Koirala's visit to Burma (March 1960).	Yes (headed by a Charge d'Affaires)	Yes	Nepal had a Consulate in Burma since 1948.
23.	Pakistan	March 1960	(i) Agreement, Trade (October 1962). (ii) Agreements, Aid and Cultural.	(i) King Mahendra's visit to Pakistan (September 1961). (ii) President Ayub's visit to Nepal (May 1963). (iii) Foreign Minister K.N. Bista's visit to Pakistan (January 1966). (iv) King Mahendra's informal visit to Pakistan (April 1967).	Yes	Yes	–

1	2	3	4	5	6	7	8
				(v) President Yhaya Khan's visit to Nepal (September 1970).			
24.	Tha Netherlands	April 1960	–	(i) King Mahendra's visit to Netherlands (April 1967)	–	–	
25.	Laos	May 1960	–	–	–	–	Relations were upgraded from Ministerial to Ambassadorial level in May 1969.
26.	Israel	June 1960	(i) Agreements, Aid	(i) Prime Minister B.P. Koirala's visit to Israel (August 1960). (ii) King Mahendra's visit to Israel (September 1963). (iii) President Shazar's visit to Nepal (March 1966).	Yes	–	–
27.	Sweden	June 1960	–	–	–	–	–
28.	Indonesia	December 1960	–	–	–	–	–
29.	Holland	December 1960	–	–	–	–	–

1	2	3	4	5	6	7	8
30.	Mongolia	January 1961	—	(i) King Mahendra's visit to Mongolia (October 1961)	—	—	—
31.	Hungary	January 1961	—	(i) Foreign Minister G.B. Rajbhandari's visit to Hungary (September 1969)	—	—	—
32.	New Zealand	May 1961	—	—	—	—	—
33.	Afghanistan	July 1961	—	(i) King Mohd. Zahir Shah's visit to Nepal (February 1969)	—	—	—
34.	Belgium	August 1963	—	—	—	—	—
35.	Lebanon	August 1963	—	—	—	—	—
36.	Iran	December 1964	—	—	—	—	—
37.	Canada	January 1966	—	—	—	—	—
38.	Argentina	September 1966	—	—	—	—	—
39.	Turkey	September 1966	—	—	—	—	—
40.	Jordan	September 1966	—	—	—	—	—
41.	Chile	September 1966	—	—	—	—	—
42.	Denmark	December 1967	—	—	—	—	—

1	2	3	4	5	6	7	8
43.	Bulgaria	April 1968	Terade and Payment Agreement on 8th October, 1969.	—	—	—	—
44.	Algeria	April 1968	—	—	—	—	—
45.	Spain	May 1968	—	—	—	—	—
46.	South Korea (Democratic People's Republic of Korea)	July 1969	—	—	—	—	—
47.	Ethiopia	—	—	—	—	—	—
48.	German Democratic Republic	—	—	—	—	—	—

Appendix IA

Nepal's Exchange of Visits with India and China*

S.No.	Name of the visiting dignitary	Date	Remarks
	(A) between Nepal and India**		
(i)	*Nepali Dignitaries Visiting India :*		
1.	Prime Minister Mohun Shumshere, JBR, Home Minister B.P. Koirala and Cabinet colleagues	8 to 15 May 1951	Discussed the composition of Cabinet with Indian leaders.
2.	Prime Minister B.P. Koirala	January 1952	
3.	King Tribhuwan, Foreign Minister D.R. Regmi and other Ministers	May 1954	Discussed foreign policy co-ordination.
4.	King Mahendra	6 November to 8 December 1955	
5.	Prime Minister tanka Prasad Acharya	4 to 7 December 1956	
6.	Prime Minister B.P. Koirala	17 to 31 January 1960	Joint Communique issued.
7.	Foreign Minister Dr. Tulsi Giri	19 to 22 January 1961	—
8.	Finance Minister Rishikesh Shah	28 December 1961	—
9.	King Mahendra	18 to 22 April 1962	Joint Communique issued.
10.	Foreign Minister Rishikesh Shah	6 to 11 September 1962	—
11.	Foreign Minister Dr. Tulsi Giri	8 to 11 December 1962	—
12.	King Mahendra	27 to 31 August 1963	Joint Communique issued.
13.	Foreign Minister K.N. Bista	24 January to 6 February 1965	-do-

S.No.	*Name of the visiting dignitary*	*Date*	*Remarks*
14.	King Mahendra	25 November to	--do- 20 December 1965
15.	Chairman Surya Bahadur Thapa	11 to 28 April 1966	-do-
16.	Defence Minister Burathoki	3 to 7 November 1966	—
17.	Foreign Minister G.B. Rajbhandari	2 to 7 May 1969	(Cut short due to President Zakir Husain's death).
18.	Foreign Minister G.B. Rajbhandari	21-24 August 1970	Information goodwill visit.
19.	King Mahendra	10 June 1971	(Informal visit, had very friendly talks with Mrs. Gandhi)
20.	King mahendra	10 to 12 November 1971	Informal.
(ii)	*Indian Dignitaries Visiting Nepal*		
1.	Prime Minister nehru	15 to 17 June 1951	—
2.	President Dr. Rajendra Prasad	21 to 24 October 1956	—
3.	Prime Minister Nehru	12 to 14 June 1959	Joint Communieque issued.
4.	Home Minister Lal Bahadur Shastri	4 to 6 March 1963	-do-
5.	President Dr. S. Radhakrishnan	4 to 8 November 1963	-do-
6.	Foreign Minister Swaran Singh	23 to 25 August 1964	-do-
7.	Prime Minister Lal bahadur Shastri	23 to 25 April 1965	-do-
8.	Prime Minister Mrs. Indira gandhi	4 to 7 October 1966	-do-
9.	Deputy prime Minister Morarji Desai	22 to 24 October 1967	-do-
10.	President Zakir Husain	12 to 16 October 1968	-do-

S.No.	*Name of the visiting dignitary*	*Date*	*Remarks*
11.	Foreign Minister Dinesh Singh	5 to 9 June 1969	-do-
12.	Maharashtra Chief Minister V.P. Naik	2 to 8 February 1970	(Informal visit. Met King Mahendra and Prime Minister K.N. Bista.)
13.	Foreign Minister Dinesh SIngh	4 to 8 February 1970	(Informal, met King Mahendra).
14.	President V.V. Giri	1 March 1970	To attend Crown Prince's Marriage.
15.	Foreign Minister Sardar Swaran Singh	3 to 5 September 1971	Joint Communique issued.
	(B) Between Nepal and China		
(i)	*Nepali Dignitaries Visiting China :*		
1.	Prime Minister Tanka Prasad Acharya	25 September to 7 October 1956	Joint Communique issued.
2.	Prime Minister B.P. Koirala	11 to 22 March 1960	(a) Joint Communique issued. (b) Boundary Agreement signed.
3.	King Mahendra 19 October 1961	26 September to	(a) Joint Communique issued.
4.	Foreign Minister Dr. Tulsi Giri	1 to 24 January 1963 (b) Protocol of the Boundary Treaty	(a) Joint Communique issued.
	signed.		
5.	Vice-Chairman Surya Bahadur Thapa	28 September to 7 October 1965	Joint Communique issued.
6.	Vice-Chairman K.N. Bista	24 Augusut to	-do- 7 September 1965
7.	Crown prince Birendra Bikram Shah	25 June to 13 July 1966	-do-

S.No.	*Name of the visiting dignitary*	*Date*	*Remarks*
8.	Foreign & Deputy Prime Minister K.N. Bista	22 May to 1 June 1968	Joint Comunique issued.
9.	Minister Rudra Prasad Giri	26 September 1969 (2 weeks)	—
10.	Princes Sharda Shah	May 1971 En-lai.	had friendly talks with Chou
(ii)	*Chinese Dignitaries Visiting Nepal :*		
1.	Prime Minister Chou En-lai	25 to 29 January 1957.	Joint Statement issued.
2.	Prime Minister Chou En-lai	26 to 28 April 1960	(a) Joint Communique issued. (b) Peace and Friendship Treaty signed.
3.	Vice-Premier Chen Yi	30 March to 3 April 1965	Joint Communique issued.
4.	Kuo Ma-jo, Vice-Chairman Standing Committee of the People's Congress.	1 to 9 March 1970	High level talks. A letter by Vice-President Ting-Pu.

Note: * Only the visits of political importance have been listed above.

** Before 1955, it was almost impossible to distinguish between an official, formal visit and an unofficial, informal visit between India and Nepal.

Appendix II

Actual Expenditure of HMG, Nepal, on Foreign Affairs and Defence, 1956-57 to 1967-68

(In Nepali Rupees, Thousands)

Years	*Foreign Affairs*	*Defence*
1956-57	1,634	9,597
1957-58*	15,034	14,154
1958-59	Not available	14,282
1959-60	2,833	14,501
1960-61	6,229	17,212
1961-62	4,925	17,515
1962-63**	6,939	23,508
1963-64	6,266	26,975
1964-65	7,400	27,495
1965-66	8,427	31,193
1966-67	7,610	39,946
1967-68**	9,4912	44,059
1968-69*	9,150	47,282
1969-70 (Estimated	10,915	50,055

* Figures for these years show Revised Estimates.

** Figures show Preliminary Actuals.

Source: tabulated from HMG, Nepal, Budgets, *Economic Data Papers*, Economic Planning Section, Program Office, US AID/Nepal, Vol. 9, No. 2, November

APPENDIX V

Treaty of "Peace and Friendship" between the Government of India and the Government of Nepal

The Government of India and the Government of Nepal recognising the ancient ties which have happily existed between the two countries for centuries;

Desiring still further to strengthen and develop these ties, and to perpetuate peace between the two countries;

Have resolved therefore to enter into a Treaty of Peace and Friendship with each other, and have, for this purpose, appointed as their plenipotentiaries the following persons, namely, THE GOVERNMENT OF INDIA, HIS EXCELLENCY SHRI CHANDRESHWAR PRASAD NARAIN SINGH, Ambassador of India in Nepal; THE GOVERNMENT OF NEPAL, MOHUN SHAMSHER JANG BAHADUR RANA, Maharaja, Prime Minister and Supreme-Commander-in-Chief of Nepal, who having examined each other's credentials and found them good and in due form have agreed as. follows :

ARTICLE 1

There shall be everlasting peace and friendship between, the Government of India and the Government of Nepal. The two Governments agree mutually to acknowledge and respect the complete sovereignty, territorial integrity and independence of each other.

ARTICLE 2

The two Governments hereby undertake to inform each other of any serious friction or misunderstanding with any neighbouring State likely to cause any breach in the friendly relations subsisting between the two Governments.

ARTICLE 3

In order to establish and maintain the relations referred to in Article 1 the two Governments agree to continue diplomatic relations with each other by means of representatives with such staff as is necessary for the due performance of their functions.

The representatives and such of their staff as may be agreed upon shall enjoy such diplomatic privileges and immunities as are customarily granted by international law on a reciprocal basis: Provided that in no case shall these be less than those granted to persons of a similar status of any other State having diplomatic relations with either Government.

ARTICLE 4

The two Governments agree to appoint Consuls-General, Consuls, Vice-Consuls and other consular agents, who shall reside in towns, ports and other places in each other's territory as may be agreed to.

Consuls-General, Consuls, Vice-Consuls and consular agents shall be provided with exequaturs or other valid authorization of their appointment. Such exequatur or authorization is liable to be withdrawn by the country which issued it, if considered necessary. The reasons for the withdrawal shall be indicated wherever possible.

The persons mentioned above shall enjoy on a reciprocal basis all the rights, privileges, exemptions and immunities that are accorded to persons of corresponding status of any other State.

ARTICLE 5

The Government of Nepal shall be free to import, from or through the territory of India, arms, ammunition or warlike material and equipment necessary for the security of Nepal. The procedure for giving effect to this arrangement shall be worked out by the two Governments acting in consultation.

ARTICLE 6

Each Government undertakes, in token of the neighbourly friendship between India and Nepal, to give to the nationals of the other, in its territory, national treatment with regard to participation in industrial and economic development of suchterritory and to the grant of concessions and contracts relating to such development.

ARTICLE 7

The Governments of India and Nepal agree to grant, on a reciprocal basis, to the nationals of one country in the territories of the other the same privileges in the matter of residence, ownership of property, participation in trade and commerce, movement and privileges of a similar nature.

ARTICLE 8

So far as matters dealt with herein are concerned, this Treaty cancels all previous treaties, agreements, and engagements entered into on behalf of India between the British Government and the Government of Nepal.

ARTICLE 9

This Treaty shall come into force from the date of signature by both Governments.

ARTICLE 10

The Treaty shall remain in force until it is terminated by either party by giving one year's notice.

Done in duplicate at Kathmandu this 31 st day of July, 1950.

(Sd.) CHANDRESHWAR PRASAD NARAIN SINGH
For the Government of India

(Sd.) MOHUN SHAMSHER JANG BAHADUR RANA
For the Government of Nepal

Letter exchanged with the Treaty

EXCELLENCY,

In the course of our discussion of the Treaties of Peace and Friendship and of Trade and Commerce which have been happily concluded between the Government of India and the Government of Nepal, we agreed that certain matters of details be regulated by an exchange of letters. In pursuance of this understanding, it is hereby agreed between the two Governments :

(1) Neither Government shall tolerate any threat to the security of the other by a foreign aggressor. To deal with any such threat, the two Governments shall consult with each other and devise effective counter-measures.

(2) Any arms, ammunition or warlike material and equipment necessary for the security of Nepal that the Government of Nepal may import through the territory of India shall be so imported with the *assistance and agreement* of the Government of India. The Government of India will take steps for the smooth and expeditious transport of such arms and ammunition through India.

(3) In regard to Article 6 of the Treaty of Peace and Friendship which provides for national treatment, the Government of India recognize that it may be necessary for some time to come to afford the Nepalese nationals in Nepal protection from unrestricted competition. The nature and extent to this protecon will be determined as and when required by mutual agreement between the two Governments.

(4) If the Government of Nepal should decide to seek foreign assistance in regard to the development of the natural resources of, or of any industrial project in Nepal, the Government of Nepal shall give first preference to the Government or the nationals of India, as the case may be, provided that the terms offered by the Government of India or Indian nationals, as the case may be, are not less favourable to Nepal than the terms offered by any other Foreign Government or by other foreign nationals. Nothing in the foregoing provision shall apply to assistance

that the Government of Nepal may seek from the United Nations Organisation or any of its specialized agencies, igs (5) Both Governments agree not to employ any foreigners whose activity may be prejudicial to the security of the other. Either Government may make representations to the other in this behalf, as and when occasion requires.

Please accept Excellency, the assurances of my highest consideration.

To

His Excellency

Shri Chandreshwar Prasad Narain Singh,

Ambassador Extraordinary and Plenipotentiary of India at the Court of Nepal, Indian Embassy, Kathmandu.

APPENDIX VI

Treaty of Peace and Friendship between the People's Republic of China and the Kingdom of Nepal

(April 28, 1960)

The Chairman of the People's Republic of China and His Majesty the King of Nepal,

Desiring to maintain and further develop peace and friendship between the People's Republic of China and the Kingdom of Nepal,

Convinced that the strengthening of good-neighbourly relations and friendly co-operation between the People's Republic of China and the Kingdom of Nepal is in accordance with the fundamental interests of the peoples of the two countries and conducive to the consolidation of peace in Asia and the world.

Have decided for this purpose to conclude the present treaty in accordance with the Five Principles of Peaceful Co-existence jointly affirmed by the two countries, and have appointed as their respective plenipotentiaries :

The (Chairman of the People's Republic of China:
Premier Chou En-lai of the State Council,
His Majesty the King of Nepal :
Prime Minister Bishweshwar Prasad Koirala.

The above-mentioned plenipotentiaries, having examined each other's credentials and found them in good and due form, have agreed upon the following :

ARTICLE 1

The Contracting Parties recognize and respect the independence, sovereignty and territorial integrity of each other.

ARTICLE 2

The Contracting Parties will maintain and develop peaceful

and friendly relations between the People's Republic of China and the Kingdom of Nepal. They undertake to settle all disputes between them by means of peaceful negotiation.

The Contracting Parties agree to develop and further strengthen the economic and cultural ties between the two countries in a spirit of friendship and co-operation, in accordance with the principles of equality and mutual benefit and of non-interference in each other's internal affairs.

ARTICLE 4

Any difference or dispute arising out of the interpretation of application of the present treaty shall be settled by negotiation through normal diplomatic channels.

ARTICLE 5

This present treaty is subject to ratification and the instruments of ratification will be exchanged in Peking as soon as possible.

The present treaty will come into force immediately on the exchange of the instruments of ratification and will remain in force for a period of ten years.

Unless either of the Contracting Parties gives to the other notice in writing to terminate the treaty at least one year before the expiration of this period, it will remain in force without any specified time limit, subject to the right of either of the Contracting Parties to terminate it by giving to the other in writing a year's notice of its intention to do so.

Done in duplicate in Kathmandu on the twenty-eighth day of April 1960, in the Chinese, Nepali and English languages, all texts being equally authentic.

(Sd.) CHOU EN-LAI
Plenipotentiary of the People's Republic of China

(Sd.) B. P. KOIRALA
Plenipotentiary of the Kingdom of Nepal

INDEX